MEASURING THE EFFICIENCY OF PUBLIC PROGRAMS

Costs and Benefits in Vocational Rehabilitation

TEMPLE UNIVERSITY PRESS   Philadelphia

MEASURING THE EFFICIENCY OF PUBLIC PROGRAMS

Costs and Benefits in Vocational Rehabilitation

Edited by Monroe Berkowitz

Temple University Press, Philadelphia 19122
Copyright © 1988 by Temple University. All rights reserved
Published 1988
Printed in the United States of America

The paper used in this publication meets the minimum
requirements of American National Standard for Information
Sciences—Permanence of Paper for Printed Library Materials,
ANSI Z39.48-1984

Library of Congress Cataloging-in-Publication Data
Measuring the efficiency of public programs.
   Includes index.
   1. Vocational rehabilitation—United States—
Cost effectiveness.   I. Berkowitz, Monroe, 1919–
HD7256.U5M44   1988   362'.0425   87-18080
ISBN 0-87722-527-3 (alk. paper)

CONTENTS

About the Authors

Edward Berkowitz is Associate Professor of History at George Washington University and Director of the Program in History and Public Policy.

Monroe Berkowitz is Professor of Economics at Rutgers University and Director of the Disability and Health Economics Section of the Bureau of Economic Research.

Frederick C. Collignon is Associate Professor of Social Policy Planning at the University of California at Berkeley and President of Berkeley Planning Associates.

David H. Dean is Assistant Professor of Economics at the University of Richmond.

Robert C. Dolan is Joseph Jennings Professor of Economics at the University of Richmond.

Ernest Gibbs is Assistant Professor of Economics at the University of Central Florida.

Anita G. Hall-Kane is Associate Manager of Rate Development at National Exchange Carrier Association, Inc.

Duncan Mann is Assistant Professor of Economics at Williams College.

William Milberg is Assistant Professor of Economics at the University of Michigan, Dearborn.

Stanley E. Portny is President of Stanley E. Portny Associates, a management consulting firm.

John D. Worrall is Associate Professor of Economics at Rutgers University, Camden, and Senior Associate of the Bureau of Economic Research.

Acknowledgments

The subject of this book has occupied economists at the Rutgers Bureau of Economic Research for more than twenty years. We owe a debt to all of the bureau's staff members who have worked on problems concerning the economics of disability and to those who have, over the years, given particular attention to the measurement of efficiency in the federal-state vocational rehabilitation program. Although we cannot call this a definitive account of the evaluation of vocational rehabilitation and other public programs—the field is too dynamic for any such summing up—it is at least a progress report. It is a look at the state of the art as we see it today.

The volume grows out of a project, "An Analysis of the Costs and Benefits in Rehabilitation," financed by the United States Department of Education (Contract No. 300-84-0259). We have, however, gone beyond the work done in that project to include results of current research from a project sponsored by the National Institutes of Disability and Rehabilitation Research, "Enhanced Understanding of the Economics of Disability" (Project No. 133AH30005). Thanks are due to many persons in the Department of Education and the National Institutes of Disability and Rehabilitation Research who have given a careful hearing to our reports and offered cogent comments.

I also wish to express my particular thanks and gratitude to Valerie LaPorte. Dr. LaPorte has served as editorial consultant to many bureau projects in the past, but in this instance, her contributions have gone beyond editorial consultation to include general supervision of the volume as a whole. Dr. LaPorte saw to it that the authors were reasonably on time with the drafts of their chapters, and she worked with individual authors to make necessary changes and improvements. In addition, because the manuscript was a collaborative effort, she revised the various chapters to bring about greater consistency in style, format, and level of technical sophistication. If we have succeeded in producing a volume that treats technical issues and yet offers the general reader some understanding of the nature and importance of those issues, Dr. LaPorte deserves much of the credit.

MONROE BERKOWITZ

INTRODUCTION

It is never easy to determine how the funds from the public purse should be divided, and in recent years the pressures of mandated budget reductions have aggravated the problem. In a democracy, the legislatures make these allocations in response to the public will as it is filtered through the media and the activities of lobbyists and as it is made known by direct communication with constituents. While some programs go along unnoticed for years at a constant level of funding, programs seeking funding in the billions of dollars sometimes become the focus of extended public debate.

The annual budgetary appropriation is only the first step. Administrators of individual programs subsequently must decide how their allocated funds should be spent. Here again, as with the basic appropriation, customary ways of doing things or the demands of constituent groups may dictate the course of action. Nevertheless, crises do arise, perhaps because of some external event, some change in the groups served, or some overall budgetary stringency. With the crises, program administrators and management and budget officials may look for some guide, some standard, or at least some rationale as they choose how and where to spend the money.

In the case of a budget cut, program personnel will want to consider how a reduction in the available dollars will affect the job the program is supposed to do. In the event of a shift in the client population, they will want to anticipate the consequences if some dollars are transferred from serving one group of clients to serving another. To ask such questions at the most general level is to inquire into the efficiency of the program. Is the program achieving its stated aims? Could some different allocation of funds within the program increase the levels of satisfaction of those being served without harming others? In the absence of functioning private markets where consumers are free to purchase or not to purchase goods as they please, efficiency is difficult to measure. In this volume, we will explore methods of evaluating the efficiency of public programs by considering one program, Vocational Rehabilitation. We will focus in particular on benefit-cost analysis and investigate its uses and its limitations as an instrument for assessing the performance of the VR program.

Our inquiry into benefit-cost methodology has three broad objectives. First, we offer a critique of the way in which this type of analysis has traditionally been conducted in the VR program. We identify deficiencies in the data maintained by the program and weaknesses in the conception of costs and benefits on which program personnel have relied. Second, we assess the *potential* value of benefit-cost analysis as a tool of program evaluation, asking to what extent the fault lies not with the method itself but with the way in which it has been applied. To resolve this issue, we experiment with different strategies for improving the measurements obtainable with benefit-cost analysis. We test possible remedies for the data deficiencies, utilizing both econometric corrections for the national data and an augmented data base at the state level, and we propose a number of modifications to the analytical model. We also raise the issue of experimental design and emphasize the use of control groups to isolate the effects of treatment on program clientele. Third and finally, our investigation into the basic validity of the benefit-cost approach leads us to reevaluate the uses of this form of analysis. We distinguish between "external evaluation"—an overall assessment of the program's returns—and "internal evaluation"—an assessment of the relative efficiency of various components of the program. The external evaluation might be used as the basis for a congressional decision to fund or not fund the program as a whole; the internal evaluation might be used as a guide by managers in allocating funds among different offices or different client groups, and by counselors who must decide on the best way to divide funds and services among clients. Having established this distinction, we go on to consider whether researchers should pursue more limited measures of internal program efficiency rather than attempt to estimate a single benefit-cost ratio for the entire program.

Before we begin our inquiry, let us look briefly at the vocational rehabilitation program, recognizing its distinctive features and, more importantly, noting how it is representative of other manpower and human service programs. It is these common features that make our findings concerning benefit-cost analysis and our evaluation of VR directly relevant to other public programs.

THE DESIGN OF THE VOCATIONAL REHABILITATION PROGRAM

The VR program was begun as a grant-in-aid program by the federal government after the First World War and has survived all of the subsequent social and economic changes. Each of the states has a vocational rehabilitation program that operates under federal guidelines and receives 80 percent of its funds from the federal government. But while the federal government has an important role in overseeing and financing the program, the states maintain broad operational discretion. They will determine how to fit the program into the structure of the state government—whether it will be located in the department of education, department of labor, or perhaps some umbrella human services agency. In addition, although the federal law makes certain stipulations about the clients accepted into the program—they must be physically or mentally impaired while showing promise of eventual return or first entrance into the labor market—the states exercise their discretion in selecting the specific type of clients admitted and the several types of services offered.

What may be most characteristic of the program as a whole is its provision of a wide variety of services. The VR program provides counseling and guidance services through its in-house counseling staff. But beyond this, the program offers a comprehensive range of purchased services, including medical restoration, education, and training. The key to the program is flexibility, and no one service or type of service predominates. Once accepted for services, the client meets with a counselor to work out an individual written rehabilitation plan that spells out the services the client is to receive and the results that are to be expected.

It is the comprehensiveness and the flexibility of the VR program that make it an interesting case example for persons interested in evaluation. Other manpower and human service delivery programs offer a fixed package of services which tend to have a very specific orientation. The Job Corps offers vocational training at its residential centers; the Work Incentive Program (WIN) offers specific types of training programs to welfare mothers; and Projects with Industry (PWI) offers particular training programs based on potential job openings with private employers. The VR program is in a sense an amalgam of these other programs, bringing together within a single organization many of the services offered individually by the others. The objection might be raised, of course, that VR is not representative of other programs because its clientele has been largely restricted to physically and mentally impaired persons. Yet this volume will argue the importance of taking into account the level of health or physical functioning that clients bring to a program when evaluating the impact of services on those clients. The practice of standardizing for health could result in more accurate evaluation of all manpower and service delivery programs.

PROGRAM CHANGES AND THE NEED FOR
NEW EVALUATION METHODS

The problem of accountability should be of particular concern at the present time to the individuals who are directly allied with vocational rehabilitation. As the opening chapter of the volume, "The Cost-Benefit Tradition in Vocational Rehabilitation," demonstrates in some detail, the VR program almost from its very inception made claims about the returns the taxpayer should expect for each dollar invested in the program. But much has changed since the early days and the time is ripe for a fresh examination of the program's direction, policies, and purposes. Over the years, the program has reached out to new clientele. At the beginning, the typical client was an industrial worker who had suffered traumatic injury. With the inauguration of the War on Poverty under President Johnson, the program was asked to serve disadvantaged persons. During the Kennedy administration, attention turned to the mentally ill, and more recently, the emphasis has shifted to severely disabled and mentally retarded persons. The present concern for the homeless has prompted the program to address the needs of this group as well.

These transformations of the client mix have in turn brought about other changes in the VR program. The stated goal of the program has always been rehabilitation, that is, restoration of a client to the labor market for a period of sixty days, but this has been interpreted in recent years to include placement in a sheltered workshop, placement as a homemaker, or placement in supported employment. Rehabilitation of severely handicapped clients has proved to be expensive, and with budgets remaining more or less constant (about $1 billion per year), the number of persons graduating successfully from the program has been declining. Because the program has traditionally prided itself on the number of persons rehabilitated, this decline is disturbing. The increasing proportion of severely handicapped persons in the case load may work to undermine the customary ways of evaluating the program. It may be that the established pattern in the program—the provision of a bundle of services to a client over a fixed period of time—may be replaced by the delivery of intermittent services to the client over an extended period of time. The evaluation system, and perhaps even the data system built up over the years, may not be able to accommodate these new patterns of service.

If changing service patterns require new methods of examining the program, other considerations also make this an opportune time for a fresh review of its activities. The VR program pioneered in providing information about its performance and in justifying its work with the rhetoric of economic analysis, but it has not kept pace with the changes in evaluation methods. In the 1920s, monitoring and reporting expenditures and results was an exciting and novel idea. But today, although the amount of information made available by the VR program compares favorably with that released by other manpower and service programs, the modeling of the evaluation process remains crude. In estimating benefits, the program has relied on simple comparisons between the economic status of individual clients as they enter the program and as they leave it, or on ad hoc modifications of these crucial variables based on limited survey data. Control group comparisons are understandably lacking, but little effort has been made to compensate for their absence.

VR is an intriguing program to examine. There is so much reported on each individual client and yet so few verifiable program results. It would seem so easy to build on what is available, to take the necessary steps to produce more accurate evaluation results, convincing not only to the friends of the program but also to those who review a multiplicity of programs with an eye to identifying the most efficient.

OUTLINE OF THE VOLUME

In Part I of this volume, the first chapter examines the cost-benefit tradition in the program, documenting the long history of reliance on what appears to be its economic justification. Chapter 2 examines the theoretical foundations of cost-benefit analysis and its relationship to welfare economics. Chapter 3 analyzes the range of benefit-cost models, how they have been applied in past studies and how they possibly could be applied in future analysis. Chapter 4 sketches a specific model based on the individual behavior of the client and the counselor.

The chapters in Part II describe the range of data about vocational rehabilitation clients reported annually by the federal government and examine the use of these data in the conduct of benefit-cost analyses. The traditional method of benefit-cost analysis used by the agency is replicated and its limitations analyzed. More complex methods are employed using various econometric and other types of corrections to compensate for the sparse information on the true level of earnings of clients at entry into and exit from the program. After doing what can be done with the information available, we conclude that some better method of evaluation is needed.

More data are available than are regularly reported to the federal government by the states. In Part III, we report on the information collected by the states and the use they make of it. With the introduction of automated data processing systems, more and more states are collecting a wide variety of information potentially useful for evaluation purposes. Unfortunately, not all of this is being amassed in forms that can be retrieved in a timely fashion, but the difficulties in access and form are probably easily remedied.

Part IV reports on some early results obtained by using an augmented data base in two selected states. Most exciting is the possibility of linking state data bases with wage information from the state employment agencies. While such information will not compensate for the lack of information about a control group, it can be used to make the internal evaluations of the program richer and more reliable.

The concluding chapter considers the possibility of linking national data with social security earning records. Although such data links have been established in the past, they have not been incorporated in a modern evaluation model.

APPLICATIONS OF THE STUDY

Our discussion of the issues of evaluation should interest all those responsible for the general oversight and administration of public programs and the allocation of public funds. The data problems we treat at length in our discussion of VR are found in most of the programs providing services to people who seek to enter or return to the labor market. All program administrators must determine the nature and extent of the data needed to manage their programs effectively, to support the delivery of services, and to assess the economic performance of the programs. They must find methods of gathering this information that disrupt the day-to-day operations of the program as little as possible, and they must motivate their staff to collect these data in a reliable and consistent fashion. In addition, administrators must find an appropriate model for analyzing the costs and benefits of the services they provide. The discussion of models in this volume will illustrate the wide range of choices and the advantages and disadvantages of particular models.

Our discussion of past and present practice in the evaluation of VR also raises a number of basic methodological problems applicable to the evaluation of other programs. We take up technical issues such as methods of correcting for deficiencies in reported earnings at time of entrance into the program, and ways and means of linking program data to earnings information available from the state employment agencies. Readers with a particular interest in methodology may find the chapters where these matters are covered especially useful.

Finally, readers interested in the vocational rehabilitation program itself will find here a comprehensive examination of the current state of benefit-cost analysis as it applies to the program. More importantly, they will find an account of specific ways in which the evaluation of the program can be improved in the future. A program that was surely the pioneer and innovator in the field of evaluation deserves to regain its premier position. It has a data base foundation that needs only modest additions, and it has the tradition of appraising itself in economic terms; what it needs now is a modern model of analysis to display its accomplishments. Its methods of evaluation can be transformed if administrators are willing to draw the lessons implicit in an examination of the program's past experience and its current problems and to undertake the steps needed to return VR to the forefront. We offer our volume as a survey of the information necessary to guide such a journey.

I

Background, Theory, and Models

Part I establishes the historical, theoretical, and conceptual contexts for the analysis presented in the volume. The first of these background chapters examines the development of cost-benefit analysis as a mode of evaluation within the vocational rehabilitation program. Edward Berkowitz chronicles the attempt to establish the economic benefits of the program, from the first fairly crude assessment of the program's returns in the 1920s to a study undertaken by the Department of Health, Education, and Welfare in 1966 that was expected to provide a more precise test of the performance of vocational rehabilitation. Berkowitz shows that the supporters of the program have represented its achievements in different terms over the years, adapting their demonstration of the program's value to changing national priorities. While the argument that the program was socially necessary and worthwhile was put forward with particular force in the 1930s, vocational rehabilitation officials in other eras placed their greatest emphasis on the fact that the program paid for itself by restoring the wage-earning capacity of disabled workers.

When program personnel pointed to the economic virtues of vocational rehabilitation, they typically backed their claims with figures suggesting that the benefits far exceeded the costs of the program. Yet, as Berkowitz observes, the analysis that yielded these impressive cost-benefit ratios was flawed on several counts. Estimates of the costs of the program were limited to formal program expenditures, and estimates of the benefits rested largely on a simple calculation of the difference between clients' earnings at the time of their acceptance into the program and their earnings at the time of closure. Follow-up data on clients was not maintained; program officials optimistically assumed that a client's earnings at closure would continue indefinitely.

This first chapter underscores the important role played by history and custom in program evaluation and helps to clarify the origins of some of the problems that beset contemporary efforts to assess the costs and benefits of vocational rehabilitation. Certain methods of selecting, recording, and analyzing client data took root early in the program, largely because they served the needs of administrators eager to demonstrate economic success. Today, analysts who seek a more realistic understanding of the program's performance must deal with the inadequacies of the data base. They must also cope with resistance to new methods of analysis that suggest a more modest record of achievement for the program.

Chapter 2 provides a different perspective on the background of benefit-cost analysis. Author William Milberg explores the theoretical basis of benefit-cost analysis in welfare economics and points to the theoretical problems that beset efforts to measuring the changes in welfare experienced by individuals or society as a whole. He reviews the traditional methods of measuring individual consumer welfare and some newer measures based on the concept of "willingness to pay." While today's cost-benefit analysis is closely allied with the concept of consumer's surplus developed in the nineteenth century, "willingness to pay" as an alternative measure of benefits has attracted new interest in vocational rehabilitation because of the developing market for private services.

Milberg also surveys the methods of aggregating individual welfare changes to measure changes in social welfare. The analyst who cites a single benefit-cost ratio for the entire VR program is actually adding up the benefits of more than 300,000 persons. Milberg analyzes the strengths and weaknesses of different methods of aggregating benefits over individuals, giving particular attention to one method of making social welfare decisions, the Kaldor-Hicks criterion, which serves as a point of departure for much benefit-cost evaluation.

If Chapter 2 is in part a critique of benefit-cost analysis, it also suggests ways to improve this form of analysis. Milberg calls for more research on the application of theory to practice and stresses the importance of striving for a logically consistent welfare measure. Implicit in his chapter is the belief that benefit-cost analysis will become more valuable as a measurement tool when the basic assumptions on which it rests are recognized.

In Chapter 3, John Worrall offers a detailed examination of the underlying designs, or models, of benefit-cost analysis. He considers first the model that is basic to the traditional analysis of the VR program and then proceeds to discuss Ronald Conley's contribution to the design of benefit-cost studies and the later variants of Conley's model. He contrasts the studies of the federal-state VR program and those of other manpower programs.

Worrall points up some of the conceptual problems involved in estimating VR program benefits—the failure of many models to account for fluctuation in the time path of wages and the difficulty of measuring nonmonetary benefits such as gains in psychological or physical functioning. Worrall devotes most of the chapter, however, to a basic weakness of all benefit-cost studies: the nonexperimental setting in which these studies have been conducted. In order to isolate the effect of participation in the program on the earnings of VR clients, researchers would have to assign persons who qualify for services to treatment and control groups on a random basis. Worrall points up the ethical dilemma involved in withholding services from eligible individuals and proposes as an alternative randomly assigning individuals to different treatment programs. The postprogram earnings increases of clients of the federal/state program could be compared to the earnings increases of individuals who had received services from, say, private rehabilitation agencies. Such an experiment would enable the analyst to judge the efficiency of the VR program relative to other kinds of treatment.

As alternatives to experimental designs, evaluation methods that rely on comparison groups and statistical controls have been adopted in the past. Worrall considers a number of such models previously used in vocational rehabilitation and other programs to estimate the effect of treatment. Particular attention is given to a set of studies linking VR case service records to Social Security Administration records in order to reveal how VR rehabilitants fared after closure from the program in comparison with individuals not accepted for services or closed out unsuccessfully.

Worrall maintains that a wholly trustworthy benefit-cost analysis of the VR program is not possible in the absence of an experimental design. He suggests that researchers might more profitably direct their efforts to an evaluation of the relative efficiency of state programs or the success of these programs in bringing about different kinds of benefits for clients.

In Chapter 4, Duncan Mann focuses on a single model designed to assess the behavior of the individual participants in the rehabilitation process rather than the overall performance of the program. Mann assumes that both client and counselor will make choices that will advance their interests or well-being. In the language of economists, client and counselor are expected to maximize their individual utility functions.

A client's utility function is based not only on expected earnings but also on possible improvements in functioning and adaptability. The client decision studied in this model centers on the length of time the individual client will remain in the program. The counselor decision concerns the mix of services to be given a client and the appropriate time for the client to leave the program. The interaction of these decisions will determine the clients to be served and the types of services to be given. These complex theoretical relationships are worked out in this chapter.

In certain respects, Chapter 4 looks back to earlier chapters in Part I and the issues raised there. Mann's model includes a control group composed of individuals who were accepted into the program but did not receive any services. Such a control group meets some of the requirements set forth in

Chapter 3, although the possibility remains that the treatment and control groups in this model differ in unobservable ways. In addition, Mann's model explains individual behavior in a manner consistent with the economic theory explored in Chapter 2 and the assumptions about human behavior on which the theory is based. Ultimately, such models promise to bring about better measurement of program impacts on clients.

1 *Edward Berkowitz*

THE COST-BENEFIT TRADITION IN VOCATIONAL REHABILITATION

Senator Chavez: What happens to rehabilitated personnel once you get them rehabilitated and, for instance, you place them in industry?
Miss Switzer: We put them to work.
Senator Chavez: Do they stay?
Miss Switzer: They stay at work. We have some rather good material on that. They not only stay at work, but they get good wages, and they pay good income taxes.
Senator Chavez: If you have some figures on that which you can place in the record it would be a good idea, because, you know, a lot of people do not understand just exactly what you are trying to do. (U.S. Senate Subcommittee on Labor-Federal Security Agency Appropriations 1951, p. 390).

On 12 January 1966, the Secretary of Health, Education, and Welfare announced the establishment of the office of the Assistant Secretary for Program Coordination. This new office sought to examine the many programs administered by the largest federal department concerned with domestic affairs. Among other tasks, it undertook the creation of a Planning-Programming-Budgeting System to help the various programs match their objectives with their expenditures. At the same time as the new office initiated PPBS, it also launched cost-benefit studies of the programs to determine which programs produced the most return for each dollar expended.

In response to the secretary's directive, statisticians in HEW planned a cost-benefit study of the vocational rehabilitation program. Unlike the other programs, vocational rehabilitation already had a long tradition of such analysis, one that had helped sustain it from the 1920s to the 1960s. Past cost-benefit analyses had demonstrated the worth of the program; now, cost-benefit analysis would serve a new purpose, that of comparing the program to other programs. HEW was confident that the program would meet the new test. They expected their study to "dramatically reveal the impressive gains to be derived from this program" (Mars 1968, p. 1).

The statisticians did, in fact, arrive at a lusty benefit-cost ratio of 35 to 1. Yet while they were issuing these very positive findings, they drew attention to some of the uncertainties attending the cost-benefit analysis of the program. Ideally, the analysis should compare all costs to all benefits of the program, but some costs and benefits eluded the analyst. Either they could not be properly quantified or they could not even be properly identified. In particular, the HEW statisticians lamented the lack of data on what happened to rehabilitated people after their rehabilitation. How many of them died, retired, or experienced new impairments? The program records were relatively silent on these questions (Mars, p. 3).[1]

This silence was understandable. The program did not operate for the convenience of the policy analyst. In fact, cost-benefit analysis had always been used as a simple demonstration of the program's net benefit to society. This demonstration helped to distinguish the program from other social welfare programs that simply transferred money from taxpayers to the poor. The analysis had never been intended to serve as a tool for policy makers charged with adjusting the total level of program expenditures or setting priorities within the program. This use of cost-benefit analysis came much later, arriving only in the middle sixties.

The program itself functioned in a way not likely to generate useful data for cost-benefit analysis. A handicapped person went to a succession of interviews with a counselor. Together they worked out a course of action to overcome the person's disability. The process resembled any training exercise: it was relatively short and had a definite beginning and end. After the program was completed, a rehabilitated person had no more reason to remain in touch with a counselor than a high school graduate did with a teacher. True, many rehabilitants stayed in touch, just as the high school often kept in touch with its alumni, particularly those who had achieved success. Many rehabilitants, however, simply dropped out of sight, their new lives totally separate from their earlier existence. Without information on the course of their careers, it was difficult to perform cost-benefit analysis.

Program officials worked with what they had available. Since it was impossible to specify and measure all of the program's benefits and costs at any given moment, program officials emphasized the most obvious and important of those benefits and costs.

A study of the history of cost-benefit analysis in the vocational rehabilitation program, therefore, reveals contemporary perceptions of the program's purpose and methods. It also shows how various customs in data gathering and analysis became established. As the program entered the modern era, these customs played a large role in determining the sort of cost-benefit analysis that modern statisticians could perform. They also tended to set the standards by which modern analysis would be judged. If the old customs generated impressive results, then modern methods tended to be accepted only when they produced similarly favorable results. In the program's traditions, therefore, is found the core of support and opposition to modern cost-benefit analysis.

ARRIVAL OF COST-BENEFIT ANALYSIS IN THE TWENTIES

Unlike other social welfare programs, vocational rehabilitation began as an economic proposition. During the late progressive era and early twenties, nearly all new social welfare programs—widows' pensions for mothers with dependent children, retirement programs for the elderly, infant and maternal health programs—were supported for their value to society. Most of these programs, however, primarily involved the maintenance of people who had come to depend on the government's support. In contrast, the proponents of vocational rehabilitation saw their program as a cure for disability rather than a means of supporting it. Instead of increasing government expenditures, vocational rehabilitation promised to reduce them. "Curing the disability is far and away the more economic procedure," said the federal agency in charge of the new program, "and in this case sound economics is clearly sound public policy" (U.S. Federal Board for Vocational Education 1921, p. 27).[2]

Vocational rehabilitation, as an outgrowth of workers' compensation, benefited from the era's interest in the concept of efficiency. Workers' compensation became the most ubiquitous social insurance program during the progressive era in part because it could be defended as a sound business investment. By forcing employers to pay the costs of the disabilities they had created, workers' compensation helped to reduce industrial accidents and so promoted the goal of efficiency. After an accident had occurred, however, workers' compensation could do little beyond maintaining the injured worker. Vocational rehabilitation carried the efficient approach to industrial disability one step further by restoring the injured worker to a condition of productivity (Berkowitz 1980a).

For whatever reason, program officials attached the rhetoric of efficiency to the program almost from its very beginnings. As early as 1922, program officials could describe vocational rehabilitation as part of the societal effort to "attain the highest possible degree of national and personal efficiency." Indeed, vocational rehabilitation formed the human counterpart of the national drive to conserve national resources. "Our only real wealth," proclaimed the program officials, "is human effort" (U.S. Federal Board for Vocational Education 1922, p. 345).

One benefit of efficiency was that it could be described numerically. "Efficiency," said the federal officials, "is the fullest possible utilization with the least expenditure of time, resources, and powers to effect a desired result" (U.S. Federal Board for Vocational Education 1922, p. 345). Such rhetoric suggested that vocational rehabilitation would pay dividends, although program officials were cautious at first. They said that vocational rehabilitation, like education, would "pay well" but warned that the "profit can not in either case be accurately delivered in dollars" (U.S. Federal Board for Vocational Education, 1921, p. 25).

By 1926 all reticence had been dropped. It was only natural, according to program officials, "to raise the question whether the investment of federal and state funds in the civilian vocational rehabilitation program brings adequate return" (U.S. Federal Board for Vocational Education 1926, p. 123). Having raised the question, program officials proceeded to answer it with a very casual form of cost-benefit analysis.

The terms of this analysis remained with the program for decades. It began with the observation that the average weekly wages for all persons rehabilitated in the United States during 1924 was $26.07. These people would, on the average, enjoy a life expectancy of at least twenty years. They would thus earn an impressive $147,004,000 during those years, an extraordinary amount compared to the slightly more than one million dollars that it took to rehabilitate them (U.S. Federal Board for Vocational Education 1926).

Such findings encouraged program officials to probe further into cost-benefit analysis. The limitations of the earliest work were obvious even to contemporary observers. Instead of following the rehabilitants through their working lives, the analysis simply assumed that they would remain employed at the same jobs until death or retirement. Moreover, the analysis failed to look into the earnings of the rehabilitants before they entered the program. Although limited by the program's short life, program officials made an attempt to correct these deficiencies with a major study of people rehabilitated between 1920 and 1924, who were followed up in the year 1927. Tracy Copp, one of the ablest federal workers employed by the program, conducted the study and wrote the final report. Even as the study was being conducted, program officials such as John Kratz, who supervised the federal office, felt confident that "this study will ultimately demonstrate scientifically and beyond question that the vocational rehabilitation in the States is permanently economically sound and socially worthwhile" (U.S. Federal Board for Vocational Education 1926, p. 127; idem 1928).

The hopes of the federal officials also revealed their anxieties. Cost-benefit analysis offered the means of solving two of the program's problems. As an experimental program, vocational rehabilitation faced the constant threat of extinction. In the twenties, unlike later eras, federal social welfare programs sometimes went out of existence; Congress simply refused to reappropriate funds. Throughout the twenties, the program's very existence was precarious, with Congress often delaying the appropriation of funds. Not until the passage of the Social Security Act in 1935 would the program become permanent. Cost-benefit analysis, therefore, gave advocates the arguments they needed to sell the program to Congress.

Not only did the analysis strengthen the program's case with Congress but it also solidified the role of the federal employees who supervised the program. These federal officials did no casework; they were not themselves involved in rehabilitating the handicapped. The role of the federal office in a program that operated on the principle of grants-in-aid to the states was just being invented. By undertaking cost-benefit analysis, federal officials were doing work that helped to boost the program, work that could not be done as effectively by the states themselves.

These considerations helped override any lingering doubts about the propriety of applying economic analysis to a social endeavor. In the 1927 annual report, the program officials included a long discussion of this matter. They distinguished between people who viewed the program as an operation in "social salvage" and those who saw it as one of "economic salvage." The former group saw the benefits of the program in the way it relieved the handicapped of their anxieties and their natural feelings of inferiority. The latter group saw the program's strength in the way it restored the handicapped to "self-supporting ability." The federal officials endorsed the economic point of view because it enabled them to apply the concept of efficiency to the program. "During the last year," they wrote, "there has been a very marked increase . . . in the acceptance of the economic point of view with a corresponding readiness to consider problems of securing the greatest social return for a dollar expended" (U.S. Federal Board for Vocational Education 1927, p. 21).

Despite the boldness of this statement, the federal officials felt an ambivalence that would continue to characterize the program. On the one hand, vocational rehabilitation represented an important entitlement, an obligation of society to handicapped individuals, regardless of whether or not those individuals repaid the investment made in them. On the other hand, the program did pay for itself and that feature made it all the more attractive.

"Vocational rehabilitation is an investment in human welfare that is wholly self-liquidating," argued program officials in 1953, even as they stressed that the program deserved support because of the "American tradition of a fair chance for all" (U.S. Dept. of Health, Education, and Welfare 1954, p. 229). There was thus a duality about vocational rehabilitation. It fell within the domain of society's charitable activities and yet it could also be justified pragmatically as a government undertaking that made economic sense. Depending on the economic conditions, the program could take on a protective coloration to suit the times.

INTERMEZZO: THE THIRTIES AND FORTIES

The thirties represented a supreme test of the program's adaptability. This depression decade decisively changed the American style of social welfare. Efficiency took second place to a more straightforward mode of social welfare that had the virtue of getting money, not training or other services, into people's hands quickly. But the earlier styles of social welfare did not disappear. Instead, the major social welfare laws of the thirties, such as the Social Security Act of 1935 and the Fair Labor Standards Act of 1938, tended to strengthen older programs even as they introduced new ones. Nevertheless, the older programs, particularly those that depended on the now much-weakened private labor market, could not easily survive in the thirties.[3]

Although cost-benefit analysis was an important asset for those who defended the validity of vocational rehabilitation, it also underwent many tests during the thirties. Program officials during the decade maintained a general silence on the results of cost-benefit studies. In 1931, however, there appeared a revealing follow-up to the studies conducted earlier. The officials made no attempt to cover up the effects of the depression on the program. For example, the thousand people in the study had no earnings before rehabilitation in 69 percent of the cases, and immediately after rehabilitation 73 percent earned over $15 a week. In the years between their rehabilitation and 1927 (the group had been rehabilitated between 1920 and 1924), the percentage earning $15 a week had risen to 80 percent. But by 1931, this percentage had slipped to 61 percent. Program officials believed that the hourly wages of most rehabilitants remained the same, but the depression had forced them to reduce the number of hours they worked (U.S. Federal Board for Vocational Education 1931, pp. 68–69).

When viewed on a more aggregate level, the numbers illustrated the effects of the depression even more clearly. The state and the federal government invested $291,000 in the rehabilitation of the thousand cases.

Their earning capacity before rehabilitation amounted only to $332,132. Immediately after rehabilitation, this capacity rose to $1,035,780 per year; by 1927, the capacity reached a high of $1,243,301 per year, and by 1931 it had slipped to $929,702 per year (U.S. Federal Board for Vocational Education 1931, pp. 68–69).

In modern times, such results might have called the entire exercise into question. The first cost-benefit studies had, in effect, posited no unemployment for the people rehabilitated and no cuts in the level of wages. The 1931 follow-up showed the vulnerability of rehabilitants to macroeconomic forces and made it quite plain that an economic downturn would reduce the benefits that accrued to rehabilitation. Such an outcome did not occur to contemporary observers. They were not attempting to fine-tune the method of policy analysis. Instead, they were demonstrating a simple point: rehabilitation paid dividends. Like any financial venture, the dividends varied from year to year, reflecting business conditions. The important point, however, was that the program continued to pay its dividends; that fact alone made the program worthy of remaining in business. Program officials decided not to follow up the group beyond 1931: "No attempt is made to predict the period of years they will continue to be productive," they wrote. The rehabilitants had already proven their worth to society: "All future production of these persons will represent so much additional return upon the original investment" (U.S. Federal Board for Vocational Education 1931, pp. 68–69).

Even when economic conditions improved in the forties, program officials launched no major new cost-benefit studies. Despite the passage of a major new rehabilitation law in 1943, program officials showed little inclination to refine their analysis. The new law in 1943, which permitted the states to pay for the physical restoration of clients with federal money, had as much to do with the exigencies of war and veterans' politics as it did with the use of cost-benefit analysis as a policy tool.[4]

Cost-benefit analysis became something of an afterthought in discussions of vocational rehabilitation. It was not represented as an important part of a continuing process of evaluation; rather, it was mentioned from year to year as an incidental demonstration of the program's value to society. The presentation for 1943 typifies the claims made by the agency during this decade. The program managed to rehabilitate 42,000 people in that year. Eighty-five percent of those people were not working just before rehabilitation; in fact, 31 percent had never worked. These 31 percent represented a segment of the population that decided to enter the labor force as a result of the expanded labor market nurtured by the war. The remaining 15 percent of the rehabilitated population had worked before rehabilitation but at marginal jobs that paid low wages. Even including welfare payments from sources like the rapidly fading Works Progress Administration (WPA), the average prerehabilitation wage for the group was $18 per week. Those conditions permitted a very broad comparison between the program's costs and its benefits. In the 1943 case, the program expenditures increased the group's earnings from $5,913,648 before rehabilitation to $65,165,828 just after. This demonstration ended the discussion, leaving people to wonder what element of the program had been responsible for these impressive returns. This year, as in the years before, the statistics tested nothing. Instead they showed that a good deed also paid (U.S. Office of Vocational Rehabilitation 1944b, p. 6).

Even as the war expanded opportunities for rehabilitation, many questions remained. In 1944, with the economy booming, the states maintained a register of 269,960 handicapped people, of whom only 145,059 received services. As many as 61,565 people were investigated but not served any further. The reasons were reported in the most vague and general of terms. Some of the people—how many was not reported—refused the services. In other cases, the services were not needed, perhaps because the wartime economy demanded little of its labor force beyond a willingness to work. In still other cases, the agency found the person not sufficiently cooperative to make rehabilitation possible. Clearly, these inconclusive investigations represented costs to the agency that yielded few benefits. The agency never pursued the matter. It did not believe its obligation extended to discovering all of the program's costs and benefits. A clear declaration of the program's value, buttressed by a statistical demonstration, remained enough (U.S. Office of Vocational Rehabilitation 1944b, p. 8).

In the forties, these demonstrations had a curiously static quality. No effort was made to compare the results from one year with the results from another year. Had program officials bothered to do so, they would have discovered that the statistics indicated a declining benefit-to-cost ratio from year to year. Since the ratio remained well above one, it did not matter. Each year the agency performed the same calculation with different numbers, and each year it came up with a glowing report on the program. Using the now standard methodology of comparing earnings before and after rehabilitation, the program officials came up with a twelve-fold increase in 1944, a six-fold increase in 1945, and a four-fold increase in 1946 (U.S. Office of Vocational Rehabilitation 1944b, p. 8; idem 1945, p. 17; U.S. Federal Security Agency 1946, pp. 219, 221).

Was the program expanding to take advantage of the disparity between marginal benefits and costs? On the contrary, the program was languishing. The pioneering generation of program administrators had been replaced by a benign but unenergetic group of federal employees. The number of rehabilitations fell from 44,000 in 1944, to 41,925 in 1945, to 36,106 in 1946. By 1946, the cost-benefit demonstration had become so half-hearted that the agency simply extrapolated data from less than half of the rehabilitants to the entire group (U.S. Office of Vocational Rehabilitation 1944b; idem 1945; U.S. Federal Security Agency 1946).

The next year, 1947, marked a transition between the pride and optimism of the twenties and the apex of the cost-benefit tradition in the fifties. For the first time in many years, the agency dressed up the rhetoric used in its annual report. A sharp increase in the number of people rehabilitated accompanied the new rhetoric. The changed rhetoric suggested a new awareness of the way in which rehabilitation related to other societal efforts. The difference between the amount expended on rehabilitation and the amount that the rehabilitants earned now represented "an increase of about $54,000,000 in the annual earned income of the nation." Not only a sense of national income accounting but also a new conception of the benefits of vocational rehabilitation appeared in the report. Rehabilitation transformed people from recipients of public funds into taxpayers. In only a short time, the cost of rehabilitation would return to the federal and state governments in the form of taxes paid by the rehabilitants. Something new had arrived on the rehabilitation analysis scene (U.S. Federal Security Agency 1947, p. 621).

TEN TO ONE: THE ULTIMATE DEMONSTRATION

The 1948 Annual Report of the Federal Security Agency, the home agency of the vocational rehabilitation program since 1939 and the forerunner of what would become the Department of Health, Education, and Welfare in 1953, included its usual report on vocational rehabilitation. One of the staples of such reports was the case history that showed the program to best advantage. In this year, the agency featured the story of a young hemiplegic who also suffered from what the agency called defective vision. Only sixteen years old, the boy faced the alternatives of a lifetime of expensive inactivity or, with the right sort of help, a career of productive employment. The boy had dropped out of high school, further diminishing his chances for a successful career. Then the agency discovered him, tested his aptitude, and paid for a course in bookkeeping and typing. Still, his attitude remained poor; he showed "personal maladjustment" and "emotional instability." He needed psychotherapy, and thanks to the 1943 law, the agency was able to get him this help. Now the newly well-adjusted boy went out and got a job, earning $75 a week as a demonstrator of home furnishings (p. 613).

If the emphasis on psychiatry was new, the example was very old. Putting the rehabilitation into uplifting human terms had always provided a counterpoint to the statistical cost-benefit demonstrations. This year, however, the agency pushed the cost-benefit demonstrations into a new realm. It emphasized that the formerly disabled hemiplegic would now pay income taxes, almost as if those taxes were a form of repayment for the advice, the training courses, and the psychotherapy received from the government.

The 1948 report contained the boldest statements the program officials had ever ventured to make. In the long run, the vocational rehabilitation program cost the federal government "nothing." Instead, it returned "pyramiding profits in what well may be termed an investment in human welfare." The hemiplegic boy, like many of his fellow rehabilitants, was quite young. The average age of rehabilitants in 1948 was only thirty-one years. That left thirty-four more years until the age established by the Social Security Act as the new standard for retirement. Assuming that the person worked 85 percent of that time, "he may be expected to return, in federal income taxes alone, approximately $10 for every dollar the federal government expends upon his rehabilitation" (p. 586).

This 10-to-1 figure soon became the new cost-benefit standard. It possessed an innate simplicity and elegance and argued powerfully for the continued expansion of the vocational rehabilitation program. Like the results of previous efforts at cost-benefit analysis, the new figure represented the outcome of a demonstration rather than of a careful analytic process. For all of that, its appeal proved to be irresistible.

What assumptions underlay the demonstration? In reality, the agency did not know how much a person made in the year after rehabilitation. All the agency had were weekly earning figures for the period immediately after rehabilitation. To obtain a yearly figure, it multiplied this weekly figure by fifty weeks. Then it made the fundamental assumption that a person would work 85 percent of the time until retirement age. Such assumptions may have overstated the level of earnings the group would obtain. A severe depression, for example, would prevent the group from working 85 percent of the time. On the other hand, the demonstration almost certainly understated the amount of federal income tax the group would pay. The agency assumed that income tax payments would not increase, that earnings would not rise, and that the group would not have more children after being rehabilitated. Still other factors affected the calculation, but in no clear direction. Earnings for farmers and housewives, for example, were not included in the estimation of benefits. All in all, the assumptions behind the calculations underscored the delicate nature of the calculations.[5]

Beyond these technical matters, the new cost-benefit demonstration owed its existence to changes in American public policy. The Second World War sharply escalated the level of federal spending. Postwar spending levels, although lower than wartime levels, never returned to the low levels of the thirties. Increased spending tended to solidify an innovation in public finance that the war had brought about: the withholding of federal income taxes from a worker's paycheck. The forced payment of income taxes during each pay period made the federal income tax much less of an abstraction and much more of a reality. To say that a social welfare program saved federal tax money suddenly meant something (Hughes 1977).

Another postwar innovation also contributed to the appearance of this new demonstration. In reporting the 10-to-1 figure to the state rehabilitation offices, Joseph Hunt, the federal official in charge of such matters in 1948, reported in passing that the calculation had been performed for the benefit of congressional committees and the Council of Economic Advisors (U.S. Office of Vocational Rehabilitation 1948). This last group had come into being under the Employment Act of 1946, and like the act itself, reflected a general societal interest in economic planning. The 1946 act owed its existence to a fear that the prosperity of the war would yield to the grim conditions that had characterized the thirties.[6] Many people believed that the federal government could act as a sort of catalyst for the economy and, by initiating macroeconomic measures such as public works, maintain the level of employment. The completed act stopped well short of the desires of committed planners, yet it established the Council of Economic Advisors as a new component of the federal bureaucracy specifically charged with keeping the President informed of economic trends. The Council became a new consumer of economic information. The vocational rehabilitation program kept this new consumer supplied with upbeat reports on its accomplishments.

Whatever the motivation for the construction of the 10-to-1 figure, it played well in Congress, where it mattered. Well into the sixties, Congress retained its tight hold over program appropriations, free from pressure to meet spending targets. It fell to program administrators to appear before the appropriation committees and make the best possible case for the program. Prospects brightened for vocational rehabilitation in 1950 when Mary Switzer took over as director. Bright, energetic, and supremely motivated, Switzer made the most of the cost-benefit demonstrations. Unlike her predecessor, Michael Shortley, Switzer came from the branch of the bureaucracy concerned with matters such as education and public health. The rhetoric of investment suited her and, in her capable hands, it became a staple of congressional testimony, helping to raise the level of program appropriations and expenditures (Berkowitz 1980b).[7]

Although Switzer might not have invented the 10-to-1 figure, she utilized it to its fullest. Early in 1955, for example, she appeared before her friend Congressman John Fogarty and recited the program's virtues. Aware that the initiative for increased appropriations had to come from the congressman, Switzer planted a question. "How much will the Federal Government get in return for every Federal dollar that we spend in rehabilitation?"

asked Fogarty. Without hesitation Switzer announced that she had the figures available. "Yes, we have that figure, and it stands up too," she said. "You ought to get back over a period of time, $10 for 1 in Federal income taxes, if our estimates are right. That's what we say."

Fogarty hastened to put the matter into even less abstract terms. He asked how much the government could expect to receive from an investment of $39 million, and Mary Switzer reassured him that the government could ultimately expect $390 million (U.S. Cong., House Committee on Appropriations 1955, p. 160).

In the congressional setting, no one bothered to correct Mary Switzer's economics. No one mentioned concepts such as the present value of $390 million; no one questioned whether it was worth more or less than the $39 million Congress would appropriate now. Nevertheless, Congress often challenged the figure itself, only to be reassured of its validity by Mary Switzer. "Everyone," she said, "is skeptical of this statement at first." To check the figure, she reported, the agency had met with the Treasury, and found that it held up (U.S. Cong., House Committee on Appropriations, 1955, p. 160). Because the congressmen were favorably disposed toward the program and eager to have a reason to appropriate money to it, they seldom pursued the matter beyond this point. Such subjects as the proper bureaucratic location for the program animated them far more than did the details of cost-benefit analysis. On occasion, however, a congressman stumbled upon a potential weakness of the analysis. Senator Dennis Chavez of New Mexico once raised the possibility that a rehabilitant might work for one day only, asking Mary Switzer if the program followed up on the work experience of rehabilitants. "We follow them up," she responded. "We have found over the years that the total group statistically works on the average of 85 percent of the time, which is pretty good" (U.S. Cong., Senate Subcommittee on Labor–Federal Security Agency Appropriations 1951, p. 393). Indeed, it was good, yet it rested on the thinnest of evidence. The appeal of rhetoric overcame all doubts. If something increased appropriations, then it worked, and the 10-to-1 figure worked.

In the early fifties, the program literature made almost constant reference to income taxes spent and saved. In 1953, for example, the program announced that "rehabilitation is more than an expenditure per se; it is an investment which produces tangible dollar returns, along with the human rewards." There followed an analysis of what had happened to the 60,000 people rehabilitated in 1952. Their earnings had increased from $17 million to $115 million. This group, it turned out, would pay $9 million in federal income taxes in the first year after their rehabilitation. Over the course of the next three years, they would completely pay for their rehabilitation, and during their lives they would return ten dollars in federal income taxes for every federal dollar spent on them (U.S. Cong., House Committee on Education and Labor 1953, p. 43). The President's Committee on Employment of the Physically Handicapped aggregated the numbers across the years. In the years between 1943 and 1955, 642,000 people were rehabilitated, increasing the national income by more than $3 billion and federal income tax revenues by more than $300 million (U.S. Office of Vocational Rehabilitation in cooperation with the President's Committee 1955, p. 7). Indeed, they had already paid for both the state and federal costs of the program. It made for a wonderfully felicitous calculus.

ANOTHER BENEFIT: ENDING DEPENDENCE

Impressive in itself, the 10-to-1 demonstration brought further benefits to the program when it was used in conjunction with another argument. As program advocates had always maintained, vocational rehabilitation transformed dependent individuals into self-supporting ones. The rehabilitants started as a net cost to society and ended as a net benefit. In the program's early years, the costs of dependency remained sketchy, as might be expected in a social welfare system that spread its programs between the public and private sectors and among the states, localities, and federal government. After the Second World War, however, these costs took the much more explicit shape of the federal-state public assistance program. Created in 1935, the public assistance program generated little controversy during the depression. After the war, however, people perceived a threatening paradox: welfare costs continued to rise even when the unemployment rate fell. The costs of dependency, as defined by the welfare program, became both more visible and more menacing (Berkowitz 1980a).

Such conditions suggested a natural comparison between the vocational rehabilitation approach, with its promise of returning ten dollars for every dollar spent, and the public assistance approach, with its continual debilitating demands on the public purse. The vocational rehabilitation program cost nothing, and in addition, it ended dependency. In the late forties and fifties, this latter feature became all the more appealing and received more frequent play from program officials.

Events strengthened this new item on the benefit side of the cost-benefit equation. The original federally assisted welfare categories included the blind, the elderly, and dependent children. In 1950, when the 10-to-1 figures began to appear frequently, Congress added a new category and began to pay welfare to the permanently and totally disabled. This action came in the middle of a protracted debate over the advisability of adding disability protection to the social security system. As the debate extended into the Korean War years, people questioned the need for handicapped people to be dependent on others when they could make obvious contributions to the war efforts. Each of these developments tended to make the problem of dependency more visible than previously (Berkowitz 1980a).

Responding to the heightened public awareness of dependency, Mary Switzer stressed the merits of rehabilitation. She often called rehabilitation "a philosophy of life," and she looked for trends that helped put social welfare policy into perspective. In 1953 she cited one such trend in a question she put before Congress. "Why do we have such a heavy relief load in most places in a period of high employment?" Part of the answer, Switzer believed, was that "a very large percentage of this welfare load of ours is due to neglected physical disability." True to the hardheaded tradition of humanitarianism in vocational rehabilitation, Switzer attached numbers to the statement. Counting the various programs, she arrived at a figure of $400 million a year to reflect the welfare-related costs of disability. That figure met only the very barest of needs (U.S. Cong., House Committee on Education and Labor 1953, pp. 9, 12).

Switzer emphasized that rehabilitation, by contrast, was "not a welfare program." It put people into jobs, rather than keeping them away from jobs. "That is the basis of it," she contended (U.S. Cong., Senate Subcommittee on Labor-Federal Security Agency Appropriations 1951, p. 393).

There followed increasingly elaborate estimates of the cost of public assistance matched with the now-standard estimates of the returns to vocational rehabilitation. In 1952, for example, the bill for public assistance came to $395 million, with Aid to Families of Dependent Children consuming the lion's share. The ADC payments created two sorts of burdens. They affected the physically disabled parent, and they spread their influence to the next generation of children who would grow up in a household marred by dependency. Children symbolized potential, and public assistance blighted that potential. The average payment for ADC amounted to $863 per family. Such expenses could continue for several years, possibly through the entire childhoods of a family. Rehabilitation, on the contrary, represented a one-time expenditure. "These facts are the simple arithmetic of rehabilitation," the federal office for vocational rehabilitation reported in 1952. "They are the hard dollar-and-cents realities which establish the . . . program on a sound economic basis" (U.S. Cong., House Committee on Education and Labor 1953, p. 37; U.S. Federal Security Agency 1952, p. 16).

On the state level, the process by which vocational rehabilitation saved money could be followed with special clarity. Officials could point to the program's accomplishments in a state such as Pennsylvania, which in the fifties maintained one of the nation's best vocational rehabilitation programs. In 1952 the Commonwealth of Pennsylvania rehabilitated 3,352 people. Of that number, 695 had been on public assistance. That meant they had received $762,684 annually in public assistance. Vocational rehabilitation ended that burden and substituted $1,406,912 for the previously negative earnings. As the state reported, "They were tax consumers through no fault of their own. Now they are taxpayers in their own right" (U.S. Cong., House Committee on Education and Labor 1953, p. 37).

It remained to determine the number of people nationwide who were removed from the public assistance rolls through rehabilitation, and by 1954 the program literature began to include that information. For fiscal 1953, one out of five disabled persons rehabilitated during the year was receiving public assistance at the time services were begun (U.S. Dept. of Health, Education, and Welfare 1954, p. 230).

Always sympathetic to the jargon of psychology, program officials portrayed the conditions of dependency in the darkest terms. At the least, dependency meant a loss of financial independence; in many cases, it led to far more serious problems. The individual on public assistance faced damaged morale and an impaired living standard. All too often, the final outcome was the "dissolution of the home and destruction of the family." The Office of Vocational Rehabilitation developed an elaborate illustration in a statement submitted to a congressional subcommittee in 1953. The statement first reflected "on the personal tragedy" that disability brought about "in one life." Then it shifted to consider the "by-products of disability," which followed one another in a kind of predetermined sequence: "Disablement is followed by loss of job, income, and savings." At this point the authors branched off from economic analysis into the realm of psychology: "As standards of living go down, emotional stress goes up. Other ills, physical or psychogenic, emerge in the family to complicate the initial disability. . . . Children deprived of the love and guidance of their parents find substitutes elsewhere—and society calls it delinquency. When the situation finally overwhelms the group, then welfare and other public agencies must take over . . ." (U.S. Dept. of Health, Education, and Welfare 1954, p. 229; U.S. Cong., House Committee on Education and Labor 1953, p. 35).

Nor would the problem go away. As the nation became older, it would face more and more problems related to dependency. Science produced wonderful gains over the course of the twentieth century, such as increasing the expected life span of an individual at birth from forty-nine to sixty-eight years, yet it also generated difficult quandaries. More older people meant more retired people, more dependent people. The ratio of productive to nonproductive workers would decline, and ever larger numbers of aged, chronically ill, and disabled people would have to be supported by those who worked. The taxpayers needed the sort of relief that rehabilitation could provide. They required the sort of technology that enabled people to be delivered from public assistance, workers' compensation, and the other public programs that threatened to grow at alarming rates. They needed to transform those dependents, remove them from institutions and other places of passivity, and convert them into taxpaying workers, allies in the struggle against dependency (U.S. Dept. of Health, Education, and Welfare 1954, p. 230).

CONCLUSION

The development of figures on dependency completed the weapons in the vocational rehabilitation arsenal and defined the terms of cost-benefit analysis until the revival of the Council of Economic Advisors and the beginnings of what might be called an econometric consciousness in the sixties. The cost side of the model remained undeveloped. The costs of the program were measured quite directly by formal program expenditures. The benefit side of the model exhibited a dynamic tendency to grow with the times. At first, benefits consisted of a worker's wages; by the fifties, the benefits had grown to encompass the income taxes paid by the rehabilitants and the welfare costs saved by the rehabilitants.

Modern observers might criticize the model on any number of grounds. To cite one obvious example, the program officials never tried to separate one rehabilitant from another. They assumed that public assistance recipients cost as much to rehabilitate and returned as much in income taxes as did other rehabilitants, yet they never tested that proposition. Working with broad averages, they lacked the technical means to complete the tests.

Before dismissing the early exercises in cost-benefit analysis as invalid or naive, however, one needs to consider their real purpose. The individuals who authorized these analyses did not seek to compare the program to similar public efforts; instead they sought to provide a rationale for their program that would demonstrate its worth and win congressional appropriations. In a more subtle sense, the demonstrations also formed a bridge between the psychologically and individually oriented process of casework and the necessities of public policy. Some programs that relied on casework, such as public assistance, lacked this sort of bridge and suffered in the appropriations process. Vocational rehabilitation grew at a much faster rate than many of its social welfare competitors. Without question, the cost-benefit demonstrations helped.

The usefulness of these calculations was underscored by Congressman Roy Wier of Minnesota, a member of a House special subcommittee looking into the vocational rehabilitation program and its needs in 1953. Congressman Wier indicated to the director of the program that it would "be well . . . if we had . . . an estimate of the people that are now drawing funds from some source because of the[ir] incapacitated condition, drawing them from relatives or drawing them from society somehow to live." The estimate would help to "substantiate the need for this program" because it could be used to demonstrate that "we will be money ahead if we can take these people off their present means of existence . . . and put them on a productive basis." Demonstrations of this kind, he observed, would enable officials "to sell this program," and to win congressional authorization for increased funding (U.S. Cong., House Committee on Education and Labor 1953, p. 27).

Congressman Wier clearly understood the exigencies of politics. Although the program continued to be run on the principles of psychological casework at the state level, it benefited at the federal level from the use of economic cost-benefit demonstrations. The analysis of dependency served to link the economic and psychological analyses to one another.

When statisticians tried to do a more modern form of cost-benefit analysis in 1966, therefore, they stepped into a program with its own set of traditions. On the one hand, program officials welcomed cost-benefit analysis and felt comfortable with it. It had, after all, served to show the program to best advantage. On the other hand, the program had developed its own form of cost-benefit analysis. This form of analysis reflected the policy environment in which the program had evolved and, while it met the needs of the program at different points in its history very effectively, it failed to keep pace with changes in the field of program evaluation. The HEW statisticians—and their successors—would have to cope with these contrasting dimensions of the legacy of cost-benefit analysis in the vocational rehabilitation program.

NOTES

1. For a general statement of the problems involved in cost-benefit analysis, see Berkowitz and Berkowitz 1983.

2. On the link between efficiency and social welfare, see Berkowitz and McQuaid 1980, Graebner 1980, and Wiebe 1967.

3. For more on these points, see Berkowitz and McQuaid 1980, and Patterson 1981.

4. For a description of the events that led up to the 1943 law, see Berkowitz 1980a.

5. On the methods of analysis used by the agency, see Office of Vocational Rehabilitation, "Processes Used to Derive Estimates of the Economic Value of the Vocational Rehabilitation Program," in U.S. Senate Subcommittee on Labor-Federal Security Agency Appropriations 1951, pp. 80–82.

6. On the 1946 Employment Act, see Graham 1974.

7. See also Walker 1985.

WORKS CITED

Berkowitz, Edward. 1980a. *Rehabilitation: The Federal Government's Response to Disability, 1935-1954.* New York: Arno Press.

———. 1980b. "Mary E. Switzer: The Entrepreneur within the Federal Bureaucracy." *American Journal of Economics and Sociology* 39:79-81.

Berkowitz, Edward, and Kim McQuaid. 1980. *Creating the Welfare State.* New York: Praeger.

Berkowitz, Monroe, and Edward Berkowitz. 1983. *Benefit-Cost Analysis.* Rehabilitation Research Review. Washington, D.C.: National Rehabilitation Information Center.

Graebner, William. 1980. *A History of Retirement: The Meaning and Function of an American Institution.* New Haven: Yale University Press.

Graham, Otis. 1974. *Toward a Planned Society.* New York: Oxford University Press.

Hughes, Jonathan. 1977. *The Governmental Habit.* New York: Basic Books.

Mars, Lawrence I. 1968. *An Exploratory Cost-Benefit Analysis of Vocational Rehabilitation.* Dept. of Health, Education, and Welfare. Rehabilitation Administration. Division of Statistics and Studies. Washington: GPO.

Patterson, James. 1981. *America's Struggle against Poverty.* Cambridge: Harvard University Press.

U.S. Dept. of Health, Education, and Welfare. 1954. *Report of the Department of Health, Education and Welfare, 1953.* Washington: GPO.

U.S. Federal Board for Vocational Education. 1921. *Annual Report, 1921.* Washington: GPO.

———. 1922. *Annual Report, 1922.* Washington: GPO.

———. 1926. *Annual Report, 1926.* Washington: GPO.

———. 1927. *Annual Report, 1927.* Washington: GPO.

———. 1928. *A Study of Rehabilitated Persons: A Statistical Analysis of the Rehabilitation of 6,391 Disabled Persons.* Civilian Vocational Rehabilitation Series 16, Bulletin 132. Washington: GPO.

———. 1931. *Annual Report, 1931.* Washington: GPO.

U.S. Federal Security Agency. 1946. *Annual Report of the Federal Security Agency: Section Three, Office of Vocational Rehabilitation, for the Fiscal Year 1946.* Washington: GPO.

———. 1947. *Annual Report of the Federal Security Agency: Section Seven, Office of Vocational Rehabilitation, 1947.* Washington: GPO.

———. 1948. *Annual Report of the Federal Security Agency: Office of Vocational Rehabilitation, 1948.* Washington: GPO.

———. 1952. *Annual Report of the Federal Security Agency: Office of Vocational Rehabilitation, 1952.* Washington: GPO.

U.S. House of Representatives. Committee on Appropriations. 1955. *Hearings on 1956 Appropriations for the Vocational Rehabilitation Program.* 84th Cong., 1st sess. Washington: GPO.

U.S. House of Representatives. Committee on Education and Labor. 1953. *Hearings Pursuant to House Resolution 115. A Resolution Authorizing the Committee on Education and Labor to Conduct Studies and Investigations Relating to Matters within*

Its Jurisdiction. Assistance and Rehabilitation of the Physically Handicapped. 83rd Cong., 1st sess. Washington: GPO.

U.S. Office of Vocational Rehabilitation. 1944a. *Charting the Way in Vocational Rehabilitation: A Progress Report.* Washington: GPO.

———. 1944b. *Annual Report for the Fiscal Year 1944.* Washington: GPO.

———. 1945. *Annual Report of the Federal Security Agency: Section Three, Vocational Rehabilitation, for the Fiscal Year 1945.* Washington: GPO.

———. 1948. "The Economic Value of Vocational Rehabilitation." Administrative Service Series, No. 9. Mimeographed.

U.S. Office of Vocational Rehabilitation in cooperation with the President's Committee on Employment of the Physically Handicapped. 1955. *Independence for the Handicapped: A Review of Progress in Rehabilitation and Employment of the Handicapped.* Mimeographed.

U.S. Senate. Subcommittee on Labor-Federal Security Agency Appropriations. 1951. *Appropriations for 1952.* 82nd Cong., 1st sess. Washington: GPO.

Walker, Martha Lentz. 1985. *Beyond Bureaucracy: Mary Switzer and Rehabilitation.* Lanham, Md.: University Press of America.

Wiebe, Robert. 1967. *The Search for Order.* New York: Hill and Wang.

2 William Milberg

WELFARE MEASUREMENT FOR COST-BENEFIT ANALYSIS

In his account of the history of cost-benefit analysis in the VR program, Edward Berkowitz demonstrated that the claims of a 10-to-1 ratio of benefits to costs proved an important part of the effort to justify the program to the legislature and the public. It is arguable that the effectiveness of this ratio as a means of promoting the program lay not only in the remarkable degree of success that the numbers seemed to indicate but also in the appeal to popular notions of cost and benefit: the "return" to the government on its "investment" in VR.

While such notions loosely describe contemporary cost-benefit analysis, developments in microeconomic theory have drawn attention to the difficulties surrounding the measurement of "returns." On the most basic level, theoreticians have emphasized the importance of distinguishing gains in individual welfare from gains in social welfare. The increase in an individual's earning capacity attributable to the receipt of VR services is not necessarily the best measure of the benefits such services bring to society. For example, a $300 annual increase in earnings may be much more beneficial to a client who earned $8000 annually before receiving VR services than it would be to a client with a $28,000 annual income. Or, to two clients with the same income, a $300 annual increase may not bring an equal increase in capacity to enjoy life. In this case the simple summation of all individual income increases attributable to VR would be a misleading measure of the increased welfare of society. Thus, although income changes resulting from the provision of services are easily observable, they are problematic as a proxy for the benefits to society.

Even in economic theory, however, the measurement of welfare raises logical problems in relation to both individual and social welfare measurement. In this chapter I outline these theoretical problems and evaluate recent attempts by economists to find solutions for them. Thus, while most of the chapters in this volume take issue with the techniques used to measure VR benefits, this chapter offers a critical appraisal of the theory underlying the analysis of benefits. By pointing up the pitfalls of welfare measurement that exist at the conceptual level, I hope to show that contemporary cost-benefit analysis is far from perfect and that research must continue in the areas of pure theory and the link between theory and practice. While applied work in cost-benefit analysis may be guided more by operational needs than theoretical concerns, practitioners of cost-benefit analysis should be motivated to seek a logically consistent welfare measure. Recognizing the theoretical shortcomings of current practices in cost-benefit analysis is a step in the right direction.

The discussion of welfare measurement entails some consideration of fundamental concepts in economic theory. The basic unit of analysis is the rational individual, whose preferences (or tastes) are assumed given (exogenous) to the economic problem. The analysis of the benefits of consumption of a good (or service, such as VR services), must take into account the subjective preferences of the consumer. For well over a century, the theory of individual consumer demand has been used to measure the benefit to an individual of consuming a good or a service such as VR. Consumer surplus, as this measure became known, was based on the idea that consumption will not occur if the price exceeds the benefit of even the "last unit" of the good consumed. This benefit of the last unit is called the marginal utility in consumption; it is assumed to decline as consumption increases.

If VR services were paid for by clients, then the amount the consumer would be willing to pay for the services presumably would reflect the consumer's benefit (welfare or utility) from "consuming" the last amount of VR services. If somehow this willingness to pay for VR could be revealed, then a dollar amount could be placed on the individual's valuation of the benefit from the services. Benefits could be weighed against costs. The model developed by Duncan Mann in Chapter 4 is based on an approach of this kind.

This chapter is divided into three sections. The first introduces the measurement problems in detail and emphasizes the importance of considering theories of individual and social welfare. The second will focus on individual welfare measurement and the theoretical problems associated with it, concluding with a discussion of some recent innovations in consumer theory that overcome or bypass these problems. The last section treats the problem of aggregating preferences over individuals to measure social welfare. The chapter concludes with an examination of the apparent popularity among cost-benefit analysts of one rule over all others.

THE SCOPE OF THE MEASUREMENT PROBLEM

The most general method of aggregating individuals' welfare changes is the social welfare function, introduced by Abram Bergson (1938) and developed later by Paul Samuelson (1950). The general form of this function is that social welfare (W) is a function of the utility levels of all individuals (U_i, where $i = 1$ to n):

(1) $W = F(U_1, U_2, \ldots, U_n)$.

To determine the change in social welfare, we take the total differential of the social welfare function:

(2) $dW = (\partial F / \partial U_1)dU_1 + (\partial F / \partial U_2)dU_2 + \ldots + (\partial F / \partial U_n)dU_n$.

In the equation above, the dU_i expressions are the changes in individual welfare described as the first part of cost-benefit analysis. The partial derivatives $\partial F / \partial U_i$ ($i = 1$ to n) can be seen as weights applied to each individual welfare change. The weights determine, in a sense, how much value society places on each individual's welfare. Depending on these weights, the specific social welfare function could take on vastly different forms. To render the social welfare function operational, the policy maker must specify both the functional form of the social welfare function and the values of the parameters (for example, weights) of that function.

While it is a normative task to specify individuals' weights in the social welfare function, this specification does not solve all the cost-benefit analyst's problems. We still must measure the individual consumer's welfare changes attributable to, say, a change in income due to VR services. Recall the decomposition of the change in social welfare, equation (2). The dU_i terms are the changes in individuals' utility. This term can itself be dissected, since an individual's direct utility is a function of commodity consumption:

(3) $U_i = U_i(X_{i1}, X_{i2}, \ldots, X_{in})$,

where X_{ij} refers to consumption of commodity j by individal i. Totally differentiating (3) gives an expression for the change in individual welfare when consumption changes:

(4) $dU_i = (\partial U_i / \partial X_{i1})dX_{i1} + (\partial U_i / \partial X_{i2})dX_{i2} + \ldots + (\partial U_i / \partial X_{in})dX_{in}.$

The Bergson-Samuelson view is to ignore this decomposition and look at dU_i as a single quantity to be measured. Another view of dU_i, however, shows the importance of its decomposition. In (3) we express utility as a function of commodity consumption; such a function is known as the direct utility function. Alternatively, we can express utility as a function of prices and income by replacing commodities with demand functions for them. This form is known as the indirect utility function:

(5) $V_i = V_i(p_1, p_2, \ldots, p_n, I_i)$

Substituting the individuals' indirect utility functions for the direct utility functions in the Bergson-Samuelson social welfare function (1) gives the following:

(6) $W = G(V_1(P, I_1), V_2(P, I_2), \ldots, V_n(P, I_n)),$

where P is a vector of all prices, and I_i is individual i's income.

Using this formulation of the social welfare function, we can express the change in social welfare due to a change in, say, income as follows:

(7) $dW = (\partial G / \partial V_1)(\partial V_1 / \partial I_1)dI_1 + (\partial G / \partial V_2)(\partial V_2 / \partial I_2)dI_2 + \ldots + (\partial G / \partial V_n)(\partial V_n / \partial I_n)dI_n.$

Comparing (7) to (2), we see that in (7) we are no longer obligated to measure individual welfare changes. The expression $(\partial G / \partial V_i)/(\partial V_i / \partial I_i)$ is the marginal social welfare change from a $1.00 change in individual i's income. Like the weights, $\partial F / \partial U_i$, in (2), the marginal social welfare change requires a normative judgment of the benefit to society of changing an individual's income. But in (7), the remaining problem is dI_i, compared to dU_i in (2). Since utility changes generally are not comparable across individuals (as discussed below), whereas income changes clearly are, the formulation of social welfare change in (7) simplifies the problem. While the normative dimension remains, the task of the cost-benefit analyst is reduced to finding monetary measures of the effect of a project on individuals. I will explore in some depth the alternative monetary measures available to the practitioner of cost-benefit analysis in the following section.

INDIVIDUAL WELFARE MEASUREMENT

Cardinal versus ordinal utility and welfare analysis

A cardinal magnitude is a variable whose measurement permits arbitrary choice only of zero-point and unit interval. An ordinal ranking is weaker than a cardinal ranking. That is, if a consumer prefers consumption bundle A to consumption bundle B in an ordinal ranking, we have no idea of the intensity of preference for A over B. A cardinal ranking specifies the exact amount by which bundle A is preferred to bundle B. Temperature is an example of a cardinal measure; Celsius and Fahrenheit scales differ, but only in the zero point and unit interval (Hirshleifer 1976). The original marginalists, such as Carl Menger (1871) and Leon Walras (1874), viewed the utility function as a way of measuring individual well-being in cardinal terms. But Pareto (1896) and Fisher (1930) recognized that cardinal utility was not necessary to a theory of demand. This argument was clearly put forth by J. Hicks in his 1937 book, *Value and Capital.* Hicks showed that all the results of utility maximization could be generated through ordinal utility only, without assuming cardinal utility.

What meaning does the ordinal/cardinal distinction have for cost-benefit analysis? Ordinal utility functions require the development of a scale, a way of measuring preferences of different people in common units. Since we cannot measure utility directly, we must find an indirect method of measuring individual intensity of preference for or against a change in economic conditions. Such measures would provide a foundation for cost-benefit analysis and be consistent with modern consumer theory.

The evolution of consumer's surplus

Before defining the Hicksian measures of individual consumer welfare, let us first discuss the traditional, and still most popular, measure—consumer's surplus. Even today, most cost-benefit analysis is largely an extension of work on consumer's surplus done by the engineer Jules Dupuit in the 1840s (see Dupuit 1844) and Cambridge economist Alfred Marshall at the turn of the century (Marshall 1890).

Dupuit's famous 1844 article, "On the Measurement of Utility of Public Works," was the first recognition that the price paid for a good is, generally, not equivalent to the value of the good to the consumer. Jean-Baptiste Say had earlier argued that price equals the average utility from consuming the goods. But Dupuit claimed the price represents not the average utility of consuming the goods but the utility gained in consumption of the last unit of the good, that is, the *marginal utility.* Dupuit assumed that individuals' preferences exhibited diminishing marginal utility. Since in the market, in the absence of price discrimination, a uniform price is charged on all goods, the price paid by the consumer represents the utility to that consumer of the last unit purchased. For other units the consumer would theoretically have been willing to pay more than the market price. Thus actual expenditure understates the total utility in consumption.

Dupuit's understanding of price as marginal, as opposed to average, value led to an interpretation of the demand curve as the marginal willingness-to-pay curve. That is, the price associated with any quantity on the consumer's demand curve is the maximum amount the consumer is willing to pay for the last unit consumed. From this, the notion of a consumer's surplus, the basis for much of contemporary applied welfare analysis, follows almost trivially. It is the aggregate of satisfaction, in dollars, achieved from the consumption of a quantity of a good, less the dollars spent to purchase this quantity.

Problems with consumer surplus

Consumer surplus is a valid measure of welfare change only under very restrictive conditions. Specifically, consumer's surplus will not always be well-defined in cases when the price of more than one good changes or when prices and income change. That is, we may generate different values for consumer surplus depending on *the order* in which we consider the various price and income changes. Consumer surplus may be sensitive to the "path of adjustment." This is the so-called path dependency problem (Just, Hueth, and Schmitz 1982).

If many prices change, the condition for the uniqueness of consumer's surplus is that the impact of the price change of good A on the demand for good B be equal to the impact of the price change of good B on the demand for good A (that is, equality of cross-price effects). When many prices change simultaneously, this condition must hold for all pairs of goods in order to obtain a unique measure of consumer's surplus. This condition is equivalent to the condition that all income effects be equal for those goods whose prices change.

The important issue is whether these elaborate conditions ever hold in the real world or whether they are approximately true. The answer is of course an empirical one, but the evidence to date is overwhelming that income effects are significantly positive and that income elasticities of demand are different for different goods. One recent contribution to the debate concludes, "Generally, the conditions for uniqueness of consumer surplus change may be so restrictive as to be unrealistic in many cases" (Just, Hueth, and Schmitz 1982, p. 80).

The nonconstancy of the marginal utility of income thus renders consumer's surplus imperfect as a measure of individual welfare change. Using consumer's surplus for this purpose is, according to Eugene Silberberg, "using the inappropriate to measure the undefinable" (1978, p. 362).

Willingness-to-pay measures of individual welfare change

In the 1940s the British economist John Hicks proposed four measures that, while still not directly linked to utility, are a direct reflection of consumer preferences. Hicks's measures are based on the concept of willingness-to-pay, that is, a monetary equivalent of the consumer's preference for or against a change in economic conditions (that is, prices and/or income).

The *compensating variation* (CV) is the change in income necessary to compensate the consumer exactly for the loss of utility due, say, to a price increase. The *equivalent variation* (EV) is the amount of income that would have to be taken from the consumer to make the consumer as well off after a price decrease.

The CV and EV can be derived using the expenditure function, also known as the cost-of-utility function. The cost-of-utility function is derived by determining the minimum expenditure (at a given set of prices) required to attain a certain level of utility. The cost-of-utility function, $E = E(P, U_0)$, thus determines, *in dollars,* how much money is needed for the consumer to attain a fixed level of satisfaction, given prices. This concept lends itself nicely to welfare analysis. The CV and EV can be calculated as the difference between two expenditure functions. That is, let P_0, U_0 be initial prices and utility conditions, and P_1, U_1 be price and utility conditions following a public investment project like VR. Then $EV = E(P_0, U_1) - E(P_0, U_0)$ and the CV $= E(P_1, U_0) - E(P_0, U_0)$ (Varian 1978).

Hicks defined two other willingness-to-pay measures of welfare change. The *compensating surplus* (CS) is defined as the increment of a single commodity that could be removed from the new consumption bundle such that the consumer would be indifferent between the modified bundle and the original bundle. The *equivalent surplus* (ES) is the increment of a single commodity that must be added to the original bundle, such that the consumer would be indifferent between the modified bundle and the new bundle (Hause 1975).

Considerable debate exists over the relative merits of the four Hicksian measures. One problem of the CS and CV measures is that they are based on the original consumption bundle and measure the money (in the case of CV) or amount of the good (in the case of CS) required to reach the new level of welfare. As a result, two different original consumption bundles that lie on the same indifference curve will bring different measures of the money or the goods needed to achieve a new welfare level. The equivalence of these measures depends on the significance of income effects. Income effects are the changes in consumption due to changes in income (which, in turn, may be due to price changes). Thus, when there are no income effects, CV = EV = consumer surplus. However, when income effects are positive, CV < consumer's surplus < EV (Varian 1978). In this case CV and EV are preferable to consumer's surplus because of the path dependency problem described above. The choice between CV and EV theory depends on whether it is more appropriate in a particular case to look at the amount the consumer would be willing to pay for a good or service (EV) or the minimum acceptable amount required to dissuade the consumer (as, for example, a VR client) from seeking the good or service (CV).

Recent innovation in welfare measurement

Robert Willig has attempted to develop bounds on the difference between the consumer surplus measure and the accurate measure of welfare change as measured by the EV or CV. Willig's article, "Consumer Surplus Without Apology" (1976), is now commonly cited as support for the use of uncompensated demand curves in applied welfare analysis. According to Willig:

> These bounds can be explicitly calculated from observable demand data, and it is clear that in most applications the error of approximation will be very small. In fact, the error will often be overshadowed by the errors involved in estimating the demand curve. . . . The results in no way depend upon arguments about the constancy of the marginal utility of income. (p. 58)

The derivation of the error bounds is mathematically complex. Basically, Willig has developed bounds that, if not exceeded, allow us to use the consumer's surplus measure with some confidence that our measurement does not diverge greatly from the CV and EV measures.

Willig argues that only in rare cases will such percentage error bounds be exceeded. But his approach has other limitations. For one, his formula assumes that the change in real income due to a price change will be a very small fraction of total income. Moreover, if the income elasticities of demand used in the formula are correctly estimated, such estimation is of a full system of demand equations. But if information exists to estimate a full system of demand equations, then the CV and EV can be calculated directly and do not have to be approximated.

While Willig's approximations have been taken as a justification for continued use of consumer's surplus in applied welfare analysis, Yrgo Vartia (1983) recently developed an algorithm for calculating compensated income (and thus CV and EV) in terms of direct demand functions. Vartia relies on the assumption that the integrability conditions hold. These commonly assumed conditions on preferences allow us to posit the existence of a well-behaved utility function. But instead of proceeding to discover this underlying function (often an impossible algebraic task), Vartia develops an algorithm to calculate directly the compensated income levels needed to make an "exact" measure of welfare change due to a change in economic conditions. This makes possible the calculation of CV and EV for classes of preferences previously excluded from applied welfare analysis. Vartia notes that the approach allows the assumption of an explicit parametric form of the utility function to be dropped. "Our paper makes it possible to work with and estimate more general forms of demand functions, adjust the estimated functions to satisfy the integrability conditions . . . in the relevant region, and carry out arbitrary ordinal welfare comparisons in this region" (pp. 92–93). This is a significant breakthrough because specific functional forms require very restrictive assumptions, such as the absence of income effects (for example, a Cobb-Douglas constant returns to scale or a constant elasticity of substitution function).

To summarize, recent efforts to use observable phenomena to calculate accurate welfare change measures have gone in two directions. Willig derived error bounds for consumer surplus as an approximation of EV or CV. Vartia, in perhaps a more fundamental innovation, found an algorithm for deriving compensated income (and thus CV and EV) from observable price and quantity data without integrating back to the explicit utility function. Use of Vartia's algorithm in the analysis would allow us to reach an unambiguous (ordinal) measure of the impact of VR services on individual clients. Unfortunately Vartia's innovation has not to date been introduced in applied welfare systems.

SOCIAL WELFARE MEASUREMENT

Aggregation for cost-benefit analysis

If the optimal measure of individual welfare is in dispute, even greater controversy exists over the method of aggregating individual welfare changes to measure changes in social welfare. At the level of individual welfare, consumer's surplus serves as a kind of benchmark to which other measures are compared. Analogously, social welfare measures are commonly compared to the principle of Pareto optimality (see, for example, the presentation in Feldman 1980).

Pareto optimality is defined as a state where no individual can improve his or her welfare without someone else's welfare being reduced. When Pareto optimality is used as a criterion for evaluating the merits of public investment (such as funding the VR program), it supports the selection of those investments that increase the welfare of at least one individual without leaving anyone else worse off.

The main weakness of the Pareto principle is that it does not provide a basis for comparing different Pareto optimal points. Generally, a decision rule that can judge the merits of all possible alternatives is called complete. The Pareto principle does not satisfy the completeness property.

In an attempt to overcome this shortcoming of the Pareto principle, Kaldor (1939) and Hicks (1939a) developed the compensation principle as a basis for social welfare decisions. The compensation principle states that a social investment should be undertaken if individuals' gains from the project exceed individuals' losses. That is, a project should be undertaken if the "winners" (those who gain from the project) could *compensate* the "losers" (those made worse off with the project) and still, after paying compensation, be better off than they would have been without the project. The Kaldor-Hicks (K-H) criterion is thus known as the compensation principle. With respect to VR, this would imply that the welfare gains made by recipients of VR services (and by those nonrecipients whose welfare increases) exceed the welfare loss suffered by members of society who bear part of the cost of the program but receive neither direct nor indirect benefits.

The link between the compensation principle and the Pareto principle is important. The compensation criterion says that a social program should be adopted if gainers could potentially make losers as well off as they would have been without the project and still be better off themselves. Appropriately, the compensation criterion is also known as the potential Pareto improvement criterion. As Hicks and Kaldor defined the criterion, whether compensation actually occurs is irrelevant. The cost-benefit analyst should, according to this rule, only point out the *potential* superiority of one state over another, not recommend that the movement to that state be made or not. If compensation takes place, then we have a Pareto improvement. The term *state* is used to describe a given situation or "state of the world." For example, one state might be the status quo. Another state might be the status quo with the exception of a much larger VR program than exists at present.

T. Scitovsky (1941) pointed out that the K-H criterion leads to reversals of social choice. That is, if state A is superior to state B by the K-H criterion, then once the move to A is made, it is possible for state B to be superior by the same criterion. The reversal arises because the status quo is compared to *all* allocations attainable from the alternative state. Scitovsky attempted to overcome the reversal problem by establishing a criterion whereby A is superior to B if A is superior to B by the K-H criterion and B is *not* superior to A by the K-H criterion.

Yet both the Scitovsky criterion and the K-H criterion it was designed to modify have been criticized on the grounds that they may lead to intransitive ranking of alternatives. That is, it is possible for A to be preferred to B and B to be preferred to C, but for C to be preferred to A (see Arrow 1951, Phlips 1974, and Sen 1970).

Paul Samuelson (1950) criticized the K-H and Scitovsky criteria essentially on these grounds and proposed an alternative. Samuelson said that even if the gainers could compensate the losers and the losers could not then profitably bribe the winners to reverse the project (that is, the K-H and Scitovsky criteria are satisfied), then we can still not determine the preferred alternative. What is required is not to compare all accessible bundles from one allocation to another bundle but to compare all accessible bundles from one allocation with all those accessible from the other allocation. Samuelson used the concept of the utility possibility frontier, or the locus of combinations of levels of utility in a given state of the world. By Samuelson's definition, an unambiguous social choice could be made between alternatives only if all the utility possibilities attainable from one state are preferred to all utility possibilities attainable from the alternative state. If the utility possibility frontiers cross, then there exist accessible distributions in each state of the world superior (by the Pareto criterion) to distributions in the other state of the world, and thus no clear superior state exists.

Figures 2.1A and 2.1B illustrate Samuelson's argument. In Figure 2.1A, b is superior to a according to the Scitovsky criterion. Samuelson calls this a "false" result because there are points on each frontier superior to some points on the other frontier. To Samuelson, the only satisfactory definition of a social improvement (in his words, "an increase in real national income") is when the utility possibility frontier is above the other frontier, as shown in Figure 2.1B. Samuelson's finding dealt another blow to the attempt to establish objective criteria for social decision making.

Which criterion for cost-benefit analysis?

Cost-benefit analysis is sometimes taken to be synonymous with the application of the K-H criterion. As we have seen, this criterion is not above criticism. Yet it is simple to apply and it is complete—that is, all alternatives can be compared. The Scitovsky and Samuelson criteria do not give much more information than the Pareto criterion, which was criticized for failing to satisfy the condition of completeness. Moreover, we saw that the social welfare function, while theoretically most general, is difficult to apply in practice because of the problematic issue of the appropriate weights. As a result, the K-H criterion is often adopted for cost-benefit analysis.

We saw that on a purely logical level, the K-H criterion suffers from potential reversals. Obviously a cost-benefit analyst should not recommend that a massive program like VR be undertaken or even enlarged and then, upon futher analysis, recommend that it be dismantled. But also from a

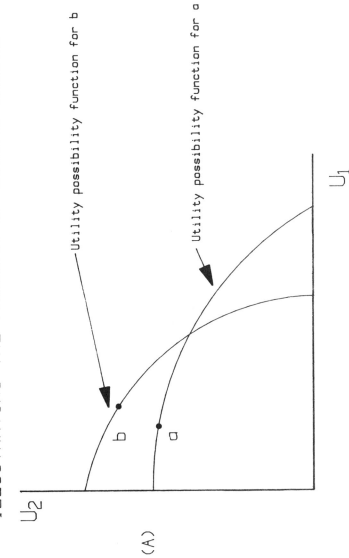

FIGURE 2.1A
UTILITY POSSIBILITY FUNCTIONS
ILLUSTRATING THE PROBLEM OF SOCIAL CHOICE

Utility possibility function for b

Utility possibility function for a

U_2

U_1

b

a

(A)

FIGURE 2.1B
UTILITY POSSIBILITY FUNCTIONS
ILLUSTRATING THE PROBLEM OF SOCIAL CHOICE

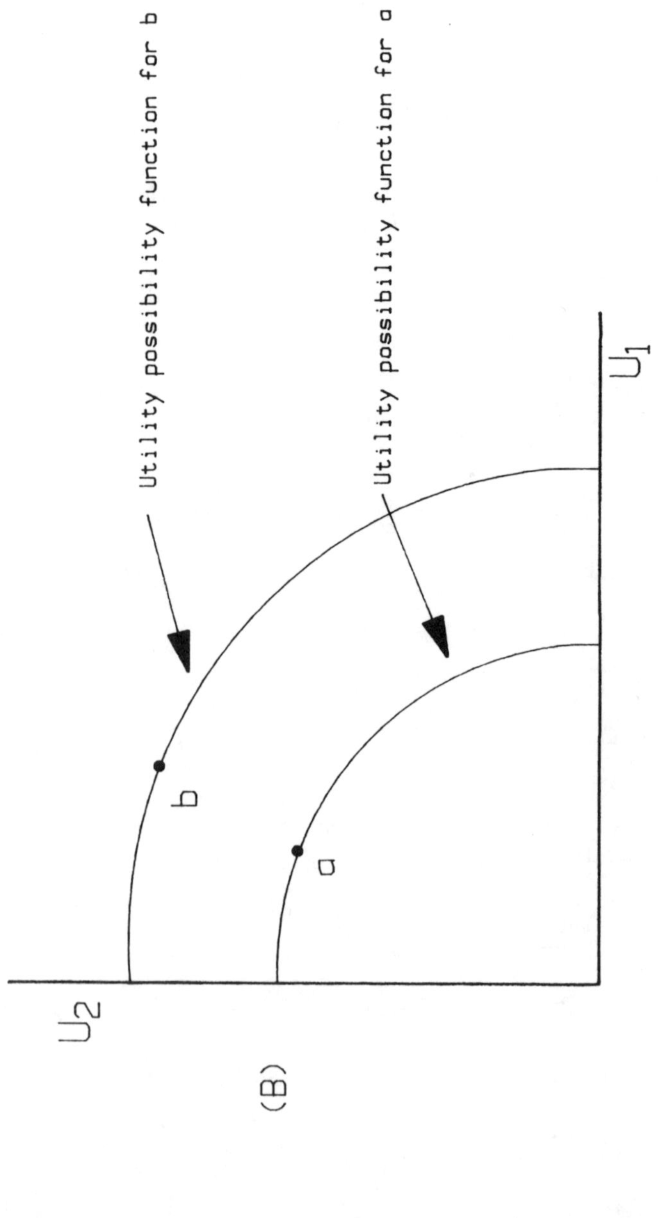

normative viewpoint, the potential Pareto improvement criterion has been criticized for ignoring the distributional impact of public investment. That is, it may rank state A over B despite the fact that the distribution of income among individuals under state A is much less egalitarian than under state B. The consideration of the distributional impact of government programs is a much-debated issue among cost-benefit analysts.

A strong tradition holds that distributional considerations are outside the proper scope of cost-benefit analysis. This view is perhaps most explicitly presented by Harberger in his article, "The Three Postulates of Applied Welfare Economics: An Interpretive Essay" (1971). The third postulate states: "when evaluating the net benefits or costs of a given action (project, program or policy), the costs and benefits accruing to each member of the relevant group (e.g. a nation) should normally be added without regard to the individual(s) to whom they accrue (p. 785)." Harberger's argument for ignoring distributional considerations is based less on logic than on tradition and pragmatism. He claims: "The three basic postulates . . . provide a de minimus answer to this need: their simplicity, their robustness and the long tradition that they represent all argue for them as the most probable common denominator on which a professional consensus on procedures for applied welfare economics can be based (p. 796)."

According to Harberger, economists are no more (or less) qualified than anyone else to make distributional value judgments. This point seems to confuse the issue, however. Economists would unanimously agree that the normative issue of a *desirable* income distribution is a societal question. Nevertheless, economists are the best qualified to estimate the distributional impact of public investment. Thus, although economists should not impose their own judgments, they should help policymakers formalize their distributional goals.

Walter Hettich (1976) and others have argued that there is no theoretical basis for ignoring distributional issues in cost-benefit analysis. Harberger implicitly assumes that the marginal utility of income is the same for all individuals. Such an assumption is difficult to accept in a model based on individualism and consumer sovereignty. Harberger has also argued that the distributional impact of a given public project is usually so small compared to the income level of affected people that such distributional consequences can be ignored without altering the cost-benefit analysis. But Hettich insists that the analyst cannot make this assumption without prior empirical analysis.

Thus the K-H criterion, because it considers only *potential* welfare gains, ignores the distributional effect of projects. For example, while a $1 billion government subsidy program to aid the automobile industry may bring greater societal welfare gains than a $1 billion increase in funding for the VR program, the distribution of gains and losses from expansion of the VR program may be much more egalitarian than that from the auto industry subsidy. If compensation is not paid by those who gain from the auto industry subsidy to those who lose by it, then, unless decision makers value gains (losses) to all individuals as equally (un)desirable, this program may satisfy the potential Pareto improvement criterion and yet emerge as socially less desirable than the VR program funding increase. Of course, if income transfers were costless, then the implicit distributional weights of the potential Pareto improvement criterion would be acceptable. Robin Boadway (1974) has, however, pointed out the difficulty (i.e. cost) of carrying out compensation. He argues that the solution to this difficulty is to analyze the same public investment project with and without compensation as two separate projects. Just, Hueth, and Schmitz (1982) agree with this view but, appropriately, see it as a distributional issue subject to normative judgments: "one of the problems with the principle is that it is based on potential rather than actual gains. Thus, in any policy context, the payment of compensation is a matter that must be decided by policy makers endowed with the authority to determine income distributional issues (p. 47)."

A final limitation of the K-H criterion, relevant to all the compensation criteria as well as the conception of the social welfare function advanced by Bergson and Samuelson, is its inclusion of *individuals' valuations* exclusively. Government decisions will in some cases override individuals' valuations. The concept of merit goods (or bads) is an attempt to deal theoretically with this phenomenon. VR services are perhaps an example of a merit good. Even if a proposal for investment in the VR program were rejected under the K-H criterion, such a cost-benefit analysis could be deemed irrelevant because of the simple imposition by society of certain "consumption patterns." Of course, even these paternalistic social values change over time, as evidenced by the constantly changing emphasis in government spending on the provision of certain social services.

Despite the limitations of the K-H criterion, it has become the starting point for cost-benefit analysis. Its prominence is largely attributable to its conceptual simplicity, its link to willingness-to-pay measures of individual welfare change, and, perhaps most important, the lack of a viable alternative. The social welfare function, of which the K-H criterion could be considered a particular form, simply was never developed into a useful tool of applied analysis.

CONCLUSION

This chapter has surveyed the microeconomic foundations of benefit, or welfare, measurement for individuals and groups of individuals. These concepts are implicit in much cost-benefit analysis of social programs such as VR. My aim has been to make the conceptual framework explicit in order to increase the precision of welfare measurement in future evaluation of social investment programs. The approach is choice-theoretic, in that it is based on individual utility-maximizing agents *choosing* consumption patterns when faced with different constraints. We saw that individual welfare measurement based on the concept of consumer surplus is problematic because of the path dependency problems, but recent theoretical innovations have attempted to overcome these deficiencies.

Perhaps more crucial for the cost-benefit analyst are the problems inherent in the process of measuring *social* welfare. We reviewed a number of the criteria that have been proposed in the economics literature, each of which has advantages and disadvantages. All of these decision rules are related to the Pareto criterion, which designates an allocation optimal if no change exists that can increase at least one individual's welfare without reducing another's welfare. An important distinction was drawn between potential and actual compensation. While in theory, potential compensation may be adequate to justify a policy, in practice, a policy that does not compensate the losers cannot be considered equivalent to a policy in which the aggregate of individual gains outweighs losses.

The basic problem is how to aggregate the welfare changes of many individuals resulting from, say, a policy change. Inevitably, society decides the relative emphasis placed on welfare gains for one individual (or group of similar individuals) as opposed to another individual. That is, distributional impacts of projects or policy changes must be accounted for in some fashion. This problem is embodied in the specification of the social welfare function. Thus, while the introduction of an explicit social welfare function into applied cost-benefit analysis may be controversial, it would clarify the link between the practice of cost-benefit analysis and policy decision making.

WORKS CITED

Arrow, Kenneth. 1951. *Social Choice and Individual Values.* Cowles Commission Monograph, no. 12.

Bailey, Martin, Mancur Olson, and P. Wonnacott. 1980. "Marginal Utility of Income Does Not Increase: Borrowing, Lending, and Friedman-Savage Gambles." *American Economic Review* 70:372-79.

Bergson, Abram. 1938. "A Reformulation of Certain Aspects of Welfare Economics." *Quarterly Journal of Economics* 52:310-34.

Boadway, Robin. 1974. "The Welfare Foundations of Cost Benefit Analysis." *Economic Journal* 84.336:926-39.

Chipman, John, and James Moore. 1980. "Compensating Variation, Consumer's Surplus and Welfare." *American Economic Review* 70:933-49.

Dupuit, Jules. 1844. "De la mesure de l'utilité des travaux publics." *Annals des Ponts et Chaussées* 2d ser. 8.
Feldman, Alan. 1980. *Welfare Economics and Social Choice Theory.* Boston: Martinus Nijhoff.
Fisher, Irving. 1930. *The Theory of Interest.* 1st ed. New York: Macmillan; New York: Augustus M. Kelly, 1970.
Friedman, Milton, and L. Savage. 1948. "The Utility Analysis of Choices Involving Risk." *Journal of Political Economy* 56:179-304.
Gorman, W. 1955. "The Intransitivity of Certain Criteria Used in Welfare Economics." *Oxford Economic Papers* 7.1:25-35.
Harberger, Arnold. 1971. "Three Basic Postulates of Applied Welfare Analysis: An Interpretive Essay." *Journal of Economic Literature* 9.3:785-97.
Hause, John. 1975. "The Theory of Welfare Cost Measurement." *Journal of Political Economy* 44:1154-78.
Hettich, Walter. 1976. "Distribution in Benefit-Cost Analysis: A Review of Theoretical Issues." *Public Finance Quarterly* 4.2.
Hicks, John. 1939a. "The Foundations of Welfare Economics." *Economic Journal* 49.196:696-712.
———. 1939b. *Value and Capital: An Inquiry into Some Fundamental Principles of Economic Theory.* Oxford: Oxford University Press.
———. 1941. "The Rehabilitation of Consumer's Surplus." *Review of Economic Studies* 8:112.
Hirshleifer, Jack. 1976. *Price Theory and Applications.* Englewood Cliffs, N.J.: Prentice-Hall.
Just, Richard, Darrel Hueth, and Andrew Schmitz. 1982. *Applied Welfare Economics and Public Policy.* Englewood Cliffs, N.J.: Prentice-Hall.
Kaldor, Nicholas. 1939. "Welfare Propositions of Economics and Interpersonal Comparisons of Utility." *Economic Journal* 49.195:549-52.
Marshall, Alfred. 1890. *Principles of Economics.* London: Macmillan; 8th ed. Philadelphia: Porcupine Press, 1920.
Mckenzie, George. 1983. *Measuring Economic Welfare: New Methods.* Cambridge: Cambridge University Press.
Menger, Carl. 1871. *Grundsatze der Volkswirthschaftslehre.* Translated as *Principles of Economics.* Trans. James Dingwall and Bert F. Hoselitz. New York: New York University Press, 1970.
Mishan, Edwin. 1982. *Cost-Benefit Analysis.* 3d ed. London: George Allen & Unwin.
Pareto, Vilfred. 1896. *Cours d'economie politique.* Vol. 2. New York: Augustus M. Kelly, 1971.
Phlips, Louis. 1974. *Applied Consumption Analysis.* Amsterdam: North-Holland Publishing Co.
Samuelson, Paul. 1950. "Evaluation of Real National Income." *Oxford Economic Papers* 2.1:1-29.
Scitovsky, Tibor. 1941. "A Note on Welfare Propositions in Economics." *Review of Economic Studies* 9.1:77-88.
Sen, Amartya. 1970. *Collective Choice and Social Welfare.* Edinburgh: Oliver & Boyd.
Silberberg, Eugene. 1978. *The Structure of Economics: A Mathematical Analysis.* New York: McGraw-Hill.

Sugden, Robert, and Alan Williams. 1978. *The Principles of Practical Cost-Benefit Analysis.* Oxford: Oxford University Press.

Tresch, Richard. 1981. *Public Finance: A Normative Theory.* Plano, Tex.: Business Publications.

Varian, Hal. 1978. *Microeconomic Analysis.* 1st ed. New York: Norton.

Vartia, Yrgo. 1983. "Efficient Methods of Measuring Welfare Change and Compensated Income in Terms of Ordinary Demand Functions." *Econometrica* 51.1:79–98.

Walras, Leon. 1874. *Eléments d'économie politique pure.* Translated as *Elements of Pure Economics.* Trans. William Jaffe. London: Richard D. Irwin, 1954.

Willig, Robert. 1976. "Consumer's Surplus without Apology." *American Economic Review* 66.4:589–97.

3 *John D. Worrall*

BENEFIT AND COST MODELS

Benefit-cost analysis of the federal-state vocational rehabilitation (VR) program has become a virtual cottage industry. There have been dozens of such studies in the last two decades, including a number which have appeared in the economics literature. These studies have differed markedly in the sophistication of their designs. This chapter reviews the analytical models used in benefit-cost evaluation of the VR program and examines some of the weaknesses of these models.

Specifically, I focus on two types of problems: measurement problems specific to the vocational rehabilitation program, and the generic problem of assessing the effects of a program on its participants in a nonexperimental context. Ideally, researchers who seek to evaluate the benefits of program participation should be able to compare the experience of clients who have undergone treatment with the experience of a control group. Estimates of the impact of treatment on future wages of VR clients should be used with caution when the subjects under study have not been randomly assigned to treatment and control groups.

Let us begin discussion of the difficulties of benefit-cost evaluation by considering the implicit designs of some of the studies of the federal-state programs. We then can proceed to contrast these models with the methods that have been recommended or applied in the evaluation of other remedial manpower programs.

THE IMPACT OF VR TREATMENT ON FUTURE WAGES

Consider a group that enters a rehabilitation program at some time (0). Assume that there are J people in the group. We observe the wages of that group at time (0) and again at some fixed point in time, (0 + k), after the application of the treatment. (a) Suppose the wage of the ith individual at time (0 + k) is greater than at (0);

$$(1) \quad W_{i0+k}^T > W_{i0}^T$$

can we deduce that the exposure to the VR program caused a wage gain? (b) Or, if the sum of the differences between wages at closure (0 + k) and at opening (0) is positive,

$$(2) \quad \sum_{i=1}^{J} W_{i0+k}^T > \sum_{i=1}^{J} W_{i0}^T$$

can we be reasonably certain that exposure to the treatment caused the wage gain? Obviously there are a host of reasons why we cannot. For example, the wages of the group may have grown over time without the application of treatment.

Suppose we attempt to guard against this obvious threat to validity by examining the wages of another group of size J that was not exposed to the treatment. We might contrast the wages of the treatment group at time (0 + k) (W_{0+k}^T) with the wages of the comparison group at the same point in time (W_{0+k}^c). If we observe that

$$(3) \quad \sum_{i=1}^{J} W_{i0+k}^T > \sum_{i=1}^{J} W_{i0+k}^c$$

we still could not be certain that the treatment caused higher wages. It might be that the wages of the treatment group (W_0^T) at time (0) were greater than those of the comparison group (W_0^c) at the same point in time. We might postulate that the wages of the comparison group were lower than those of the treatment groups at time (0) and (0 + k) because of some unchanging characteristic (such as gender) of both groups. Perhaps we could control for this unchanging characteristic or fixed effect, as well as for the effect of the passage of time, with some differencing technique,

$$(4) \quad \sum_{i=1}^{J} (W_{i0+k}^T - W_{i0}^T) - \sum_{i=1}^{J} (W_{i0+k}^c - W_{i0}^c)$$

such as that given in (4), where the difference in differences might be attributed to the treatment effect. The choice of (2), (3), or (4) as an estimate of wage gain reflects the researcher's belief about the nature of the decision made by the treatment and comparison groups to participate in the VR program,[1] and the time path of wages.

RANDOM ASSIGNMENT

If eligible applicants for VR services were randomly assigned to a treatment group (T) or a control group (C), then the decision to participate would truly be controlled and the two groups could be considered homogeneous. The wage gain, if any, estimated by (3) above would serve as the true measure of treatment effect at time $(0 + k)$.[2] In such a researcher's paradise, it would appear that all of our measurement problems would be solved.

Although random assignment, and hence participation, is the ideal, access to social service programs in general, and the VR programs in particular, is not granted on the basis of the desires of program evaluators. Denial of service on such bases might be unethical. I suggest some "moral" designs below, but first let's consider some potential problems with measurement even with random assignment.

The population served by the VR program is a young one. It is not unusual to find a rehabilitant in her twenties who leaves the program at time $(0 + k)$. She may have a life expectancy of more than fifty years, the bulk of which she may choose to spend in the labor force. Suppose her wage is typical of the rest of her treatment group and we can use it as the mean of the other $J - 1$ subjects. If her wage at time $(0 + k)$, $(\overline{W}_{0+k}^{T})$ exceeds that of the mean of the control $(\overline{W}_{0+k}^{c})$, we still do not know if or how long the effect of the treatment will last. Our data is right censored. The time paths of W^{T} and W^{C} may converge, diverge, or continue along parallel paths. (See Figure 3.1.[3]) In Figure 3.1, we use t* as the end of the treatment period and $(0 + k)$ as the time at which group wage differences are measured. In many studies of the VR program, the elapsed time from the end of treatment to the time of measurement of the wage gap $(0 + k) - (t*)$ is either sixty days (recent studies) or thirty days (older studies). Suppose we assume that the wage gain will remain constant from $(0 + k)$ to $(0 + r)$ where r is the date of retirement. How do we value the aggregate wage gain over this time period? What interest rate do we use to discount this gain to present value? We do not know with perfect certainty.

We might also question whether the control group had been contaminated (see Orr 1983) by exposure to the agency (VR) administering the treatment. I shall return to these and related issues below.

MORAL DESIGNS

Although services currently are not denied on a random basis, clients who are found eligible for VR services can be randomly assigned to different treatments, and the efficacy of the VR program can be analyzed. Clients

FIGURE 3.1

WAGE TIME PATHS

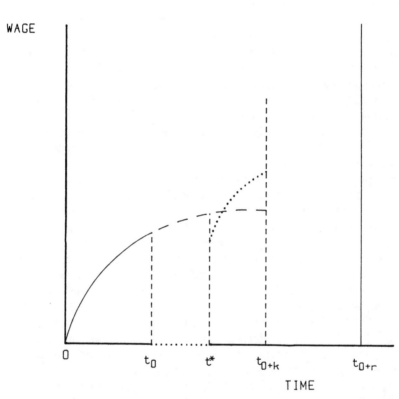

WAGE

0   t_0 t^* t_{0+k} t_{0+r}

TIME

⟋   = both treatment and control (equal by random assignment)

⋰····   = treatment, assumed zero during the period of treatment

⟋ ⁻   = control, assumed to have an aggregated time effect

t_0 = beginning of treatment

t^* = end of treatment

t_{0+k} = end of observation period

t_{0+r} = retirement

could be assigned to the treatments by a disinterested third party or university group. Treatment groups might consist of:

Group 1 = Federal/state program
Group 2 = Private rehabilitation practices
Group 3 = Voucher tied to purchase of rehabilitation services
Group 4 = Cash payment equal to an estimate of the value of foregone service.[4]

Although such a design would provide a rudimentary measure of the *relative* efficiency of the VR program, many problems in addition to the time path of wages measurement problem would remain. The gains from the program are not limited to the pecuniary ones. Researchers have not been successful in measuring psychic gains from the program (see Cardus, Fuhrer, and Thrall 1982). A design that allowed those eligible for services to purchase them would yield the *rehabilitation client's* evaluation of the monetary equivalent of the pecuniary and nonpecuniary gain associated with the program.

If group 4 were given the cash equivalent of foregone services and denied service, a fifth group could be given the same payment and given no instruction about what to do with their cash award. Subjects in different, *randomly* chosen areas could be presented with price schedules for various rehabilitation services that are designed to derive demand schedules for such services. The cost of this design would be miniscule in comparison with the cost of the income maintenance experiments or the billions of dollars that have been spent in the federal/state VR program since its inception.

It is not clear that random denial of services need be immoral. It has never been established, in any scientific sense, that the VR program is cost-beneficial, or that the individuals who participate in the program actually have their productivity (and wages), health status, or net utility increased by program participation. There is evidence that the program is cost-beneficial, in an intuitive sense, from the perspective of program participants. Millions of people with work disabilities have revealed their preference by program participation. Their expected utility gains outweighed the opportunity cost of their time. Society, in some loose sense, has also revealed its preference, through its elected representatives and their willingness to support the program over time.[5]

NONRANDOM ASSIGNMENT

Much of the research that has been done has been directed toward determining an absolute benefit-cost ratio for the VR program. The program evaluators have never had the luxury of a randomly assigned treatment and control group; hence, they have had to resort to nonexperimental designs in their attempts to fashion comparison (or quasi-control) groups. Some of these quasi-controls have been quite crude when gauged against the potential threats to internal and external validity.

I shall follow Bassi (1984, pp. 36–43) and LaLonde (1984) and set out a simple taxonomy of estimates of treatment effects, specification, and assumptions. I shall consider the principal findings of LaLonde's comparison of these estimators with known treatment effects, Bassi's suggested statistical tests and findings, and Long, Mallar, and Thornton's application (1981) of one of the techniques to an evaluation of the Job Corps. The problem is to estimate *one* of the benefit components in a benefit-cost analysis of the VR program, wage gain. The primary difficulty is that we do not know if program participation is random. Rehabilitation clients may differ in both observed characteristics (such as gender) and unobserved characteristics (such as the propensity to return to work after multiple nonwork spells). Program participation may vary systematically with these characteristics. Such characteristics may be fixed or may change over time. The specification that is chosen will affect the properties of the estimators.

LaLonde has demonstrated that most of the specifications considered below provide poor estimates of the treatment effect, especially for males, of the National Supported Work Demonstration. Nonexperimental methods generally understated the value of the treatment effect for males, frequently producing negative estimates of wage gain when the wage gain was actually positive.[6] The nonexperimental methods provided more accurate estimates of the treatment effect for women, but the range was quite wide depending upon the comparison group and the earnings and participation specification chosen.[7] We turn to LaLonde's model of earnings and participation.[8]

Suppose we hypothesize that an individual's earnings at time t depend upon whether that individual received vocational rehabilitation services (V_{it}) at time j, and a set of exogenous characteristics (X_{1it}). We could specify this earnings equation as:

(5) $Y_{it} = \beta_1 X_{1it} + \delta V_{it} + \epsilon_i + \epsilon_t + \epsilon_{it}$

where ϵ_i is an individual fixed effect

ϵ_t is a time specific effect

and ϵ_{it} is a serially correlated error, with

(6) $\epsilon_{it} - \rho\epsilon_{it-1} = \nu_{it}$, $E(\nu_{it}) = E(\nu_{is}\,\nu_{it}) = 0$, and $E(\nu_{it}^2) = \sigma^2$

and s denotes pretreatment time.

Suppose that we further hypothesize that participation in the VR program is a function of a set of exogenous variables, X_{2it}, and current and past income. We could specify the participation equation as:

(7) $V_{it} = \beta_2 X_{2it} + \lambda_0 Y_{it} + \ldots + \lambda_g Y_{it-g} + \Upsilon + \eta_{it}$

   where Υ is an individual fixed effect,

   and η_{it} is a serially uncorrelated error, with

   $E(\eta_{it}) = E(\eta_{is}, \eta_{it}) = 0, E(\epsilon_{it} \eta_{it}) = 0.$

(8) If $^vis \leq v$, $V_{it=1}$ for $t \geq j$, and $V_{it=0}$ for $t \leq j.$

   If $^vis \geq v$, $V_{it=0}$ for all t.

Both LaLonde (pp. 16-17) and Bassi (p. 37) assume either the absence of serial correlation or a first order autoregressive scheme. LaLonde makes explicit the assumption that η_{it} and v_{it} are uncorrelated for the cases he considers. Bassi warns her readers that the first order autoregressive scheme may be too simple to capture the unobservables. Finally, LaLonde notes that X_{1it} or a subset may be in X_{2it}, and that the participation variable is probably a reflection of supply and demand interaction.[9]

AGGREGATE AND INDIVIDUAL DATA

The need for aggregate data—summary or mean data of all cases—or individual data for the measurement of wage gain and for VR benefit-cost analysis depends upon the structure given in (5)-(8) above. Any attempts to estimate the treatment effect with econometric techniques, given nonrandom program participation, require individual client and control observations.

Many of the earliest studies of the VR program adopted the estimator given in (2) above. They assumed that program participation was random, or that if it were nonrandom it was a function of an individual fixed effect—that is, an individual-specific unchanging component of the error term. Rewriting (2), for convenience, in terms of earnings and dividing by J, will yield

(2') $\overline{Y}_t^T - \overline{Y}_{j-1}^T$

as the estimate of earnings gain attributable to the program, given the assumptions above. The Federal Board for Vocational Education adopted this estimator in its 1926 *Annual Report,* with the *further assumption that* $\overline{Y}_{j-1}^T$ *and the social rate of discount were zero.* This, however, was followed rapidly by federal evaluations that not only attempted to control for $\overline{Y}_{j-1}^T$ but also were concerned with the time path of wages.

The Federal Board's 1931 *Annual Report* measured the earnings change from opening (1920-1924) to the 1927-1931 period. The Board did not assume that Y_{j-1}^T was zero, and they examined changes in unemployment over time. This measurement of wage gain for *specific individuals* over such a long period of time has not been duplicated, and the mapping of the time paths of individual earnings was unmatched until the SSA-RSA data-link studies of the 1970s. (See discussion of the data-link studies below.) Although the 1931 *Annual Report* showed insight into the problem of the time path of wages and attempted to control for fixed effects,[10] it did not allow for the wage gain that might occur independently of the program with the passage of time (aggregate time effect).

It still implicitly adopted (2). If the board had extended its concern with the time path of wages to a comparison group and allowed earnings to be a function of an aggregate time component, they would have had (4') as their estimate of the program's effect.[11]

Rewriting (4) for convenience, with the necessary aggregations and divisions, will yield

(4') $(\overline{Y}_t^T - \overline{Y}_{j-1}^T) - (\overline{Y}_t^c - \overline{Y}_{j-1}^c)$

the difference in differences (see LaLonde, p. 18) that, together with more elaborate specifications, has been the basic model of more recent benefit-cost studies of the VR program. These efforts have been ad hoc attempts to get estimators in the (4') family. Typically, as a control group is not available, investigators will attempt to adjust the Y^T stream to net out Y^c.

The work of Ronald W. Conley (1965, 1969) has served as the basis for most of the VR benefit-cost studies of the last two decades. The most sophisticated extensions are currently being used to evaluate various state VR programs. Perhaps the most widely used extension of Conley's model applied to aggregate data is the Berkeley Planning Associates (BPA) model developed by Frederick C. Collignon and his associates.[12] The BPA model reduces the stream by adjusting wages at opening by one-third to reflect transitory low-wage effects and then reduces the benefit attributable to the program by 20 percent to capture a portion of the change in earnings streams that was not caused by the program. The earnings stream is projected using age-earnings profiles constructed from census data. Gains attributed to the program are also subject to a decay function. The BPA model is used to estimate a benefit-cost ratio for the entire program as well as for various aggregate subgroups. Numerous adjustments are made to the benefit and cost estimates in order to provide realistic estimates, and the adjustments are subjected to sensitivity analysis.

Cardus, Fuhrer, and Thrall (1982) adopt the methodology of the BPA model for estimating the monetary portion of benefits and costs of the VR program. However, the authors propose the more ambitious analysis of all benefits—monetary and nonmonetary. In defining such nonmonetary benefits, they point out that those who receive the VR treatment may have improved physiological, psychological, and interpersonal functioning (BEN 2), and that the program may promote independent living (BEN 3). They propose measuring BEN 2 by observing the change in a group of items on the Minnesota Functional Assessment Inventory (FAI) and BEN 3 by observing the change in a group of items on the Life Functional Index (LFI). Identifying BEN 1 as the monetary benefit of VR, they want to map the net benefit flow from BEN 1, 2, and 3 into a single number (see Cardus, Fuhrer, and Thrall 1982, pp. 11, 15–17; and Cardus, Fuhrer, and Thrall 1980, pp. 29–41, 63–71). The authors suggest using the program manager's value judgments to determine the weights necessary to map the net benefit vector into the single value number.

Bellante (1972) used data from the R-300 tapes to compute earnings gains. The R-300 tapes are computer tapes containing data drawn from the case service records of all clients of the federal-state VR program. Bellante regressed the earnings gains on a set of socioeconomic variables in order to produce estimates of stratified benefits. Worrall (1978) used a similar method to arrive at benefit-cost ratios stratified by the age, disabling condition, and race of the program participants. Worrall used a crude method in an attempt to construct a quasi-comparison group and control for time effects. He used the mean wages of all those who had wages before the VR treatment and were either accepted or rejected for treatment. He estimated that mean wages were one quarter higher than median wages. He used the mean wages to construct cross-section age-earnings profiles, controlling for education, sex, race, and disabling condition. Using a method introduced by Becker (1964) and applied by Conley (1969), Worrall dynamized these cross section *pretreatment* age-earnings profiles. He followed the same procedure to construct posttreatment age-earnings profiles. However, he used *median* wages to adjust the posttreatment flows to further reduce gains attributable to the program. He regressed the difference in the present value of the earnings streams on a set of socioeconomic variables to retrieve estimated benefit variables for stratified benefit-cost ratios.

Each of the studies of the VR program discussed above was hampered by its lack of a control group. Methodologically, all were seriously flawed. The BPA studies and the Worrall paper, for example, all but explicitly stated the belief that the program participation decision and earnings function were related through both fixed effects and transitory components of income. The BPA group offered the transitory income components explanation as part of the rationale for adjusting wages at opening. Without control groups and micro data, neither the BPA nor the Worrall paper could have instrumented the VR participation variable or controlled for it through elaboration of specifications in the (4′) family. LaLonde reviews these specifications, so we can be brief in our discussion of them here.

With individual observations on both a treatment and comparison group, (4) can be specified as

(4A) $Y_{it} - Y_{is} = \partial V_{it} + \beta_1(X_{1it} - X_{1is}) + (\epsilon_{it} - \epsilon_{is})$

This specification allows for the fixed effect and its negative correlation with V, as well as an aggregate time effect and changes in exogenous characteristics between the pretreatment and posttreatment period. Unrestricted versions of (4A), such as

(4B) $Y_{it} = \partial V_{it} + \beta_1 X_{1it} + R_1 X_{2is} + B_3 Y_{is} + \epsilon_{it}$ or

(4C) $Y_{it} = \partial V_{it} + \beta_1 X_{1it} + B_3 Y_{is} + \epsilon_{it}$

can also be estimated. Choosing (4B) allows for the impact of a transitory component of income on participation, and (4C) extends this to control for the impact of exogenous factors in the program participation decision. LaLonde has demonstrated that consistent estimates can be retrieved with (4B) and (4C). (See LaLonde pp. 22–30.) LaLonde has also demonstrated that consistent estimates of the treatment effect can be retrieved from the reduced form (4D) or with instrumentation of the treatment variable from structure (4E).

(4D) $Y_{it} = \partial V_{it} + \beta_1 X_{1it} + R_1 X_{2is} + B_3 Y_{is} + \epsilon_{it}$

(4E) $Y_{it} = \partial V_{it} + \beta_1 X_{1it} + \epsilon_{it}$

There has been one study of the treatment effect of the VR program that had individual data on the treatment and comparison groups. The Rutgers University Bureau of Economic Research drew a random sample of those who were referred to or applied for services but did not receive such services. The sampling frame was the New Jersey Federal-State R-300 tape of 1975 fiscal year case service records. The Bureau hired rehabilitation counselors, who were employed by the New Jersey program, to interview the sample of those who did not receive services. All interviews were conducted after the counselors' normal working hours.

Nowak (1983) used the Rutgers interview results, the Survey of Health and Work Adjustment, to form a comparison group to contrast with a treatment group drawn from a random sample of New Jersey clients who received services and were closed in fiscal year 1975. To estimate the treatment effect, she estimated the parameters of

(9) $Y_{it} - Y_{is} = \partial V_{it} + \beta_1 X_{1it} + (\epsilon_{it} - \epsilon_{is})$.

This attempt to estimate the effect of the VR program represented an improvement over earlier studies, but even this specification can lead to both biased and inconsistent parameter estimates, if the error structure and participation decision assumption is incorrect.

If Nowak believed that participation was random after controlling for a set of exogenous characteristics, she could have simply regressed Y_{it} on V_{it},

X_{1it}, and ϵ_{it}. If she believed that there was a fixed effect, she could have used the specification given in (4A) above, and then only age need appear in the X vector. Suppose there are no higher-order age effects and age is a good instrument for the change in age, then using Nowak's specification would be equivalent to estimating (4A), and the rest of the X vector should have no influence on the change in earnings. Nowak does not report joint F statistics but does report individual t statistics. When she discounts earnings flows at 10 percent, two of her four age variables and two of the eleven other variables in X are significant. With a 5 percent discount rate, three of the age dummies, and only one of the remaining eleven dummies are significant. Nowak does not believe that the participation decision is random (see Nowak, p. 23); however, she did not attempt to estimate the specifications given in (4B) to (4E), although data were available for some tests.

The Survey of Health and Work Adjustment did not have information on at least one key variable, disabling condition. Consequently, Nowak omitted this variable from her regressions.[13] Worrall (1978), using maximum likelihood techniques, found a significant relationship between seven of the eleven disability conditions he studied and the successful completion of the program. If the participation decision varies systematically with the disability condition, and there are transitory income effects, estimation of specification (4C), (4D), or (4E) with data from the Survey of Health and Work Adjustment may not be possible without the disability condition variables.

Worrall (1976) also tested the hypothesis that application for VR treatment varied systematically with disabling condition. He found that seven of the eleven disabling condition variables were significant in a probit analysis of the probability of application for VR services. In general, he found that the incremental probability of application varied directly with expected wage gain. His right-hand-side variables, with the exception of the disability conditions, were nearly identical with those used by Nowak in her 1983 study.

Bassi (1984) suggests that the fixed effects model (4A) above is not likely to hold for the Comprehensive Employment and Training Act program (CETA). Her observation can be readily extrapolated to the vocational rehabilitation program. She pointed out that there may be self-selection into the CETA program on the basis of nonconstant unobservables—for example, failing health. Or there may be creaming—the selection of the easiest cases— as administrators have incentive to choose those with negative transitory error terms (see Bassi, p. 37). Worrall and Berkowitz (1975) have found that the probability of acceptance into the VR program varies systematically with age, the unemployment rate, referral source, and disabling condition. Nine of eleven disability variables were significant in their probability of acceptance runs. Given this kind of evidence, it is difficult to believe that participation is random.

Bassi (1984) suggests a hierarchy of tests to be used when estimating treatment effects in the face of nonrandom selection. She recommends starting with the estimation of

(10) $Y_{is} = X_{is}\beta + V_{it}\beta_s + \mu_{is}$

with β_s providing a test of the correlation between participation and the error term and a Chow test providing a test of earnings function structure. If these preprogram random effects tests are passed, that is, $\beta_s = 0$ and the earnings functions of the treatment and comparison groups are the same in the absence of the treatment, then the VR treatment effect could be estimated with a random effects model. Simply estimating (5) with ordinary least squares would yield maximum likelihood estimates (see Bassi, p. 38). If the tests are failed, a fixed effects model might be appropriate.

Bassi then applied the same tests to a fixed effects model. She conducted her error and structure tests with the base year one year before training and with the base year two years before training. This provided her with information on the incidence of creaming. If, as she found with her minority women sample, the error and structure tests can be rejected with a base period one year before training but cannot be rejected with the base period two years before training, there is reason to suspect creaming.[14]

Bassi integrated a first order autoregressive scheme into the fixed effects model (4A above) and illustrated a recursive scheme for retrieving point estimates of the treatment effect when creaming is present. The tests of homogeneous earnings function and common structure are also applied to this specification.

Long, Mallar, and Thornton (1981) retrieved structural estimates of the effect of Job Corps treatment on earnings. (See model 4E above.) They chose their comparison group in a way that enabled them to identify the participation decision. They began by attempting to limit treatment contamination. They eliminated geographic areas that were near treatment centers or where program publicity, outreach, and recruitment were strong. They then matched the characteristics of program sites and comparison sites and drew a random sample of the comparison sites. Finally, they selected a sample of individuals who were similar to program participants but who had never applied to the program.[15] They were able to use distance from the treatment centers, knowledge of the program, and access to publicity to identify the participation decision.

THE SOCIAL SECURITY ADMINISTRATION-
REHABILITATION SERVICES ADMINISTRATION DATA-LINK:
SUGGESTED MODELS OF TREATMENT MEASUREMENT

The SSA-RSA Data-Link provided the data that would have made it possible to estimate models in the (4') family above. Unfortunately, such estimation was not undertaken, the data-link has been discontinued, and the data-link computer tapes are not available. I shall briefly describe this merger of client records and suggest how it could be reinstituted and applied to systematic VR program evaluation.

The data-link involved a comparison of the R-300 case service records of those who were closed in fiscal year 1971 with the Social Security Administration's Earnings Summary Record (ESR) and Master Beneficiary Record (MBR). The Rehabilitation Service Administration (RSA) provided SSA with a computer tape containing 756,716 FY 1971 records. SSA was able to match 639,900 of these to the MBR and ESR. Of those VR clients whose records were matched, 34 percent had completed the program successfully (closure status 26), 11.5 percent had been accepted for services but had not successfully completed the program (closure statuses 28 and 30), and 50.6 percent had not been accepted for services (closure statuses 00–08).[16] The ESR provided the history of wages and self-employment income reported to SSA, and the MBR provided a monthly record of cash benefits paid under the Old Age, Survivors, and Disability Insurance program (OASDI).

The data-link was used to contrast the wages and employment percentages of successful closures, nonsuccessful closures, and those not accepted for services. This research effort is summarized in two excellent articles by Joseph Greenblum (1977, 1979). SSA and RSA realized that the participation decision might not be random (see Greenblum 1977), but the participation decision was not explicitly modeled. Instead, the main focus of the analysis was shifted to comparisons of successful and nonsuccessful closures, on the assumption that a control would be provided by virtue of the fact that both groups were participants. This method may provide a partial control, but both groups have received the treatment, albeit with different intensities.

Some of the "nonsuccesses" may have received the full treatment and not been employed when their cases were closed. If they found employment subsequent to closure, no benefit would have been attributed to the treatment. In the data-link studies, the earnings from the year before referral, which varied for individuals, through 1972 or the year after closure, were used. RSA defined successful program completion as having been employed for thirty days or more.[17]

Greenblum realized that there were factors, some exogenous, that would affect the level of wages. He assumed that these factors were not as likely to affect the probability of employment. Consequently, not only were the level of wages of rehabilitation clients contrasted but the percentages employed were also contrasted. Greenblum (1979) also provided cross section age-earnings profiles by sex-race-education and by disability condition for both successful and nonsuccessful VR clients, as well as for those not accepted for services. Although interaction effects were considered in the data-link studies, no full multivariate analysis was undertaken.

IRS CONFIDENTIALITY AND PROGRAM EVALUATION

A new data-link would provide the data necessary to estimate models (4) through (4E) and to conduct the tests suggested by Bassi. However, SSA earnings records are subject to the confidentiality requirements of the United States Internal Revenue Service. These confidentiality requirements are designed to prevent the identification of any individual taxpayer. Models such as (4C), (4D), and (4E) require a full vector of X variables. Consider that the X vector might contain age, race, sex, education, marital status, family size, disability condition code, referral source, and the presence of severe or multiple disabilities. If these variables were cast as polytomies and an investigator were parsimonious, with six age, two race, two sex, five education, two marital status, three family size, eleven disability conditions, and five referral source categories, there would be 39,600 distinct combinations of these variables. Even at the national level, it would be highly likely that individual clients could be identified.[18] Individual state program evaluation by persons other than social security investigators would clearly violate IRS confidentiality requirements. However, estimation of fixed effects models such as (4A) and (4B) require only a few variables and are not likely to result in violations of the IRS confidentiality requirements.

Estimation of (4A) and its elaborators and their related tests suggested by Bassi (1984) would require only age and disability variables. For aggregate evaluation of the program, the age variable alone would suffice. The disability variables would enable benefit-cost ratios to be derived by disability group. Estimation of model (4B), which allows for both fixed effects and *transitory* error effects, requires no data on exogenous variables (other than the treatment) for an aggregate program evaluation. Provision of the age and disability variables would allow for stratified benefit-cost analysis.

In order to apply Bassi's test, the earnings data provided by the new data-link would have to be provided for a period beginning at least three periods before referral.[19] In addition, although few VR clients will exceed the earnings limits for the payment of Social Security taxes, if the earnings streams were provided on a quarterly basis, maximum likelihood techniques could be used to provide earnings estimates for the entire year.

Use of information from a data-link may obviate some of the problems in estimating the VR treatment effect; however, many problems and questions remain. I conclude with some of these.

SOME PROBLEMS AND QUESTIONS

We have seen that the data-link would allow us to apply econometric techniques to consider individual fixed effects, aggregate time effects, and transitory income effects. We can also test for the appropriateness of the models that we are using. However, the research of LaLonde should convince us that the application of these techniques is not foolproof. He found that they did not necessarily provide a good measure of the treatment effect. Bassi found that none of the models we could estimate without violating the confidentiality requirements was appropriate for an evaluation of the CETA treatment effect in white males. Although LaLonde's results with the National Supported Work treatment and Bassi's findings with her CETA treatment need not be generalizable, they should give us pause.

Nowak has come the closest to applying the method I recommend. She computed benefit-cost ratios using *some* of variable cost only. Casual observation suggests that if her denominators were leveraged to reflect the full cost of the treatment (that is, to arrive at average benefit-cost ratios), the benefit-cost ratios could fall below one. Even if modern econometric methods indicated that the benefit, as measured by the earnings gain, did not exceed the cost, we could not demonstrate that the program is not cost-beneficial from a social perspective. None of the methods suggested above provides for an estimation and valuation of full utility gains as a result of the treatment. Nonetheless, we should employ the methods suggested and contrast them with the estimates derived from the ad hoc methods employed by Conley, Bellante, Collignon, and Worrall.

Full benefit-cost analysis of the VR system may ultimately not be possible. We might consider turning to less ambitious program evaluation goals. Perhaps we should investigate the relative efficiency of the various state programs, examining what they achieved in the production of multiple outputs—for example, earnings, employment, and health—as compared with what they could have achieved if they had followed "best practice." The research of Cavin and Stafford (1985) on frontier production and cost functions and their application to an evaluation of the Employment Service (ES) points the direction for such work.

NOTES

1. I use the decision to participate as if it were a utility-maximizing choice on the part of a person with a work disability. Actually, the process is far more complicated because it also involves a decision on the part of a helping professional (that is, a program counselor) to accept the client for services.

2. And we could apply the classical statistical tests of the difference in means of the two groups, calculate confidence intervals for the wage gains, etc.

3. Many subjects earn wages while receiving the rehabilitating "treatment." I show the typical age-earnings profile in Figure 3.1, that is, concave. LaLonde (1984), using the National Supported Work Demonstration data, found wage gaps that decreased from t* to (0 + k).

4. If those in group 4 received a cash payment of $10,000 each and were not

permitted to participate in the VR program, they would provide a measure of a pure income effect.

5. I realize that for individuals participating in the program, expectations are frequently not met. Fully one-third are not successfully closed, for example. Hence, "participation" cannot be used as proof that the program is cost-beneficial. Similarly, the fact that a coalition of voters or legislators reveal their preference for a program cannot be used as a proof of its cost-beneficiality without additional knowledge. (See Chapter 2 in this volume.)

6. The mean earnings gain measured from experimental data was $886 with a standard error of $476. (See LaLonde 1984, Table 2-8, p. 45.) Hence, the 95 percent confidence interval includes zero (−$46 treatment effect $1,818). However, many of the estimators from the econometric techniques were large and negative. These nonexperimental estimates ranged from −$15,578 to $1,466. (See LaLonde's Table C.1, p. 68).

7. The mean earnings gain measured from experimental data for females was $851, with a standard error of $307. (See LaLonde 1984, Table 1.8, p. 22.) The 95 percent confidence interval for the treatment effect is ($246 treatment effect $1,456). Nonexperimental estimates of the treatment effect ranged from $3,575 to −$3,363 with 95 percent confidence intervals of ($3,023 treatment effect $4,130) and (−$3,993 treatment effect − $2,733), respectively. These confidence intervals have been derived from LaLonde's Table 1.8. The figure there for the highest estimate differs by $3 from that reported in his Table C.1 (p. 68).

8. I have changed the notation slightly. See LaLonde (1984, p. 16).

9. Although the Arkansas R & T Center has done work on client-counselor interaction, I know of no benefit-cost analysis of the VR system that has modeled the applicant and gatekeeper side. The analysis usually proceeds with the implicit assumption of a utility-maximizing process on the part of the applicant. Attempts to make this process explicit and to specify a model have been very sophisticated. See Crawford and Killingsworth (1984).

10. Edward Berkowitz discusses this and other earlier efforts herein in Chapter 1, "The Cost-Benefit Tradition in Vocational Rehabilitation."

11. Formula (3) above rewritten as (3′) would be $\overline{Y}_t^T - \overline{Y}_t^c$. Although (3′) allows for the aggregate component, it assumes that participation is random.

12. See Frederick C. Collignon, Richard B. Dodson, and Gloria Root (1977) for a clearer exposition of the model.

13. See Yatchew and Griliches (1985) for a discussion of specification error in probit models.

14. See Bassi (1984), p. 40, and Table 1.

15. Mallar (1979) outlines the design, estimation technique, some econometric issues and results.

16. The remaining 3.9 percent were for clients whose closure status was unknown. See Greenblum (1979), p. 37.

17. Crawford and Killingsworth (1984) suggest a model that takes advantage of information on the intensity of the treatment to measure the impact of the VR program.

18. If a dummy variable for the state general program were included, there could be far more unique variable combinations than VR clients in any individual year.

19. Bassi (1984) used Y_{it-3} as an instrument for Y_{it-1} to eliminate correlation with V_{it} and Y_{is} in her fixed effects model with a first order autoregressive scheme. It is crucial to have a good instrument to begin to solve her model recursively; see her footnote 9.

WORKS CITED

Bassi, Laurie J. 1984. "Estimating the Effect of Training Programs with Non-Random Selection." *The Review of Economics and Statistics* 66.1:36-43.

Becker, Gary S. 1964. *Human Capital.* New York: National Bureau of Economic Research.

Bellante, Donald M. 1972. "A Multivariate Analysis of a Vocational Rehabilitation System." *The Journal of Human Resources* 7:226-41.

Cardus, David, Marcus J. Fuhrer, and Robert M. Thrall. 1980. *A Benefit-Cost Approach to the Prioritization of Rehabilitation Research.* Report Grant HEW 12-P-59036/6-03. Houston: Institute for Rehabilitation Research, Baylor College of Medicine.

———. 1982. *A Benefit Cost Model for the State Vocational Rehabilitation Program.* Houston: Institute for Rehabilitation and Research, Baylor College of Medicine.

Cavin, Edward S., and Frank P. Stafford. 1985. "Efficient Provision of Employment Service Outputs: A Production Frontier Analysis." Princeton: Mathematica Policy Research. Mimeographed.

Collignon, Frederick, Richard B. Dodson, and Gloria Root. 1977. "Benefit-Cost Analysis of Vocational Rehabilitation Services Provided by the California Department of Rehabilitation." Berkeley, Ca.: Berkeley Planning Associates.

Conley, Ronald W. 1965. *Economics of Vocational Rehabilitation.* Baltimore, Md.: Johns Hopkins University Press.

———. 1969. "A Benefit-Cost Analysis of the Vocational Rehabilitation Program." *Journal of Human Resources* 4:226-52.

———. 1973. *The Economics of Mental Retardation.* Baltimore, Md.: Johns Hopkins University Press.

Crawford, David L., and Mark R. Killingsworth. 1984. "Toward a Strategy for the Measurement of VR Program Impacts." Revised. New Brunswick, N.J.: Rutgers University. Mimeographed.

Greenblum, Joseph. 1977. "Effect of Vocational Rehabilitation on Employment and Earnings of the Disabled: State Variations." *Social Security Bulletin* 40:3-16.

———. 1979. "Effect of Rehabilitation on Employment and Earnings of the Disabled: Sociodemographic Factors." *Social Security Bulletin* 42.8:11-37.

LaLonde, Robert J. 1984. "Evaluating the Econometric Evaluations of Training Programs with Experimental Data." Working Paper No. 183. Princeton, N.J.: Industrial Relations Section.

Long, D. A., Charles D. Mallar, and Craig Van Doren Thornton. 1981. "Evaluating the Benefits and Costs of the Job Corps." *Journal of Policy Analysis and Management* 1:56-76.

Mallar, Charles D. 1979. "Alternative Econometric Procedures for Program Evaluations: Illustrations from an Evaluation of Job Corps." *Proceedings of the Business and Economic Statistics Section.* American Statistical Association. Pp. 317-21.

Nowak, Laura. 1983. "A Cost-Effectiveness Evaluation of the Federal/State Vocational Rehabilitation Program—Using a Comparison Group." *American Economist* 27:23-29.

Orr, Larry L. 1983. "The Use of Experimental Methods to Evaluate Demonstration Projects." Presented at the 96th annual meeting of the American Economics Association, San Francisco, December 1983.

Worrall, John D. 1976. "Some Economic Aspects of the Vocational Rehabilitation Program." Ph.D. diss. Rutgers University.

———. 1978. "A Benefit-Cost Analysis of the Vocational Rehabilitation Program." *Journal of Human Resources* 13:285-98.

———, and Monroe Berkowitz. 1975. *Severe Disability and the Vocational Rehabilitation Program: Some Empirical Findings.* Washington, D.C.: WDIS, Inc. Mimeographed.

Yatchew, Adonis, and Zvi Griliches. 1985. "Specification Error in Probit Models." *Review of Economics and Statistics* 67.1:134-39.

4 Duncan Mann

A MODEL BASED ON INDIVIDUAL BEHAVIOR

This chapter develops a theoretical model of client participation and individual program design in a state vocational rehabilitation (VR) program. Both client and counselor are assumed to make choices that are in their own best interests—choices that will promote their individual welfare. This structure facilitates the empirical analysis of client and counselor decisions regarding program participation, the intensity and duration of services, and the like. The model provides a framework within which the measurement of the costs and benefits of a VR program can be better understood. To a large extent the discussion of client behavior builds upon unpublished work by Crawford and Killingsworth (1983).

The benefits from a vocational rehabilitation program are varied and difficult to measure. Better health and improved job skills for program participants are the obvious outcomes. In an important sense, however, gains in utility and productivity constitute a more appropriate measure of benefit: how much better off are individual VR clients, their friends and families, and society as a whole because of the services provided by the program? Enhanced health may allow clients to enjoy life more and directly increase their well-being. In addition, improvements in health and in the ability to function on the job may have an indirect effect by enabling clients to increase their earnings and raise their level of consumption. The relatives and friends of a client may also realize utility gains from VR program services to the extent that the improved health and functioning of the client are important to them. Healthy individuals who can perform satisfactorily in productive jobs are a benefit to society as a whole; they will require less supportive care, and their work or output is in itself valuable.

Capturing the direct effect of health gains on client welfare or any external benefits is exceedingly difficult if not impossible. Improved health may be very important to one person and only moderately so to another. Although quantitative measures of health gains for individuals may be derivable from data, the value of these improvements is subjective and summing these valuations across individuals problematic. This difficulty is similar to that encountered by the analyst in using the sum of changes in consumer's surplus as an indicator of social welfare—a problem that is discussed in Chapter 2.

In all, it may be significantly easier to estimate the impact of VR program services on an individual's productivity. Competitive labor markets can translate a client's productivity gains into higher wages and earnings. These income gains are measurable and, furthermore, can sometimes be legitimately construed as a direct measure of benefit and added across individuals as a measure of aggregate benefit (again, see Chapter 2).

The client population considered here includes individuals who satisfy two conditions: each individual has been accepted into the VR program and is slated to receive a specific set of individualized program services, and each carries out the agreement to begin the program. Individuals who have been accepted into the program but who for one reason or another have not received any program services constitute a "control group." This collection of individuals provides a population with observable and unobservable characteristics that closely approximate those of the client population. The benefits of program participation that arise from increased productivity or wage income can then be isolated by subtracting the wage gains of the control group from the wage gains of the client population.

It should be noted that such a control group is not the ideal since there is presumably something that differentiates this group from the client population. If there is an unobservable systematic difference between these two groups, our measurement of benefits could be poor. It is the case, however, that individuals are identified with the control group for a variety of reasons. Individuals who have been accepted into a VR program often do not receive services because of random events such as a move out of state. The data need to be analyzed carefully for any suspected unobservable differences.

The difficulties of extracting consistent, unbiased estimates of a treatment effect with nonrandom assignment are discussed in Chapter 3. My approach here is evolutionary regarding this issue in that I believe the control group identified is a distinct improvement over past studies.

A client's decision to begin a VR program implies that the expected utility of participation is greater than the client's status quo position or reservation utility level. Furthermore, since a client does not bear the actual cost of program services, he or she has greater reason to believe that the benefits of participation will be positive. The utility consequences of particular employment situations will vary with the individual client. The transition from sheltered workshop to supported employment to competitive labor market may be a source of anxiety for some individuals and therefore detract from the client's well-being. For others, these moves may be welcome and utility-enhancing.

A client's decision consists of how long to remain in the VR program. The client also agrees to the particular type or intensity of services in the individualized program. From a client's perspective, remaining in the VR program entails both benefits and costs. The benefits of continued participation include incremental gains to health and work skill levels. The opportunity cost of remaining in the VR program consists of foregone income; the client might earn more in wages in the labor market than he or she receives in compensation within the VR program. This tradeoff can be formulated and analyzed as a problem of choosing the optimal time to leave the program.

The counselor's decisions include selecting the type and intensity of services that each client should receive and determining the time when each client should leave the program. Although the counselor will have little, if any, control over the makeup of the client population, the counselor must choose the best way to allocate limited agency resources to that population. In making these choices, the counselor may be serving humanitarian and social-service goals or self-interested goals or all of these.[1]

Some decisions will involve the participation of both counselor and client. The determination that a client should leave the program reflects the judgment of both individuals as to the minimum length of time appropriate for program participation. The client must also agree to the program of services prescribed by the counselor. This program is not presented to the client with instructions to "take it or leave it"; the client may in fact work with the counselor to design and plan the service package. (Both individuals are operating, of course, within budgetary and other constraints.)

The next two sections analyze the optimization problems of both client and counselor.

CLIENT

Each client is assumed to have a utility function that depends on levels of consumption (c) and health (h). For simplicity, the utility a client enjoys at a given point in time is assumed to take a particular form

(1) $U(c(t), h(t)) = bc(t) + g(h(t))$

where t represents time, b is a positive number and g is an increasing function. Over a period of time, say from t_1 to t_2, utility can be represented as

(2) $\int_{t_1}^{t_2} \{bc(t) + g(h(t))\} \, e^{-qt} \, dt$

where q is the client's discount factor.

At any time a client can purchase a level of consumption that is constrained by his or her current income.[2] Clients' income may come from nonwage sources, I, as well as wage sources, w. Nonwage income is assumed to be fixed at a level I over time. A client participating in the VR program is assumed to have a fixed level of maintenance income and thus consumption, $\bar{c}$. This fixed level of income and consumption is net of any direct expenses or indirect costs of participating in the program. It was noted earlier that a client's utility may change, depending on the structure of the work environment. For simplicity, these differences are assumed to be constants and may be positive or negative. These transition costs can then be embedded into $\bar{c}$.

The benefits of participation in the VR program are described by changes in the health and adaptability status of individual clients. Better health is of direct interest to clients since it is an argument in their utility function. Individuals in good health are better able to enjoy life. Health is also important to a client for its influence on earnings. The clear positive relationship between health and earnings is well documented in the literature.

Adaptability is here construed to mean basic skills necessary for functioning on a job. The level of adaptability achieved by clients will influence their earnings when employed. A wage or earnings equation for an individual can be written as

(3) $w(t) = \phi + \phi_a a(t) + \phi_h h(t)$.

I further suppose that the effect of the substance or intensity, s, and duration, d, of an individual client's program participation adaptability and health takes the form[3]

(4)

$a(t) = a_0 e^{(\gamma_a s_a - \delta_a)d}$

$h(t) = h_0 e^{(\gamma_h s_h - \delta_h)d}$

The initial levels of health and adaptability are h_0 and a_0. Parameters λ_h and λ_a represent the rate at which a level of services translates into gains in health and adaptability. The parameters δ_h and δ_a are "depreciation" factors for health and adaptability. Notice that it is assumed that different intensities of health and adaptability augmenting services may be received, s_h and s_a.[4]

The client's problem is to choose the optimal time to leave the VR program:

$$(5) \quad \max_{d} \int_{0}^{d} \{bc(t) + g(h(t))\}e^{-qt}\,dt + \int_{d}^{T} \{bc(t) = g(h(t))\}e^{-qt}\,dt$$

s.t.
$$c(t) = \begin{cases} \bar{c} + I & t < d \\ I + w(t) & t \geq d \end{cases}$$

$$w(t) = \phi + \phi_a a(t) + \phi_h h(t)$$

$$h(t) = \begin{cases} h_0 e^{(\gamma_h s_h - \delta_h)t} & t < d \\ h_0 e^{(\gamma_h s_h d - \delta_h t)} & t \geq d \end{cases}$$

$$a(t) = \begin{cases} a_0 e^{(\gamma_a s_a - \delta_a)t} & t < d \\ a_0 e^{(\gamma_a s_a d - \delta_a t)} & t \geq d \end{cases}$$

All of the constraints can be substituted directly into the objective function to yield an unconstrained maximization problem. The necessary condition for an optimum is

$$(6) \quad 0 = -\{b(I+\phi+\phi_h h_0 e^{(\gamma_h s_h - \delta_h)d} + \phi_a a_0 e^{(\gamma_a s_a - \delta_a)d} + g(h_0 e^{(\gamma_h s_h - \delta_h)d}))\}e^{-qd}$$

$$+ \{b(I+\bar{c}) + g(h_0 e^{(\gamma_h s_h - \delta_h)d})\}e^{-qd}$$

$$+ \int_{d}^{T} \{b(\gamma_h s_h \phi_h h_0 e^{(\gamma_h s_h d - \delta_h t)} + \gamma_a s_a \phi_a a_0 e^{(\gamma_a s_a d - \delta_a t)}) + g'\gamma_h s_h h_0 e^{(\gamma_h s_h d - \delta_h t)}\}e^{-qt}\,dt$$

This expression simplifies to

$$(7) \quad d = \frac{\log(m(0)) - \log[\dfrac{b\gamma_h s_h \phi_h + g'\gamma_h s_h}{\delta_h + q}e^{(\gamma_h s_h - \delta_h)} + \dfrac{b\gamma_a s_a \phi_a a_0}{\delta_a + q}e^{(\gamma_a s_a - \delta_a)}]}{1 - q}$$

where $m(0) = b[\phi + \phi_h h_0 + \phi_a a_0 - \bar{c}]$ is the "cost" of participating in the program at time zero. This simplification also assumes that the time horizon that the client considers in making a decision is sufficiently long that nothing is lost in equating T to infinity.

The first two terms in (6) represent the consumption losses incurred by a client because of the presumably low fixed compensation received while in the program, compared to a market wage reflecting health and adaptability levels at time d. This cost could be negative; for example, a person with a recent severe injury may be virtually unemployable before receiving adequate rehabilitative services. The third term measures how incremental consumption and health gains from further participation affect future utility levels.

Counselors must decide how to allocate a limited amount of rehabilitative services across the client population. (The process by which individuals are deemed to be eligible clients is assumed to have occurred already and is not addressed in this model.) Each counselor is assumed to have access to a fixed dollar level of services, $\bar{k}$. The number and type of clients each counselor deals with are also exogenously given. The counselor's utility function is assumed to be monotonically increasing in the number of "successful" cases.[5] This effect on utility could result from increases in future compensation or less quantifiable gains associated with helping others or from a combination of these. Although the counselor's interests will coincide to an extent with those of the client, it is clear that counselors are not perfect agents for clients. The analysis that follows assumes only that counselors are motivated to some degree by the number of closures.

A counselor can select (subject to the approval of the client) the substance or intensity level of services related to health (s_h) and adaptability (s_a) for each client. The counselor may also determine the duration of participation (d') for each client.[6] It is assumed that the counselor's choices are made at the start of a client's participation and are not modified through time. The probability that a particular client becomes a successful closure is assumed to be a function of the levels of health and adaptability that the client takes to the labor market.

(8) $\quad \Pr(i = 1 | a_{0i}, h_{0i}, s_{ai}, s_{hi}, d_i') = \sigma + \sigma_h h_{0i} e^{(\eta_h s_i - \delta_h) d_i'} + \sigma_a a_{0i} e^{(\eta_a s_i - \delta_a) d_i'}$

$\quad$ for $i = 1 \ldots n$

The counselor's budgetary constraint is

(9) $\quad \displaystyle\sum_{i=1}^{n} (w_a s_{ai} + w_h s_{hi})\, d_i' \leq \bar{k}.$

The prices of adaptability and health related services are w_a and w_h, respectively. The objective function of a counselor can now be written as

(10) $\quad \displaystyle\max_{s_{ai},\, s_{hi},\, d_i'} \sum_{i=1}^{n} (\sigma + \sigma_h h_{0i} e^{(\eta_h s_{hi} - \delta_h) d_i'} + \sigma_a a_{0i} e^{(\eta_a s_{ai} - \delta_a) d_i'})$

$\quad$ s.t. $\displaystyle\sum_{i=1}^{n} (w_a s_{ai} + w_h s_{hi}) d_i' \leq k.$

The first order conditions to this problem can be manipulated to yield a relation between the substance or intensity of health and adaptability services for an individual client:

$$(11) \quad \frac{\eta_a \sigma_a a_{0i} e^{(\eta_a s_{ai} - \delta_a)}}{\eta_h \sigma_h h_{0i} e^{(\eta_h s_{hi} - \delta_h)}} = \frac{w_a}{w_h}$$

This "efficiency" condition is interpreted as equating the ratio of productivity in adaptability and health services to the relative prices of those services. Notice that, other things being equal, a reduction in a client's initial health (adaptability) status would be reflected in an increase in the intensity or substance of health (adaptability) services. Other comparative statics are easily obtained. This comparative static can be identified directly from this relation because the first order conditions for s_{ai} and s_{hi} do not involve any of the other choice variables—in particular these conditions are independent of d_i.

The duration a counselor would choose for different clients satisfies the next relation, also derived from the first order conditions:

$$(12) \quad d_i' - d_j' = \log[(\eta_h s_{hj} - \delta_h)\sigma_h h_{0j} e^{(\eta_h s_{hj} - \delta_h)} + (\eta_a s_{aj} - \delta_a)\sigma_a a_{0j} e^{(\eta_a s_{aj} - \delta_a)}]$$

$$- \log[(\eta_h s_{hi} - \delta_h)\sigma_h h_{0i} e^{(\eta_h s_{hi} - \delta_h)} + (\eta_a s_{ai} - \delta_a)\sigma_a a_{0i} e^{(\eta_a s_{ai} - \delta_a)}].$$

This equation explains differences in the length of program participation chosen by the counselor. The endogenous selections of s_{ai}, s_{aj}, s_{hi}, and s_{hg}, as well as parameters, affect these duration choices. Other things being equal, clients with relatively lower levels of health and adaptability would be given longer periods of service.

The third equation of interest is the counselor's budget constraint, which determines the absolute levels and durations of services received by clients. The actual duration of program participation by a particular client is the minimum of the client's own choice, d_i, and the counselor's choice, d_i'.

This chapter provides a framework for analyzing client and counselor decision making that is consistent with microeconomic theory. The client and counselor choices described above have testable implications. The model suggests the role that formal analysis can play in understanding VR program outcomes.

NOTES

1. Researchers might investigate the decisions regarding duration and substance or intensity that would be made by a social planner maximizing a social welfare function. Mechanisms or incentive schemes that make client and counselor decisions congruent with the judgments of a social planner could be taken under consideration.

2. Borrowing is ruled out. This restriction could easily be relaxed although it

would seem likely that individuals in a state VR program do not have significant opportunities to moderate their income fluctuations.

3. Simpler or more complicated functional relationships are possible for these effects as well as other effects described. These are manageable and capture the important elements of choice. I hope that they also yield results that can be tested empirically.

4. It may be desirable to disaggregate the VR population into two groups. Preliminary discussion suggests that there may be a large group of individuals who receive primarily health related services and another group who receive mostly adaptability related services. Further analysis of the data and discussion of this issue are needed.

5. The definition of a successful case is arbitrary. Here it is assumed to coincide with sixty continuous days of employment. Alternative goals such as maximizing the sum of clients' earnings increases yield similar results, since earnings as well as successful cases are assumed to depend on levels of health and adaptability.

6. If the counselor can choose distinct lengths for health and adaptability services, d_h' and d_a', respectively, the expressions derived later relating choice variables to parameters are significantly simplified.

WORK CITED

Crawford, David L., and Mark R. Killingsworth. 1983. "Toward a Strategy for the Measurement of VR Program Impacts." Mimeographed. Rutgers University.

II

Benefit-Cost Analysis Using the Reported Data

We have seen that the benefit-cost analyses performed over the years in the vocational rehabilitation program were of a very simple kind. Program officials most often calculated benefits as the difference between wages at acceptance and closure and, in addition, they rather naively assumed that this wage difference would continue into the future. The information base that underlay these efforts at program evaluation was essentially the same as the one available to researchers today. In the following four chapters, the authors test the limits of the information base and investigate whether the application of a more sophisticated methodology will lead to better measures of program performance. The basic questions at issue here are: What can be done with the existing data? Are the data adequate for the purposes of evaluation? Are there econometric adjustments that can be made to the data that will improve the estimation of program costs and benefits?

It is our inability to conduct an evaluation of the program in a true experimental setting that makes the issue of data so crucial. As John Worrall observed in Chapter 3, the economic analyst does not have the advantage of comparing the experience of VR clientele to the experience of a control group. It is therefore difficult to know what would have happened to clients had they not come into contact with the program. The adjustments to the data that the authors make in Part II are, in a sense, a statistical attempt to compensate for the absence of information about a control group. If no one can know for certain the fate of these persons had they not participated in the program, the analyst can at least standardize for the variables that are likely to affect the way the program impacts upon their lives. Persons of different ages with different educational attainments and work experience will fare differently in the program. The objective in making use of statistical controls is the same as the objective in making use of a control group—to isolate the effects of treatment and to determine how the services provided, apart from all other factors, will affect the client's chances of returning to the labor market. In Part III, some alternative methods of adjusting the data will be discussed in the context of a review of state evaluation practices; these methods, like those illustrated in Part II, can be seen as a strategy to compensate for the lack of an experimental design.

Ernest Gibbs opens Chapter 5 with an examination of the national data base. He singles out elements of the information applicable to program evaluation and explains how each can be used in the actual calculation of costs and benefits. He then uses the 1982 data to replicate the traditional method of benefit-cost analysis. The next step introduces a series of econometric corrections. In an effort to work out a more precise measure of benefits, Gibbs uses different methods of compounding estimated earnings gains over the lifetime of individuals and different methods of assigning wages to those who report zero wages at referral. He also stratifies clients by cohorts according to age, sex, race, education, and disabling condition, and calculates benefits and costs separately for each cohort.

The discussion and analysis in this chapter highlight deficiencies in the data base. What is most regrettable from the standpoint of evaluation is the lack of information about client earnings for extended periods of time before and after the receipt of rehabilitation services. The benefit-cost ratios computed by Gibbs vary significantly, depending on the assumptions he makes about wages at referral. While Gibbs is dissatisfied with the ratios he arrives at, he does indicate that some fairly certain observations can be made about the way in which such variables as age, education, and sex will affect the ratios. Moreover, this analysis shows that the existing data are sufficient to allow researchers to reach conclusions about the probability of successfully rehabilitating certain subgroups of clients. Findings of this kind are clearly of value to program administrators who must make choices about program services and the allocation of resources.

Chapter 6 focuses more intensively a data base problem raised in the preceding chapter: the misleading information on client earnings at referral recorded in the national data set. Anita Hall-Kane and Ernest Gibbs, pointing to the large number of VR clients who report that they are not earning wages at the time of their referral to the program, argue that it is unrealistic to conclude that these clients have no earnings capacity. It is at least possible that some of the clients reporting zero earnings are only temporarily out of the labor market and might return at some later time, even without the program's services. The authors go on to suggest that, in the light of the frequency with which clients report zero earnings, the practice of comparing client earnings at referral and closure as a measure of program benefits may overestimate the actual impact of VR services.

The data problem explored in Chapter 6 could presumably be solved if a control group existed and the analyst could compare the experience of the group that received the treatment with the experience of the group that did not. In the absence of a control group, however, other solutions must be found. In Chapter 5, the assumption was adopted that those persons who reported zero wages at referral would have eventually earned the same mean wage as those who reported positive wages at referral. In Chapter 6, Hall-Kane and Gibbs follow a different, and probably a better, course by estimating the earnings capacity of those clients who reported zero wages. They assign these individuals an entering wage derived from an analysis of the wages of comparable applicants with the same demographic and human capital characteristics who do report positive wages. Their approach is based on work done by James Heckman and involves the use of a two-step selection-bias correction technique.

The technique leads to an interesting result: it predicts wages for non-working male and female VR clients that are significantly higher than the wages for clients working at referral. The authors look for an explanation in the disincentive effects of disability transfers and other transfer payments. Clients who report zero wages at referral may have chosen not to enter the labor market because the wage they could command in the labor market is less than the value they attach to their leisure, together with the value of their transfers.

Like the preceding chapters in Part II, Chapter 7 deals with the limitations of the data and the questionable interpretations of these data in the past. Benefit-cost analysis has traditionally assigned zero benefits to those clients who are judged "not rehabilitated" and closed in status 28. David Dean and Robert Dolan suggest that it is inappropriate to assume that these clients have received no benefit from VR services while the expenses incurred in serving these clients are fully taken into account in the calculation of costs. These clients are classified as not rehabilitated because they are not earning wages sixty days after they leave the program; as the authors observe, a more sustained tracking of their earnings might show significant postclosure earnings.

Dean and Dolan use a technique similar to that used by Hall-Kane and Gibbs in the preceding chapter to impute benefits to persons closed as not rehabilitated. They estimate earnings for the unsuccessful closure that are somewhat lower than those for the successful closure but still substantial. They suggest too that inclusion of earnings for this cohort would add significantly to any measure of the effectiveness of the VR program.

5 *Ernest Gibbs*

THE VOCATIONAL REHABILITATION DATA BASE AND THE ESTIMATION OF BENEFIT-COST RATIOS

The information source basic to all evaluation of the vocational rehabilitation program is the R-300 or RSA-911 data set.[1] Compiled annually by the Rehabilitation Services Administration, the R-300 set provides statistical information on all individuals closed from the program. In this chapter, I survey the kinds of information that are available in the R-300 set,[2] and then proceed to conduct benefit-cost analysis of the vocational rehabilitation program using the national data for the fiscal year 1982. Other authors in this volume have argued that past analyses of the program's cost effectiveness—analyses that drew on the same national data base—were seriously flawed and yielded results of questionable validity. My purpose here is to determine if it is possible to refine the use of the data so as to arrive at more credible conclusions about the costs and benefits of vocational rehabilitation.

THE R-300 DATA

The information that the RSA gathers each year about the client population is, from many points of view, fairly comprehensive. The vocational rehabilitation program pioneered in the production of useful information about program services and results and, even in recent years, has published more information than other remedial manpower programs.

The R-300 data set for fiscal year 1982 contains information on 720,612 vocational rehabilitation clients. This information is drawn from the reports of state rehabilitation agencies serving all eligible clients and specialized rehabilitation agencies serving the blind. The agencies record information on every case closed from the rehabilitation program, whether closed out successfully or unsuccessfully, in one of the several nonsuccessful closure categories.

Because I will refer to these closure categories in my analysis, I offer some brief definitions at this point:

1. An individual is closed in status 08 who fails to meet the eligibility requirements for vocational rehabilitation services. The eligibility

requirements specify (a) the presence of a physical or mental disability; (b) the existence of a substantial handicap to employment; (c) a finding that a reasonable expectation exists that vocational rehabilitation services may be of benefit in enhancing employability. Closure status 08 applies to all persons not accepted into vocational rehabilitation, whether closed from referral, from applicant status, or from extended evaluation.

2. Closure status 30 applies to all cases closed after acceptance for vocational rehabilitation services but before receipt of services.
3. Closure status 28 applies to all cases closed "not rehabilitated" after receipt of services.
4. Closure status 26 applies to all successfully rehabilitated clients. The criterion for successful closure is employment for a minimum of sixty days, except in the case of homemaker placements.

The agencies maintain information on all individuals in these four categories from the time they are referred to the program to the time they are closed out. This information includes such items as demographic characteristics, a classification of the disabling condition, a record of services received, wages at opening, and wages at closure. When the data from the reporting agencies are compiled by the RSA and issued as the national R-300 data set, they offer a considerable body of information that is of use in benefit-cost analysis of the program. Let us examine the elements of the data that are most relevant to program evaluation. In each case, note how the particular element or variable figures in benefit-cost analysis and, in addition, note how the absence of certain information limits the ability of the program analyst to arrive at precise measures of costs and benefits.

Age at referral

The age of the client at referral is recorded as a continuous variable. Most clients are between eighteen and sixty-five years of age with an average age at referral of thirty-three years. Age is an important variable when analyzing the benefits of VR because of the correlation between age and earnings. The relationship of earnings to age over time increases, then at some point in time, flattens and begins to decrease. We will calculate these "age-earnings profiles" to examine the relationship between age and earnings later.

Client gender

Sex of a client is included when determining the benefits of VR because of its possible role in the determination of wages. Also, many women are closed as unpaid homemakers and thus have zero wage at closure.

Client race

The client's race may have a significant bearing on the probability of success in the VR program and on the benefits attributable to the VR program. Traditionally, because of better labor conditions, whites have had higher benefits than nonwhites. Later, in the multivariate benefit-cost analysis, we will compare benefits and costs for only the white and black racial groups, since most of the clients fall into one of these two classifications.

Client marital status

The marital status variable is often used to capture effects such as motivation, effort, and the stability of the client—factors that may ultimately have an impact on the rehabilitation outcome. Some regression equations include variables to measure the effects of marital status on the probability of successful completion of the program.

Education

The highest grade completed by clients educated under a regular educational system is recorded in a continuous format. In the case of clients who report mental retardation as a major or secondary disabling condition, the highest grade completed is not recorded as zero but as a separate, easily identifiable code. In the stratified benefit-cost analysis, I use three broad education classifications: less than eight years of education, eight to twelve years of education, and more than twelve years.

Three personal characteristics—the level of education, current age, and major disabling condition—are often used as proxies to measure the rehabilitation client's aptitude or ability to work.

Disability as reported at referral: major disabling condition

The variables pertaining to disabling conditions are organized in seven broad condition categories. It is not possible to assess the *actual* severity of a client's major disabling condition by referring to the condition classifications. Two persons with identical conditions may fare quite differently in the labor market because of differences in the severity of their conditions. The R-300 data set provides no information about specific functional limitations or limitations in motor movements that might affect a client's performance in the labor market. Such information would be useful in efforts to predict successful closure from VR or to estimate the benefits and costs attributable to VR participation.

Nevertheless, through a variable recorded at the time of closure from the VR program (the federal special program identifier variable), a counselor will designate a client as severely disabled if the definition of severe disability as defined in the *RSA Manual* is met. This provides a general measure of severity of impairments.

In the stratified benefit-cost analysis, I make an alternative specification of the disability classifications to reduce the required number of explanatory variables in a regression equation. I combine the Visual (RSA codes 100-150) and Hearing (200-230) Impairments into one "sensory" limitation, and the Orthopedic (300-399) and Amputation (400-449) Impairments into a "physical" impairment. I split the Mental, Psychoneurotic, and Personality Disorders category into two classifications—a "mental illness" variable (500-522) and a "mental retardation" variable (530-534)—and then place the remaining disability groups into the "other" classification.

Client weekly earnings

Client weekly earnings at referral and at closure are intended to provide actual data on the cash earnings of the client in the week of referral (or closure) regardless of earnings prior to the week of referral (or closure).

To calculate benefits, we seek to learn how much of a gain in client weekly earnings from referral to closure can be attributed to participation in the VR program. This objective, however, is not easily accomplished. Various methods have been suggested in the literature, but all are less than perfect because of the lack of an ideal comparison or control group. A researcher who works with the R-300 data set can only draw conclusions based on the success of a client (status 26) relative to the remaining nonsuccessfully rehabilitated clients (statuses 08, 28, 30). Chapters 3 and 4 of this volume addressed aspects of this control group problem.

A selection-bias problem is introduced in the analysis because all clients, whether or not successfully rehabilitated, have made a decision to participate in the VR program. Here, the problem is that individuals who decide to participate in a rehabilitation program have characteristics that differentiate them from individuals who have decided against participation.

Cost of case services

A major portion of the total costs estimated in the benefit analysis of the VR program are case service costs. The R-300 case service record indicates the amount of case service costs to the vocational rehabilitation agency for each client.

Services provided by the VR agency

The R-300 data includes information on services provided that enables researchers to determine the usage frequency for each type of service or training. With the aid of categorical variables, researchers can then evaluate how much of an influence (or lack of it) each service or training type is likely to have on the client's anticipated success in the program.

CALCULATION OF SIMPLE BENEFIT-COST RATIOS

Let us proceed to use the R-300 data set for fiscal year 1982 to calculate benefit-cost ratios for the vocational rehabilitation program. We begin by replicating the simple method that the RSA has traditionally employed. Following this demonstration, we will go on to consider ways of improving the method.

Computation of cost

The major costs of the VR program consist of program costs—case service costs, which are variable costs; and overhead costs, which can be considered a fixed cost. Overhead costs cover operating and administrative expenses, as well as the costs associated with providing such in-house services as placement and counseling. When estimating the total costs in the benefit-cost ratio, we must take both cost categories into account. To estimate the total case service costs, we take the average costs of clients with positive case service costs and then aggregate to attain a total cost figure.

The total case service cost for the 215,569 clients successfully rehabilitated (closure status 26) in the population was $253.9 million. However, of the 215,569 clients, only 154,338 clients incurred a case service cost of at least one dollar. It was from these clients that the non-zero cost of case services was computed. The non-zero mean cost of case services for the 215,569 clients in the population who were successfully rehabilitated was approximately $1,645 (see Table 5.1).

Next, we estimate the case service cost for those clients who (1) failed to report a case service cost, or (2) incurred zero case service cost. The second group would be made up of clients who received only in-house VR services. Our procedure is to assign both groups the non-zero mean rehabilitation cost. (I acknowledge, however, that the procedure will tend to overestimate costs for those who report zero case service costs.[3]) Assuming the same mean rehabilitation cost of $1,645 for the remaining 61,231 successfully rehabilitated clients in the population yields $100.7 million. Thus the grand total case service cost for all 215,569 successfully rehabilitated clients is $354.6 million (see Table 5.2).

These total expenditures are still incomplete because they omit cost for services received by clients whose cases were closed "not rehabilitated" and by others who were not accepted for VR services (that is, closure statuses 08, 28, 30). The method outlined above was used to estimate the total case service cost of these persons. The non-zero mean of case service costs of each closure status was assigned to the clients in that status (see Table 5.2).

TABLE 5.1

TOTAL AND MEAN CASE SERVICE COSTS
BY CLOSURE CODE

Closure Code	Number Closed	Number Reporting Positive Costs	Total Case Service Costs	Non-Zero Mean of Service Costs
08	369,681	110,081	$24,961,504	$226.75
26	215,569	154,338	$253,870,873	$1,644.90
28	98,935	70,439	$93,138,765	$1,322.26
30	36,427	23,679	$5,971,811	$252.20
TOTAL	720,612	358,537	$377,942,953	

Given this method of computing costs, the estimated case service costs on all cases closed in fiscal year 1982 was $578.4 million. The estimated cost figure overestimates the service costs as reported by the RSA in their annual program cost report. In this report, the total case service expenditure for all individuals was $521.6 million.

TABLE 5.2

ESTIMATION OF TOTAL CASE SERVICE COSTS
BY CLOSURE CODE

Closure Code	Total Reported Service Costs	Total Costs For Services Received By Those Not Reporting or Reporting Zero*	Total Case Service Cost
08	$24,961,504	$58,866,896	$83,828,400
26	$253,870,873	$100,718,872	$354,589,745
28	$93,138,765	$37,679,121	$130,817,886
30	$5,971,811	$3,215,046	$9,186,857
TOTAL**	$377,942,953	$200,479,934	$578,422,887

----

* These costs are estimated using the RSA methodology. The total costs for those who did not report or did not incur any costs is calculated by multiplying the number reporting either zero or not reporting any by the non-zero mean.

** Totals may not add due to rounding

As I suggested above, another major cost area in the provision of rehabilitation services consists of overhead expenditures. Data contained in the RSA cost report indicated that these costs were 55.3 percent of all rehabilitation expenditures in fiscal year 1982. The remaining 44.7 percent of total expenditures represented the case service costs reported on cases closed in fiscal year 1982. Therefore, the grand total cost of services rendered to clients can be obtained by dividing the total case service cost of 578.4 million by .447. For the population, this yields a grand total of $1,294 million. Again this figure overestimates the $1,166 million cited in the RSA cost report as the total obligation.

Computation of long-term improvement in earnings

In this benefit-cost model, the benefits of the VR program are defined as the difference of wages at closure and at referral. The annual increase in weekly earnings of all clients rehabilitated in 1982 is $1,207.6 million (see Table 5.3). This is calculated by taking the difference in the mean weekly earnings of clients from referral to closure and aggregating over all rehabilitated persons, including those with zero earnings. This figure is then raised to aggregate annual earnings changes by multiplying by fifty.

The aggregate earnings improvement is then discounted over a thirty-year period. The thirty-year period is chosen because the average age of rehabilitated clients is approximately thirty-five, which would leave thirty working years until the assumed retirement age of sixty-five. The discounting function used was 12 percent. The present value of one dollar received annually for thirty years discounted at 12 percent per year is $8.055. Multiplying this factor by $1,207.6 million yields $9,727.2 million. This is the projected lifetime improvement in earnings accumulated over thirty years that program officials attribute to vocational rehabilitation intervention.

Dividing the discounted lifetime earnings aggregates by the total cost of the rehabilitation produces a benefit-cost ratio of $7.52 ($9,727.2/$1,294 = $7.52) for the entire population (see Table 5.4).[4]

STRATIFIED BENEFIT-COST ANALYSIS

The traditional method of computing benefit-cost ratios has the advantage of being simple, but its weaknesses are manifest. In this section, I apply some of the corrections discussed in Chapter 3 in an effort to arrive at more realistic estimates of the costs and benefits of the program. I complicate the simple analysis carried out in the preceding section by using multivariate methods of measurement and by using regression analysis to estimate benefit-cost relationships for subgroups or cohorts of clients in the vocational rehabilitation program.

TABLE 5.3

MEAN WEEK EARNINGS OF SUCCESSFULLY
REHABILITATED CLIENTS AT REFERRAL
AND CLOSURE PROJECTED AT ANNUAL RATES

Number of Clients	Mean Weekly Earnings:		Annual Aggregate Earnings(in thousands): (3)		Difference Between Referral and Closure Earnings (in thousands)
	At Referral (1)	At Closure (2)	At Referral	At Closure	
215,569	$24.22	$136.26	$261,054	$1,468,672	$1,207,618

(1) includes those reporting no weekly earnings at referral

(2) includes homemakers

(3) weekly earnings were annualized by multiplying by 50 and then by the total number of rehabilitations

TABLE 5.4

BENEFIT-COST RATIOS
PRESENT VALUE OF IMPROVED EARNINGS
PROJECTED FOR FIVE TO THIRTY YEARS
AND DISCOUNTED AT 12% PER YEAR

Time Period	Present Value of One Dollar Discounted at 12 %	Future Earnings Discounted at 12 % Per Year	Benefit- Cost Ratio
=========	==============	================	========
5 years	$3.605	$4,353,461,224	$3.36
10 years	$5.650	$6,823,039,090	$5.27
15 years	$6.811	$8,225,083,051	$6.36
20 years	$7.469	$9,019,695,391	$6.97
25 years	$7.843	$9,471,344,351	$7.32
30 years	$8.055	$9,727,359,269	$7.52

I stratify the clients on the R-300 data set by age, race, sex, education, and disabling condition. There are many possible ways to stratify individuals and thousands of possible combinations of characteristics. In this study, I use five age classes, three education groups, five disability classifications, two race groups, and two sex groups. Table 5.5 shows the method and categories used to stratify the data set. It is now possible to analyze the impact of, say, additional education, while controlling for disabling condition, age, race and sex.

Using this method of stratification gives a total of 300 cohorts or cells. Table 5.6 shows the frequency of individuals in each cohort.

Methodology for stratified benefit-cost ratios

The basic methodology for the stratified benefit-cost analysis using regression methods was set forth by Bellante (1972). The model is described below.

The benefit-cost ratios in this chapter are computed with the following formula:

$$[P_s(B_s) + (1-P_s)B_n]/[P_s(C_s) + (1-P_s)C_n]$$

TABLE 5.5

VARIABLE DEFINITIONS
PROBABILITY OF SUCCESS

NAME	CODE	VALUE
AGE	AGE 00	= 1 if 14 - 24, 0 otherwise
	AGE 25	= 1 if 25 - 34, 0 otherwise
	AGE 35	= 1 if 35 - 44, 0 otherwise
	AGE 45	= 1 if 45 - 54, 0 otherwise
	AGE 55	= 1 if 55 - 64, 0 otherwise
SEX	SEXM	= 1 if Male, 0 otherwise
	SEXF	= 1 if Female, 0 otherwise
RACE	RACEW	= 1 if White, 0 otherwise
	RACEB	= 1 if Black, 0 otherwise
EDUCATION	ED8	= 1 if 0 - 8th grade, 0 otherwise
	ED9	= 1 if 9th - 12th grade, 0 otherwise
	ED13	= 1 if 13+, 0 otherwise
DISABLING CONDITION	SENSORY	= 1 if sensory, 0 otherwise(1)
	ORTHO/AMPUT	= 1 if orthopedic or amputation 0 otherwise(2)
	MILL	= 1 if mentally ill, 0 otherwise(3)
	MRET	= 1 if mentally retarded, 0 otherwise(4)
	OTHER	= 1 if other, 0 otherwise(5)

----

(1) SENSORY incluses disablilty codes 100 to 229.
(2) ORTHO/AMPUT includes disability codes 300 to 449.
(3) MILL includes disability codes 500 to 529.
(4) MRET includes disability codes 530 to 534.
(5) OTHER includes disability codes greater than 600.

where P_s = the probability that an individual with given characteristics will be successfully rehabilitated;

$(1 - P_s)$ = the probability that the individual will not be rehabilitated;

B_s = the estimated lifetime benefits generated from the successful rehabilitation of a client with given characteristics;

B_n = the benefits attributed to the rehabilitation process for a client who is unsuccessfully rehabilitated after acceptance into the program (in this analysis, B_n is assumed to be zero; in Chapter 7 we impute earnings to persons closed out in statuses 28 and 30);

C_s = the estimated cost of rehabilitation of a client with given characteristics who is successfully rehabilitated;

TABLE 5.6

FREQUENCY OF SUCCESSFUL
REHABILITATIONS BY COHORTS

WHITE MALES

COHORT/AGE	15-24	25-34	35-44	45-54	55+	TOTAL
0 - 8 YEARS EDUCATION						
SENSORY	205	179	229	430	1,590	2,633
ORTHO/AMPUT	609	801	1,006	940	573	3,929
MENTAL ILL	1,403	787	624	445	231	3,490
OTHER	734	534	594	764	558	3,184
9 - 12 YEARS EDUCATION						
SENSORY	1,472	752	675	681	1,718	5,298
ORTHO/AMPUT	7,192	5,849	3,448	1,774	847	19,110
MENTAL ILL	6,268	4,889	2,209	1,098	359	14,823
OTHER	4,945	2,059	1,323	1,146	706	10,179
13+ YEARS EDUCATION						
SENSORY	272	393	176	158	425	1,424
ORTHO/AMPUT	1,172	2,293	993	469	237	5,164
MENTAL ILL	696	2,252	1,170	577	184	4,879
OTHER	647	833	368	359	207	2,414

Table 5.6--Continued

BLACK MALES

0 - 8 YEARS EDUCATION

COHORT/AGE	15-24	25-34	35-44	45-54	55+	TOTAL
SENSORY	72	49	56	97	210	484
ORTHO/AMPUT	118	152	268	263	220	1,021
MENTAL ILL	399	272	182	122	44	1,019
OTHER	156	111	150	214	169	800

9 - 12 YEARS EDUCATION

	15-24	25-34	35-44	45-54	55+	TOTAL
SENSORY	310	220	147	93	93	863
ORTHO/AMPUT	780	893	541	297	109	2,620
MENTAL ILL	1,442	1,589	640	194	53	3,918
OTHER	743	532	319	188	73	1,855

13+ YEARS EDUCATION

	15-24	25-34	35-44	45-54	55+	TOTAL
SENSORY	34	57	32	15	16	154
ORTHO/AMPUT	107	261	105	48	23	544
MENTAL ILL	120	390	152	44	9	715
OTHER	98	118	63	33	15	327

TABLE 5.6--Continued

WHITE FEMALES

COHORT/AGE	15-24	25-34	35-44	45-54	55+	TOTAL
0 - 8 YEARS EDUCATION						
SENSORY	205	279	229	430	1,590	2,633
ORTHO/AMPUT	272	330	411	620	564	2,197
MENTAL ILL	607	519	441	409	131	2,107
OTHER	501	543	737	918	770	3,469
9 - 12 YEARS EDUCATION						
SENSORY	1,472	752	675	681	1,718	5,298
ORTHO/AMPUT	3,828	2,757	2,436	1,889	1,054	11,964
MENTAL ILL	4,554	4,635	2,798	1,443	402	13,832
OTHER	4,360	2,961	2,025	1,461	829	11,636
13+ YEARS EDUCATION						
SENSORY	272	393	176	158	425	1,424
ORTHO/AMPUT	835	1,156	676	442	224	3,333
MENTAL ILL	798	1,957	949	485	143	4,332
OTHER	604	710	360	210	92	1,976

Table 5.6--Continued

BLACK FEMALES

0 - 8 YEARS EDUCATION

COHORT/AGE	15-24	25-34	35-44	45-54	55+	TOTAL
SENSORY	44	48	59	158	440	749
ORTHO/AMPUT	59	77	111	195	232	674
MENTAL ILL	168	153	127	90	26	564
OTHER	104	111	235	389	302	1,141

9 - 12 YEARS EDUCATION

	15-24	25-34	35-44	45-54	55+	TOTAL
SENSORY	246	216	142	221	290	1,115
ORTHO/AMPUT	383	534	544	427	223	2,111
MENTAL ILL	907	1,109	531	223	46	2,816
OTHER	697	892	801	610	226	3,226

13+ YEARS EDUCATION

	15-24	25-34	35-44	45-54	55+	TOTAL
SENSORY	37	58	23	39	44	201
ORTHO/AMPUT	86	164	114	72	31	467
MENTAL ILL	145	294	117	58	7	621
OTHER	140	172	103	55	20	490

MENTALLY RETARDED

	15-24	25-34	35-44	45-54	55+	TOTAL
WHITE MALE	7,205	1,750	737	399	194	10,285
BLACK MALE	3,841	420	117	56	24	4,458
WHITE FEMALE	4,489	1,366	606	329	146	7,336
BLACK FEMALE	2,321	405	149	59	15	2,949
TOTAL	70,160	51,220	31,850	22,691	16,875	192,796

C_n = the total estimated cost associated with a client with a given set of characteristics who is closed unsuccessfully after acceptance into the program (closure status 28 or 30).

P_s: *the probability of success*

P_s, the probability of success, is determined by regressing the dichotomous dependent variable of success or lack of success on the given characteristics of each individual.

Success is defined as closure in status 26. To estimate the probability of success, I converted the categorical independent variables, listed in Table 5.5, as well as the dependent variable, to dummy variables. The regression for probability of success was run over the entire population of 350,931 clients. The ordinary least squares results of the regression are presented in Table 5.7.

The average probability of success of the basis group, those individuals having a zero value for all of the dummy variables, is given by the intercept term. The estimated probability that an individual with a given set of characteristics will be successfully rehabilitated, P_s, can be calculated by summing the coefficients for the selected characteristics and adding this result to the intercept value. The probability of success for each cohort is reported in Table 5.8.

Costs for success and nonsuccess

I estimated the costs for success, C_s, and the costs for nonsuccess, C_n, by regressing case service costs on the same set of independent variables. The regression of C_s was run over the 192,796 successful rehabilitants; the regression of C_n was run over only the 158,135 nonrehabilitants. The results of these regressions yield the estimated predicted case service costs. In addition to computing these costs, we must assign fixed overhead costs. The estimated case service costs are multiplied by the same factor used in the simple benefit-cost ratio in order to estimate the total cost figure.

The results of the regressions on costs for successful and unsuccessful cases are given in Table 5.7. The total cost for any client with a given set of characteristics can be estimated by summing the dollar amounts of the coefficients of the desired characteristics and adding these to the intercept term. Estimated costs for successful and unsuccessful cases are reported in Tables 5.9 and 5.10. These values will yield the values of C_s and C_n, which are used in the benefit-cost ratio. To compute the expected costs of a client with a particular set of characteristics, we can add the product of the probability that the client will be rehabilitated and the estimated total cost of success to the product of the probability that the client will not be rehabilitated and the estimated cost of nonsuccess. That is, $P_s(C_s)$ +

TABLE 5.7

RESULTS OF REGRESSIONS

VARIABLE CODE	SUCCESS	COST (SUCCESS)	COST (NONSUCCESS)
AGE 00 (basis)	0	0	0
AGE 25	0.0004	-949.82	-429.27
AGE 35	0.0081	-1237.39	-672.40
AGE 45	0.0172	-1489.11	-911.45
AGE 55	0.1047	-2446.82	-1167.61
SEXF (basis)	0	0	0
SEXM	-0.0625	-444.65	-84.45
RACEB (basis)	0	0	0
RACEW	0.0719	585.44	193.69
ED8 (basis)	0	0	0
ED9	0.0349	-444.65	-209.24
ED13	0.0821	-165.32	4.03
MRET (basis)	0	0	0
SENSORY	0.0121	1266.56	1285.79
ORTHO/AMPUT	-0.0954	914.11	596.86
MILL	-0.1639	-516.10	-471.13
OTHER	-0.0357	586.64	29.51
INTERCEPT	0.6294	4044.36	2498.97

$(1 - P_s)C_n$ is the expected cost of a client. This expected cost figure is the denominator of the benefit-cost ratio.

Benefits

In this analysis, we can measure the benefits of vocational rehabilitation to clients as simply the difference of earnings at closure and earnings at

TABLE 5.8

PROBABILITY OF SUCCESS

WHITE MALES

DISABILITY/AGE	15-24	25-34	35-44	45-54	55+
0 - 8 YEARS EDUCATION					
SENSORY	0.65	0.65	0.66	0.67	0.76
ORTHO/AMPUT	0.54	0.54	0.55	0.56	0.65
MENTAL ILL	0.47	0.48	0.48	0.49	0.58
MENTAL RET	0.64	0.64	0.65	0.66	0.74
OTHER	0.60	0.60	0.61	0.62	0.71
9 - 12 YEARS EDUCATION					
SENSORY	0.69	0.69	0.69	0.70	0.79
ORTHO/AMPUT	0.58	0.58	0.59	0.60	0.68
MENTAL ILL	0.51	0.51	0.52	0.53	0.61
MENTAL RET	0.67	0.67	0.68	0.69	0.78
OTHER	0.64	0.64	0.65	0.66	0.74
13+ YEARS EDUCATION					
SENSORY	0.73	0.73	0.74	0.75	0.84
ORTHO/AMPUT	0.63	0.63	0.63	0.64	0.73
MENTAL ILL	0.56	0.56	0.57	0.57	0.66
MENTAL RET	0.72	0.72	0.73	0.74	0.83
OTHER	0.69	0.69	0.69	0.70	0.79

Table 5.8--Continued

BLACK MALES
0 - 8 YEARS EDUCATION

DISABILITY/AGE	14-24	25-34	35-44	45-54	55+
SENSORY	0.58	0.58	0.59	0.60	0.68
ORTHO/AMPUT	0.47	0.47	0.48	0.49	0.58
MENTAL ILL	0.40	0.40	0.41	0.42	0.51
MENTAL RET	0.57	0.57	0.57	0.58	0.67
OTHER	0.53	0.53	0.54	0.55	0.64

9 - 12 YEARS EDUCATION

	14-24	25-34	35-44	45-54	55+
SENSORY	0.61	0.61	0.62	0.63	0.72
ORTHO/AMPUT	0.51	0.51	0.51	0.52	0.61
MENTAL ILL	0.44	0.44	0.45	0.46	0.54
MENTAL RET	0.60	0.60	0.61	0.62	0.71
OTHER	0.57	0.57	0.57	0.58	0.67

13+ YEARS EDUCATION

	14-24	25-34	35-44	45-54	55+
SENSORY	0.66	0.66	0.67	0.68	0.77
ORTHO/AMPUT	0.55	0.55	0.56	0.57	0.66
MENTAL ILL	0.49	0.49	0.49	0.50	0.59
MENTAL RET	0.65	0.65	0.66	0.67	0.75
OTHER	0.61	0.61	0.62	0.63	0.72

TABLE 5.8--Continued

WHITE FEMALES

0 - 8 YEARS EDUCATION

DISABILITY/AGE	14-24	25-34	35-44	45-54	55+
SENSORY	0.71	0.71	0.72	0.73	0.82
ORTHO/AMPUT	0.61	0.61	0.61	0.62	0.71
MENTAL ILL	0.54	0.54	0.55	0.55	0.64
MENTAL RET	0.70	0.70	0.71	0.72	0.81
OTHER	0.67	0.67	0.67	0.68	0.77

9 - 12 YEARS EDUCATION

	14-24	25-34	35-44	45-54	55+
SENSORY	0.75	0.75	0.76	0.77	0.85
ORTHO/AMPUT	0.64	0.64	0.65	0.66	0.75
MENTAL ILL	0.57	0.57	0.58	0.59	0.68
MENTAL RET	0.74	0.74	0.74	0.75	0.84
OTHER	0.70	0.70	0.71	0.72	0.81

13+ YEARS EDUCATION

	14-24	25-34	35-44	45-54	55+
SENSORY	0.80	0.80	0.80	0.81	0.90
ORTHO/AMPUT	0.69	0.69	0.70	0.71	0.79
MENTAL ILL	0.62	0.62	0.63	0.64	0.72
MENTAL RET	0.78	0.78	0.79	0.80	0.89
OTHER	0.75	0.75	0.76	0.76	0.85

Table 5.8--Continued

BLACK FEMALES

DISABILITY/AGE	14-24	25-34	35-44	45-54	55+
0 - 8 YEARS EDUCATION					
SENSORY	0.64	0.64	0.65	0.66	0.75
ORTHO/AMPUT	0.53	0.53	0.54	0.55	0.64
MENTAL ILL	0.47	0.47	0.47	0.48	0.57
MENTAL RET	0.63	0.63	0.64	0.65	0.73
OTHER	0.59	0.59	0.60	0.61	0.70
9 - 12 YEARS EDUCATION					
SENSORY	0.68	0.68	0.68	0.69	0.78
ORTHO/AMPUT	0.57	0.57	0.58	0.59	0.67
MENTAL ILL	0.50	0.50	0.51	0.52	0.61
MENTAL RET	0.66	0.66	0.67	0.68	0.77
OTHER	0.63	0.63	0.64	0.65	0.73
13+ YEARS EDUCATION					
SENSORY	0.72	0.72	0.73	0.74	0.83
ORTHO/AMPUT	0.62	0.62	0.62	0.63	0.72
MENTAL ILL	0.55	0.55	0.56	0.56	0.65
MENTAL RET	0.71	0.71	0.72	0.73	0.82
OTHER	0.68	0.68	0.68	0.69	0.78

TABLE 5.9

COSTS OF SUCCESS

WHITE MALES

0 - 8 YEARS EDUCATION

DISABILITY/AGE	14-24	25-34	35-44	45-54	55+
SENSORY	5,452	4,502	4,214	3,963	3,005
ORTHO/AMPUT	5,099	4,149	3,862	3,610	2,652
MENTAL ILL	3,669	2,719	2,432	2,180	1,222
MENTAL RET	4,185	3,235	2,948	2,696	1,738
OTHER	4,772	3,822	3,534	3,283	2,325

9 - 12 YEARS EDUCATION

DISABILITY/AGE	14-24	25-34	35-44	45-54	55+
SENSORY	5,007	4,057	3,770	3,518	2,560
ORTHO/AMPUT	4,655	3,705	3,417	3,166	2,208
MENTAL ILL	3,224	2,275	1,987	1,735	778
MENTAL RET	3,741	2,791	2,503	2,251	1,294
OTHER	4,327	3,377	3,090	2,838	1,880

13+ YEARS EDUCATION

DISABILITY/AGE	14-24	25-34	35-44	45-54	55+
SENSORY	5,286	4,337	4,049	3,797	2,840
ORTHO/AMPUT	4,934	3,984	3,697	3,445	2,487
MENTAL ILL	3,504	2,554	2,266	2,015	1,057
MENTAL RET	4,020	3,070	2,782	2,531	1,573
OTHER	4,606	3,657	3,369	3,117	2,160

Table 5.9--Continued

BLACK MALES

0 - 8 YEARS EDUCATION

DISABILITY/AGE	14-24	25-34	35-44	45-54	55+
SENSORY	4,866	3,916	3,629	3,377	2,419
ORTHO/AMPUT	4,514	3,564	3,276	3,025	2,067
MENTAL ILL	3,084	2,134	1,846	1,595	637
MENTAL RET	3,600	2,650	2,362	2,111	1,153
OTHER	4,186	3,237	2,949	2,697	1,740

9 - 12 YEARS EDUCATION

DISABILITY/AGE	14-24	25-34	35-44	45-54	55+
SENSORY	4,422	3,472	3,184	2,933	1,975
ORTHO/AMPUT	4,069	3,119	2,832	2,580	1,622
MENTAL ILL	2,639	1,689	1,402	1,150	192
MENTAL RET	3,155	2,205	1,918	1,666	708
OTHER	3,742	2,792	2,504	2,253	1,295

13+ YEARS EDUCATION

DISABILITY/AGE	14-24	25-34	35-44	45-54	55+
SENSORY	4,701	3,751	3,464	3,212	2,254
ORTHO/AMPUT	4,349	3,399	3,111	2,859	1,902
MENTAL ILL	2,918	1,968	1,681	1,429	471
MENTAL RET	3,434	2,485	2,197	1,945	988
OTHER	4,021	3,071	2,784	2,532	1,574

TABLE 5.9--Continued

WHITE FEMALES

DISABILITY/AGE	14-24	25-34	35-44	45-54	55+
			0 - 8 YEARS EDUCATION		
SENSORY	5,896	4,947	4,659	4,407	3,450
ORTHO/AMPUT	5,544	4,594	4,307	4,055	3,097
MENTAL ILL	4,114	3,164	2,876	2,625	1,667
MENTAL RET	4,630	3,680	3,392	3,141	2,183
OTHER	5,216	4,267	3,979	3,727	2,770
			9 - 12 YEARS EDUCATION		
SENSORY	5,452	4,502	4,214	3,963	3,005
ORTHO/AMPUT	5,099	4,149	3,862	3,610	2,652
MENTAL ILL	3,669	2,719	2,432	2,180	1,222
MENTAL RET	4,185	3,235	2,948	2,696	1,738
OTHER	4,772	3,822	3,534	3,283	2,325
			13+ YEARS EDUCATION		
SENSORY	5,731	4,781	4,494	4,242	3,284
ORTHO/AMPUT	5,379	4,429	4,141	3,889	2,932
MENTAL ILL	3,948	2,999	2,711	2,459	1,502
MENTAL RET	4,464	3,515	3,227	2,975	2,018
OTHER	5,051	4,101	3,814	3,562	2,604

Table 5.9--Continued

BLACK FEMALES

DISABILITY/AGE	14-24	25-34	35-44	45-54	55+
0 - 8 YEARS EDUCATION					
SENSORY	5,311	4,361	4,074	3,822	2,864
ORTHO/AMPUT	4,958	4,009	3,721	3,469	2,512
MENTAL ILL	3,528	2,578	2,291	2,039	1,081
MENTAL RET	4,044	3,095	2,807	2,555	1,598
OTHER	4,631	3,681	3,394	3,142	2,184
9 - 12 YEARS EDUCATION					
SENSORY	4,866	3,916	3,629	3,377	2,419
ORTHO/AMPUT	4,514	3,564	3,276	3,025	2,067
MENTAL ILL	3,084	2,134	1,846	1,595	637
MENTAL RET	3,600	2,650	2,362	2,111	1,153
OTHER	4,186	3,237	2,949	2,697	1,740
13+ YEARS EDUCATION					
SENSORY	5,146	4,196	3,908	3,656	2,699
ORTHO/AMPUT	4,793	3,843	3,556	3,304	2,346
MENTAL ILL	3,363	2,413	2,126	1,874	916
MENTAL RET	3,879	2,929	2,642	2,390	1,432
OTHER	4,466	3,516	3,228	2,977	2,019

TABLE 5.10

COSTS OF NONSUCCESS

WHITE MALES

DISABILITY/AGE	14-24	25-34	35-44	45-54	55+
0 - 8 YEARS EDUCATION					
SENSORY	3,894	3,465	3,222	2,983	2,726
ORTHO	3,205	2,776	2,533	2,294	2,037
MENTAL ILL	2,137	1,708	1,465	1,226	969
MENTAL RET	2,608	2,179	1,936	1,697	1,441
OTHER	2,638	2,208	1,965	1,726	1,470
9 - 12 YEARS EDUCATION					
SENSORY	3,685	3,255	3,012	2,773	2,517
ORTHO	2,996	2,567	2,323	2,084	1,828
MENTAL ILL	1,928	1,499	1,255	1,016	760
MENTAL RET	2,399	1,970	1,727	1,488	1,231
OTHER	2,428	1,999	1,756	1,517	1,261
13+ YEARS EDUCATION					
SENSORY	3,898	3,469	3,226	2,987	2,730
ORTHO	3,209	2,780	2,537	2,298	2,042
MENTAL ILL	2,141	1,712	1,469	1,230	974
MENTAL RET	2,612	2,183	1,940	1,701	1,445
OTHER	2,642	2,212	1,969	1,730	1,474

Table 5.10--Continued

BLACK MALES
0 - 8 YEARS EDUCATION

DISABILITY/AGE	14-24	25-34	35-44	45-54	55+
SENSORY	3,700	3,271	3,028	2,789	2,533
ORTHO	3,011	2,582	2,339	2,100	1,844
MENTAL ILL	1,943	1,514	1,271	1,032	776
MENTAL RET	2,415	1,985	1,742	1,503	1,247
OTHER	2,444	2,015	1,772	1,533	1,276

9 - 12 YEARS EDUCATION

	14-24	25-34	35-44	45-54	55+
SENSORY	3,704	3,062	2,819	2,793	2,323
ORTHO	3,015	2,373	2,130	2,104	1,635
MENTAL ILL	1,947	1,305	1,062	1,036	567
MENTAL RET	2,419	1,776	1,533	1,507	1,038
OTHER	2,448	1,806	1,562	1,537	1,067

13+ YEARS EDUCATION

	14-24	25-34	35-44	45-54	55+
SENSORY	3,491	3,275	3,032	2,580	2,537
ORTHO	2,802	2,586	2,343	1,891	1,848
MENTAL ILL	1,734	1,518	1,275	823	780
MENTAL RET	2,205	1,989	1,746	1,294	1,251
OTHER	2,235	2,019	1,776	1,323	1,280

TABLE 5.10--Continued

WHITE FEMALES

DISABILITY/AGE	14-24	25-34	35-44	45-54	55+
0 - 8 YEARS EDUCATION					
SENSORY	3,978	3,549	3,306	3,067	2,811
ORTHO	3,290	2,860	2,617	2,378	2,122
MENTAL ILL	2,222	1,792	1,549	1,310	1,054
MENTAL RET	2,693	2,263	2,020	1,781	1,525
OTHER	2,722	2,293	2,050	1,811	1,555
9 - 12 YEARS EDUCATION					
SENSORY	3,769	3,340	3,097	2,858	2,602
ORTHO	3,080	2,651	2,408	2,169	1,913
MENTAL ILL	2,012	1,583	1,340	1,101	845
MENTAL RET	2,483	2,054	1,811	1,572	1,316
OTHER	2,513	2,084	1,841	1,601	1,345
13+ YEARS EDUCATION					
SENSORY	3,982	3,553	3,310	3,071	2,815
ORTHO	3,294	2,864	2,621	2,382	2,126
MENTAL ILL	2,226	1,796	1,553	1,314	1,058
MENTAL RET	2,697	2,267	2,024	1,785	1,529
OTHER	2,726	2,297	2,054	1,815	1,559

Table 5.10--Continued

BLACK FEMALES

DISABILITY/AGE	14-24	25-34	35-44	45-54	55+
0 - 8 YEARS EDUCATION					
SENSORY	3,785	3,355	3,112	2,873	2,617
ORTHO	3,096	2,667	2,423	2,184	1,928
MENTAL ILL	2,028	1,599	1,355	1,116	860
MENTAL RET	2,499	2,070	1,827	1,588	1,331
OTHER	2,528	2,099	1,856	1,617	1,361
9 - 12 YEARS EDUCATION					
SENSORY	3,576	3,146	2,903	2,664	2,408
ORTHO	2,887	2,457	2,214	1,975	1,719
MENTAL ILL	1,819	1,389	1,146	907	651
MENTAL RET	2,290	1,860	1,617	1,378	1,122
OTHER	2,319	1,890	1,647	1,408	1,152
13+ YEARS EDUCATION					
SENSORY	3,789	3,360	3,116	2,877	2,621
ORTHO	3,100	2,671	2,427	2,188	1,932
MENTAL ILL	2,032	1,603	1,359	1,120	864
MENTAL RET	2,503	2,074	1,831	1,592	1,335
OTHER	2,533	2,103	1,860	1,621	1,365

referral. This wage gain is then compounded over the client's work life. However, the data concerning many clients' earnings, at referral and closure, are incomplete. To correct for this, we must make assumptions about the future earnings of these individuals.

Wage at referral

From the R-300, we have information on the wage of the client at referral, which is defined as the wage the individual earned during the week before entry into the program. Thus, if the individual was unemployed during this period, the wage at referral would be zero. One assumption that could be made is that those individuals who had zero earnings at referral would have continued to have zero earnings if they had not entered the VR program. In our analysis, the first measure of the benefits of VR follows this assumption.

This assumption, however, could lead to a gross overestimation of benefits. It is unrealistic to assume that persons who report no earnings at referral would continue without earnings for the rest of their lives. One alternative is to assume that those persons who reported zero wage at referral would have eventually earned the same mean wage as persons in their cohort with positive wages, even without the intervention of the VR program. In the remaining two measures of benefits, we will follow this assumption. A third way to deal with the problem of zero reported earnings at referral would be to use a two-stage selection bias method to impute earnings for these particular clients. This work is done in the next chapter.

Wages at closure

Wages for successful rehabilitants reported on the R-300 data set are based on the wage they earned after sixty days on their job. However, some rehabilitants, especially homemakers, are placed in unpaid positions. To attain a measure of their value in the marketplace, I assigned these individuals the mean wage of their cohort.

The wages at referral and at closure are not assumed to remain constant over the work life of the rehabilitant. They must be adjusted for several factors, which include unemployment, productivity, and mortality. The future wages must also be discounted by an appropriate social discount rate.

To account for periods of unemployment, wages at closure are adjusted downward by 20 percent in each of the measures of benefits. In the last two measures of benefits, where the mean wage at referral was assigned to those clients who reported zero earnings, wages at referral were adjusted downward by 30 percent.

To account for the productivity growth of labor over time, I adjusted by a productivity growth factor. In the ratios involved, I used growth rates of 2.5 and 3 percent.

Another factor that must be accounted for is mortality, because not all rehabilitants will live until the normal retirement age, which is assumed to be sixty-five. Therefore, the projections of wages at referral and closure are adjusted in accordance with the mortality rates found in the *Life Tables for the United States.*

Future wage gain must be discounted by an appropriate social discount rate. The choice of a discount rate is important, since it can crucially affect the resulting benefit-cost ratios. The present analysis uses discount rates of 10 and 12 percent.

Wage projections

After accounting for these adjustments, we must project wages over the work life of the clients to compute a measure of lifetime earnings. In the first two models, the following formula is used to project wages and calculate benefits:

$$B = {}_{N = A}[(WC_N)\,(M_N)\,(U_N)\,(1 + P)^{N - A + 0.5}]/(1 + R)^{N - A + 1}$$

$$B - {}_{N = A}[(WR_N)\,(M_N)\,(U_N)\,(1 + P)^{N - A + 0.5}]/(1 + R)^{N - A + 1}$$

where: B = the discounted benefit stream;

WC_N = the client's wage at closure;

WR_N = the client's wage at referral;

M_N = the mortality adjustment;

U_N = the unemployment adjustment;

P = the productivity adjustment;

R = the social discount rate;

A = the client's age.

In the first measure of benefit, I assigned the mean wage at closure to those clients with zero wage at closure but did not assign the mean wage to those who reported no wage at referral. In the second measure, I assigned the mean wage to all clients who reported zero wage, either at referral or closure.

For both of these measures of benefits, I conducted sensitivity analyses to examine the effects of different productivity growth rates and social discount rates. The benefit variables and combinations of productivity increases and discount rates associated with them are as follows:

Benefit Variable	Productivity Rate	Discount Rate
Ben1.11*	0.025	0.10
Ben1.12	0.025	0.12
Ben1.21	0.03	0.10
Ben1.22	0.03	0.12
Ben2.11†	0.025	0.10
Ben2.12	0.025	0.12
Ben2.21	0.03	0.10
Ben2.22	0.03	0.12

*Ben1 denotes those benefit variables estimated using the first assumption.
† Ben2 denotes those benefit variables estimated using the second assumption.

Age-earning profiles

This type of projection method is one of simple compounding. Another method to project earnings would assume that the wages of an individual would follow an age-earnings profile. The methodology of using an age-earnings profile to project wages in benefit-cost analysis is set forth by Conley (1973) and Worrall (1978). I use the mean earnings of the stratified cohorts to calculate the estimated future mean earnings of a worker, age eighteen, as the worker moves into successive age groups. Thus we are able to convert the cross sectional data into a time series. The formula used to dynamize the cross section is

$$V = W (1 + P)^{n - 18} [1 + (1 + P) + (1 + P)^2 + \ldots + (1 + P)^{i - 1}]/ i$$

where W = the mean earnings in the age interval in 1982;

n = the lowest age in interval;

i = number of years in age interval;

P = the productivity adjustment.

To construct the age-earnings profile for wages at closure, I used the mean wage of the stratified cohorts. I adjusted all earnings downward by an assumed 20 percent unemployment rate. The age-earnings profile for each cohort is reported in Table 5.11. Figure 5.1 illustrates the shape of some of the estimated age-earnings profiles.

In a third measure of benefit, I use these age-earnings profiles to project wages at closure. I assume that the earnings of the individual over the course of a lifetime will follow the shape of the relevant cohort's age-earnings profile. I also assume a constant difference between the individual's wage and the mean wage of the cohort. In this method of computing benefits, we

TABLE 5.11

EXPECTED FUTURE EARNINGS
FOR AN EIGHTEEN-YEAR-OLD
(In Dollars)

WHITE MALES

DISABILITY/AGE	15-24	25-34	35-44	45-54	55+
0 - 8 YEARS EDUCATION					
SENSORY	3,827	5,776	7,629	8,820	5,647
ORTHO/AMPUT	4,897	7,923	10,655	11,730	9,225
MENTAL ILL	5,815	7,934	10,821	12,419	13,475
OTHER	5,053	6,910	10,100	12,234	11,728
9 - 12 YEARS EDUCATION					
SENSORY	7,802	9,449	11,665	11,718	7,799
ORTHO/AMPUT	8,014	11,015	13,878	15,323	11,612
MENTAL ILL	6,741	9,698	12,421	15,038	15,916
OTHER	7,518	9,668	12,989	16,112	16,864
13+ YEARS EDUCATION					
SENSORY	9,694	12,073	14,705	17,396	10,487
ORTHO/AMPUT	10,026	12,314	16,022	18,269	17,792
MENTAL ILL	7,580	10,410	14,106	18,372	19,947
OTHER	9,822	11,091	15,975	21,042	25,546

Table 5.11-Continued

BLACK MALES

DISABILITY/AGE	15-24	25-34	35-44	45-54	55+
0 - 8 YEARS EDUCATION					
SENSORY	4,205	5,724	4,684	5,874	4,859
ORTHO/AMPUT	5,057	5,342	8,102	9,081	6,188
MENTAL ILL	5,550	7,358	9,295	11,969	10,983
OTHER	5,448	6,817	8,525	9,543	9,981
9 - 12 YEARS EDUCATION					
SENSORY	6,399	7,432	7,789	6,300	4,335
ORTHO/AMPUT	6,469	8,398	10,453	10,987	9,101
MENTAL ILL	5,873	8,230	11,239	13,178	13,900
OTHER	6,281	8,005	10,157	12,154	14,015
13+ YEARS EDUCATION					
SENSORY	7,242	8,614	12,734	13,186	5,503
ORTHO/AMPUT	7,800	10,812	13,674	16,090	11,208
MENTAL ILL	6,632	9,415	12,879	17,430	21,019
OTHER	7,288	9,304	12,488	17,291	17,311

TABLE 5.11--Continued

WHITE FEMALES

DISABILITY/AGE	15-24	25-34	35-44	45-54	55+
0 - 8 YEARS EDUCATION					
SENSORY	2,348	3,217	3,079	2,895	1,367
ORTHO/AMPUT	3,066	3,836	5,996	5,760	4,032
MENTAL ILL	4,042	4,979	5,927	6,674	5,319
OTHER	3,216	4,205	5,184	5,667	4,428
9 - 12 YEARS EDUCATION					
SENSORY	5,528	5,474	6,187	5,744	2,415
ORTHO/AMPUT	6,192	6,777	8,232	8,720	6,474
MENTAL ILL	5,571	7,085	8,755	9,816	9,696
OTHER	5,595	5,847	7,397	8,319	7,501
13+ YEARS EDUCATION					
SENSORY	6,863	8,772	8,419	10,858	3,197
ORTHO/AMPUT	7,670	9,392	11,067	12,987	11,365
MENTAL ILL	6,757	8,816	11,261	13,142	12,711
OTHER	7,283	8,719	11,022	13,109	13,094

Table 5.11--Continued

BLACK FEMALES

0 - 8 YEARS EDUCATION

DISABILITY/AGE	15-24	25-34	35-44	45-54	55+
SENSORY	2,403	3,101	3,232	2,394	1,655
ORTHO/AMPUT	2,244	4,383	5,093	5,291	2,931
MENTAL ILL	3,946	4,928	5,976	4,986	5,497
OTHER	3,528	4,324	5,353	5,062	4,990

9 - 12 YEARS EDUCATION

	15-24	25-34	35-44	45-54	55+
SENSORY	5,104	4,987	5,281	3,758	2,146
ORTHO/AMPUT	6,337	6,571	7,593	6,670	5,617
MENTAL ILL	5,323	6,575	7,572	8,110	9,100
OTHER	5,184	5,896	7,034	7,187	6,968

13+ YEARS EDUCATION

	15-24	25-34	35-44	45-54	55+
SENSORY	5,923	8,118	11,136	8,988	3,729
ORTHO/AMPUT	7,280	8,367	10,670	10,258	6,654
MENTAL ILL	6,568	7,916	9,833	11,021	14,302
OTHER	6,363	7,136	10,346	11,473	8,112

MENTALLY RETARDED

COHORT/AGE	15-24	25-34	35-44	45-54	55+
WHITE MALE	4,155	4,249	4,333	4,059	4,743
BLACK MALE	4,993	5,355	5,976	7,204	6,457
WHITE FEMALE	2,858	3,003	3,327	3,450	2,943
BLACK FEMALE	3,257	4,222	4,969	5,666	5,088

FIGURE 5.1

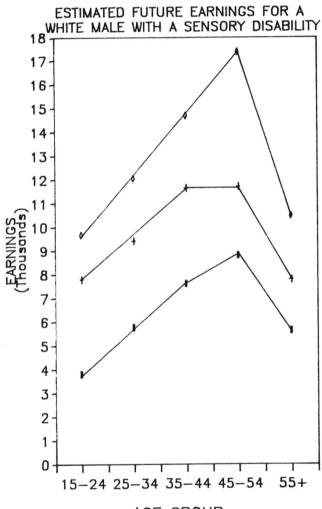

ESTIMATED FUTURE EARNINGS FOR A
WHITE MALE WITH A SENSORY DISABILITY

AGE GROUP

Years of Education:

ı Less than 8 years
ı 9 to 12 years
◊ 13 or more years

can also construct age-earnings profiles to project wages at referral. Here those clients who reported zero wage at referral are assigned the non-zero mean wage of their cohort at referral and a 30 percent unemployment rate for wages at referral is assumed. This measure of benefit was derived using a 2.5 percent productivity growth rate and a 10 percent discount rate. This measure of benefits is denoted as ben3.

I regressed these benefit values on the same set of independent variables in Table 5.5. The results of these regressions are reported in Table 5.12. To compute the estimated benefits for an individual with a particular set of characteristics, the coefficients of the selected characteristics were added or subtracted to the intercept value. This yielded the value of B_s that is used in the benefit-cost ratio.

To calculate the expected lifetime benefits, we can simply multiply P_s, the probability of success, by B_s, the estimated benefit. This is the numerator of the benefit-cost ratio. The expected cost of a client, the denominator of the benefit-cost ratio, is simply $P_s(C_s) + (1 - P_s)C_n$. Dividing the numerator by the denominator yields the benefit-cost ratio. Selected benefit-cost ratios of the three models are reported in Tables 5.13, 5.14 and 5.15.

CONCLUSIONS

The adjustments suggested here may improve the calculation of benefit-cost ratios but they do not solve the problem of providing an unambiguous measure that would be widely accepted. The benefit-cost ratios calculated in this chapter are very sensitive to the assumptions concerning zero wages at referral and to the specification of the productivity growth rate and social discount rate.

In my analysis, I made use of two assumptions concerning clients who reported zero wages at referral. Initially, I arrived at a measure of benefits by assuming that clients who reported a zero wage at opening would, in fact, have continued to be without earnings if they had not entered the vocational rehabilitation program. In the second and third measures of benefits, I assumed that clients who reported a zero wage would eventually earn the non-zero mean wage of their cohort. The weighted average of the stratified benefit-cost ratios derived using the first measure of benefits ranged from a ratio of 9 to 1 to a ratio of 12 to 1. As I indicated above, these ratios are exaggerated because they tend to overestimate the wage gain of rehabilitants. In the second measure of benefits, the average benefit-cost ratios ranged from a ratio of 3 to 1 to a ratio of 4 to 1, depending on the discount and productivity rates used. This measure of benefit may underestimate the wage gain of rehabilitants. In the last measure of benefits, where the age-earnings profiles were used to project benefits, the overall average was approximately

TABLE 5.12

RESULTS OF
BENEFIT REGRESSIONS

VARIABLE CODE	BEN1.11	BEN1.12	BEN1.21	BEN1.22	BEN2.11	BEN2.12	BEN2.21	BEN2.22	BEN3
AGE 00 (basis)	0.0	0.0	0.0	0.0	0.0	0.0	0.0	0.0	0.0
AGE 25	-10387.4	-7613.9	-11407.5	-8205.3	-3205.3	-2368.1	-3575.9	-2556.0	-34104.1
AGE 35	17341.3	-12003.8	-19300.4	-13148.9	-5781.4	-4057.2	-6411.4	-4427.7	-45800.1
AGE 45	-32527.6	-23495.6	-35683.9	-25487.1	-13911.2	-10663.7	-15017.7	-11384.8	-67388.3
AGE 55	-51990.4	-40388.7	-55869.0	-42989.2	-19255.8	-15461.4	-20509.1	-16311.1	-71690.4
SEXF (basis)	0.0	0.0	0.0	0.0	0.0	0.0	0.0	0.0	0.0
SEXM	17551.3	14642.3	18463.9	15304.9	377.3	409.9	359.4	403.9	30024.0
RACEB (basis)	0.0	0.0	0.0	0.0	0.0	0.0	0.0	0.0	0.0
RACEW	3405.4	2886.5	3564.4	3005.4	-3697.5	-2973.0	-3935.3	-3135.8	7431.0
ED8 (basis)	0.0	0.0	0.0	0.0	0.0	0.0	0.0	0.0	0.0

Table 5.12--Continued

VARIABLE CODE	BEN1.11	BEN1.12	BEN1.21	BEN1.22	BEN2.11	BEN2.12	BEN2.21	BEN2.22	BEN3
ED9	13211.2	11038.8	13893.6	11532.9	3730.7	3058.1	3946.3	3210.5	8725.6
ED13	22300.1	18700.6	23418.2	19523.1	4380.2	3621.2	6220.5	3793.7	31163.0
MRET (basis)	0.0	0.0	0.0	0.0	0.0	0.0	0.0	0.0	0.0
SENSORY	2650.7	1399.2	3103.6	1674.4	-11687.5	-9768.8	-12295.9	-10203.0	-31964.3
ORTHO/AMPUT	20241.4	16407.4	21478.1	17275.4	-2243.7	-1736.6	-2421.3	-1847.3	14494.0
MILL	17002.4	13852.5	18011.4	14567.3	-4700.2	-3678.9	-5048.6	-3904.8	43179.1
OTHER	12548.6	10083.0	13355.4	10637.9	-5938.4	-4713.6	-6346.4	-4987.5	27167.2
INTERCEPT	32928.3	25988.3	35262.5	27532.8	26733.8	21448.6	28480.3	22632.3	20161.3

TABLE 5.13

BENEFIT-COST RATIOS
(BEN1.12)

	WHITE MALES			BLACK MALES		
			0 - 8 YEARS EDUCATION			
DISABILITY/AGE	25-34	35-44	45-54	25-34	35-44	45-54
SENSORY	5.87	5.60	3.93	5.47	5.21	3.52
ORTHO/AMPUT	8.08	8.09	6.74	7.66	7.74	6.42
MENTAL ILL	10.81	11.34	9.83	10.72	11.58	10.27
MENTAL RET	10.30	10.39	8.40	10.35	10.60	8.56
OTHER	6.81	6.59	4.61	6.59	6.41	4.33
			9 - 12 YEARS EDUCATION			
SENSORY	8.72	8.62	6.92	8.43	8.38	6.48
ORTHO/AMPUT	11.37	11.66	10.36	11.14	11.58	9.92
MENTAL ILL	16.37	17.87	16.96	17.23	19.67	17.58
MENTAL RET	15.23	15.91	14.10	16.02	17.16	14.75
OTHER	10.41	10.50	8.54	10.56	10.83	8.41
			13+ YEARS EDUCATION			
SENSORY	10.00	9.97	8.37	9.79	9.82	8.39
ORTHO/AMPUT	12.58	12.90	11.67	12.43	12.90	12.20
MENTAL ILL	17.49	18.86	17.96	18.33	20.45	22.14
MENTAL RET	16.53	17.21	15.57	17.37	18.47	17.70
OTHER	11.69	11.84	10.06	11.91	12.24	10.83

8 to 1. The variation in these ratios underscores the significance of the assumption concerning zero wages at referral.

Ideally, stratified benefit-cost analysis would enable program evaluators to determine which cohorts had the highest benefit-cost ratios and thus to conclude which groups are economically efficient to rehabilitate. But the need to rely on certain assumptions in measuring the benefits of the program makes this a rather uncertain enterprise. In addition to the assumption concerning wage at referral, an assumption must be made concerning the method of projecting the wage gain of clients throughout their work lives. In my analysis, I used two measures: in the first, I applied a simple compounding method to project wage gain, and in the second, I assumed that the wage gain of a subgroup would follow the age-earnings profile of that cohort.

Table 5.13--Continued

	WHITE FEMALES			BLACK FEMALES		
			0 - 8 YEARS EDUCATION			
DISABILITY/AGE	25-34	35-44	45-54	25-34	35-44	45-54
SENSORY	3.56	3.08	1.22	3.17	2.67	-2.45
ORTHO/AMPUT	5.84	5.59	3.97	5.49	5.27	0.38
MENTAL ILL	7.46	7.37	5.23	7.31	7.33	-0.17
MENTAL RET	4.58	4.00	1.40	4.26	3.64	-4.21
OTHER	5.79	5.42	3.38	5.56	5.21	-1.03
			9 - 12 YEARS EDUCATION			
SENSORY	5.99	5.62	3.68	5.69	5.32	-0.43
ORTHO/AMPUT	8.65	8.58	6.93	8.45	8.46	2.95
MENTAL ILL	11.83	12.28	10.27	12.30	13.16	4.30
MENTAL RET	8.14	7.82	5.11	8.20	7.94	-1.22
OTHER	9.00	8.85	6.77	9.08	9.03	1.94
			13+ YEARS EDUCATION			
SENSORY	7.27	6.97	5.15	7.02	6.75	1.22
ORTHO/AMPUT	9.85	9.83	8.29	9.72	9.78	4.53
MENTAL ILL	13.13	13.61	11.82	13.64	14.49	6.63
MENTAL RET	9.65	9.46	7.04	9.84	9.74	1.44
OTHER	10.27	10.20	8.29	10.43	10.46	3.89

Despite this drawback, multivariate benefit-cost analysis can be useful when examining the VR program. If we cannot compare the benefit-cost ratios of particular cohorts with any real confidence, we can at least estimate the probability that a client in a particular cohort will be successfully rehabilitated. The estimation of the probability of success is independent of the assumptions made concerning the wage at referral. The results in this chapter show that the probability of success is positively related to the age of the clients and to the level of education. Examining the race of the client, while controlling the other variables, shows that whites have a higher probability of success than blacks. Men were more likely to be successfully rehabilitated than women.

In addition to these findings, certain results from the estimated benefit-cost ratios hold, regardless of the assumptions made. The first result is that the benefit-cost ratios are generally inversely related to age. The older age

TABLE 5.14

BENEFIT-COST RATIOS
(BEN2.21)

	WHITE MALES			BLACK MALES		
			0 - 8 YEARS EDUCATION			
DISABILITY/AGE	25-34	35-44	45-54	25-34	35-44	45-54
SENSORY	1.06	0.86	-0.28	1.55	1.39	0.27
ORTHO/AMPUT	2.28	2.21	1.20	2.75	2.76	1.81
MENTAL ILL	2.79	2.79	1.32	3.62	3.85	2.49
MENTAL RET	2.64	2.53	0.98	3.55	3.59	2.04
OTHER	3.13	3.10	1.89	3.89	3.99	2.83
			9 - 12 YEARS EDUCATION			
SENSORY	1.77	1.59	0.32	2.37	2.26	0.98
ORTHO/AMPUT	3.20	3.19	2.08	3.83	3.95	2.78
MENTAL ILL	4.28	4.50	2.87	5.61	6.31	4.42
MENTAL RET	3.97	3.98	2.25	5.28	5.57	3.68
OTHER	4.34	4.41	3.10	5.40	5.69	4.25
			13+ YEARS EDUCATION			
SENSORY	1.85	1.68	0.43	2.46	2.35	1.14
ORTHO/AMPUT	3.26	3.24	2.14	3.90	3.99	3.05
MENTAL ILL	4.21	4.35	2.79	5.43	5.93	4.96
MENTAL RET	3.94	3.92	2.27	5.17	5.38	3.89
OTHER	4.31	4.35	3.08	5.32	5.54	4.48

groups (forty-five years old and above) have lower benefit-cost ratios than the younger age groups (below forty-five). We also see that when we control for the other variables, the size of the benefit-cost ratio is positively related to the level of education. Finally, we see that, in all cases, males have higher benefit-cost ratios than females but the size of the difference varies, depending on the assumptions of the model.

These ratios can only be taken as rough averages of the benefits and costs of the vocational program. If the objective is to measure the efficiency of the program—to determine if the expenditure of the marginal dollar yields more than a dollar of benefits—these measures fall short. Such a conclusion comes as no surprise; it is the same conclusion reached earlier in our examination of the models.

Table 5.14--Continued

	WHITE FEMALES				BLACK FEMALES		
	0 - 8 YEARS EDUCATION						
DISABILITY/AGE	25-34	35-44	45-54		25-34	35-44	45-54
SENSORY	1.00	0.78	-0.35		1.49	1.33	-0.71
ORTHO/AMPUT	2.23	2.13	1.11		2.74	2.71	0.81
MENTAL ILL	2.64	2.58	1.12		3.49	3.61	0.71
MENTAL RET	3.47	3.42	2.04		4.43	4.52	1.75
OTHER	2.10	1.95	0.68		2.81	2.74	0.31
	9 - 12 YEARS EDUCATION						
SENSORY	1.67	1.48	0.23		2.28	2.15	-0.16
ORTHO/AMPUT	3.09	3.05	1.93		3.76	3.82	1.65
MENTAL ILL	3.97	4.06	2.44		5.25	5.68	2.20
MENTAL RET	4.83	4.90	3.39		6.17	6.49	3.28
OTHER	3.07	2.97	1.57		4.00	4.05	1.25
	13+ YEARS EDUCATION						
SENSORY	1.75	1.56	0.34		2.36	2.23	-0.03
ORTHO/AMPUT	3.14	3.08	1.98		3.81	3.84	1.72
MENTAL ILL	3.91	3.95	2.42		5.09	5.40	2.17
MENTAL RET	4.77	4.80	3.34		6.02	6.26	3.22
OTHER	3.08	2.98	1.63		3.98	3.99	1.32

TABLE 5.15

BENEFIT-COST RATIOS
(BEN3)

	WHITE MALES				BLACK MALES		
	0 - 8 YEARS EDUCATION						
DISABILITY/AGE	25-34	35-44	45-54		25-34	35-44	45-54
SENSORY	-1.33	-3.43	-7.67		-2.52	-4.79	-9.34
ORTHO/AMPUT	5.87	4.44	0.87		4.74	3.25	-0.52
MENTAL ILL	14.48	13.75	9.70		13.55	12.97	8.61
MENTAL RET	11.35	9.73	4.85		10.39	8.64	3.13
OTHER	4.46	2.47	-2.25		3.21	0.98	-4.35
	9 - 12 YEARS EDUCATION						
SENSORY	0.05	-2.24	-7.04		-1.33	-3.85	-8.86
ORTHO/AMPUT	8.38	6.93	2.94		7.24	5.70	1.34
MENTAL ILL	20.31	20.19	15.91		20.22	20.69	14.52
MENTAL RET	15.87	14.42	8.95		15.38	13.90	7.21
OTHER	7.15	5.07	-0.29		5.94	3.58	-2.53

Table 5.15--Continued

	WHITE MALES			BLACK MALES		
		13+	YEARS EDUCATION			
SENSORY	4.06	2.13	-2.21	2.82	0.72	-4.06
ORTHO/AMPUT	12.25	11.13	7.60	11.26	10.13	6.65
MENTAL ILL	25.01	25.36	22.06	25.27	26.32	25.46
MENTAL RET	20.91	20.02	15.49	20.91	20.17	15.86
OTHER	11.70	10.14	5.56	10.88	9.20	4.22

	WHITE FEMALES			BLACK FEMALES		
		0 - 8	YEARS EDUCATION			
DISABILITY/AGE	25-34	35-44	45-54	25-34	35-44	45-54
SENSORY	-6.04	-8.45	-12.96	-7.36	-10.01	-15.72
ORTHO/AMPUT	1.24	-0.62	-4.61	0.09	-1.93	-7.06
MENTAL ILL	7.80	5.99	0.92	6.63	4.62	-2.58
MENTAL RET	-1.40	-4.31	-10.37	-3.23	-6.67	-15.05
OTHER	3.81	1.80	-2.76	2.59	0.33	-5.84
		9 - 12	YEARS EDUCATION			
SENSORY	-5.29	-7.95	-13.03	-6.86	-9.84	-16.42
ORTHO/AMPUT	2.97	0.97	-3.50	1.71	-0.49	-6.41
MENTAL ILL	11.64	9.91	4.11	10.79	8.89	0.15
MENTAL RET	0.56	-2.66	-9.68	-1.45	-5.37	-15.54
OTHER	6.24	4.12	-1.00	5.04	2.64	-4.51
		13+	YEARS EDUCATION			
SENSORY	-1.28	-3.58	-8.20	-2.69	-5.23	-11.22
ORTHO/AMPUT	6.84	5.19	1.20	5.76	3.99	-1.28
MENTAL ILL	16.54	15.45	10.77	16.17	15.16	8.33
MENTAL RET	5.95	3.45	-2.52	4.57	1.65	-6.83
OTHER	10.63	8.96	4.50	9.81	8.00	1.84

NOTES

1. For a number of years, each state vocational rehabilitation agency has reported to the federal Rehabilitation Services Administration (RSA) information on each case closed during the year. In the last several years, there has been much discussion among the states, the RSA, and the federal Office of Management and Budget (OMB) about the need for such information in general and more particularly, for certain individual data items. Information is currently being collected and sent to the RSA on form RSA-911. The data are comparable but not exactly the same as the data on the R-300 form. The analysis in this chapter and in many of those that follow is

based on the R-300 data and it is this term that will be used throughout the volume to denote the national data base.

2. Anita Hall-Kane assisted in the preparation of this account of the information contained in the national data set.

3. These clients are assigned the non-zero mean rehabilitation cost on the theory that they have received services paid for by other agencies. See the discussion of the "similar benefits" issue in Chapter 10 of this volume, "Using a Better Measure for Services."

4. In this crude model, we can replicate results using a random 1 percent sample. There has been some reluctance to use a less expensive sampling method, but little difference could be detected in the results when a random 1 percent sample was used. In the sample of 7,193 clients, the total case service cost for the 2,169 successfully rehabilitated clients was $3,849,478; and the total case service cost for all closures was approximately $6 million. With overhead and administrative costs, the total cost is $13.6 million. The lifetime improvement in earnings aggregated over the thirty year period is $100.1 million. Dividing the lifetime earnings aggregates by the total cost of the rehabilitation produces a benefit-cost ratio of $7.34, which appears to be similar to the ratio for the population of $7.52.

WORKS CITED

Bellante, Donald M. 1972. "A Multivariate Analysis of a Vocational Rehabilitation System." *Journal of Human Resources* 7:226–41.

Conley, Ronald W. 1973. *The Economics of Mental Retardation.* Baltimore, Md.: Johns Hopkins University Press.

Worrall, John D. 1978. "A Benefit-Cost Analysis of the Vocational Rehabilitation Program." *Journal of Human Resources* 13:285–98.

6   *Anita G. Hall-Kane and Ernest Gibbs*

CORRECTING FOR ZERO WAGES
AT REFERRAL

Ronald Conley has observed that a "striking measure of the economic value of the rehabilitation program is obtained by comparing the increase in estimated annual earnings of rehabilitants between time of acceptance and time of closure relative to the costs of the program" (1964, p. 55). One significant problem that arises with the use of this measure, however, is *how* to measure client earnings at acceptance.

The overwhelming majority of persons accepted into the program report that they were not working at the time of application and so were not earning any wages. Although there is no reason to doubt the truth of their assertion, it may be that they withdrew from the labor market because of their decision to apply to the program. Had they not chosen to apply, it is possible that they could have entered the labor market and commanded some wage greater than zero. It is also possible that individuals who report zero wages do in fact have a history of work experience but have not been able to find employment for some period of time before applying to the program. A third possibility is that individuals who report zero wages have not pursued competitive employment because their leisure time, with the support of their disability transfer payments, seems to them more desirable than the wage they could command in the labor force. In the language of economists, the reservation wage (the value of time in the home) exceeds the market offer wage (the value of time in the labor force). In all cases, if we adopt the assumption that the zero wages reported by such clients are a true reflection of their earnings power, then any positive wage they report at closure will suggest that program participation yields infinite benefits. In this chapter, we review some earlier attempts to compensate for this problem and present a method of imputing earnings to clients who do not report earnings at referral.

RSA EFFORTS TO ALLEVIATE THE DATA PROBLEM

On average, 88 percent of all accepted VR cases did not report earnings at acceptance during the fourteen-year period from 1945 to 1958 (see Table 6.1). Over the next five years, the Rehabilitation Services Administration (RSA)

TABLE 6.1

PERCENTAGE OF VR CLIENTS REPORTING EARNINGS AT ACCEPTANCE
1945 - 1963

Year	Number of Cases Accepted	Number with Earnings at Acceptance	Percentage
1945	86,826	10,056	11.58%
1946	80,380	8,770	10.91%
1947	68,692	10,420	15.17%
1948	88,357	12,337	13.96%
1949	99,202	12,626	12.73%
1950	92,009	11,938	12.97%
1951	90,603	11,512	12.71%
1952	88,922	11,241	12.64%
1953	84,397	10,946	12.97%
1954	78,045	9,622	12.33%
1955	82,269	9,331	11.34%
1956	93,555	10,421	11.14%
1957	104,125	11,863	11.39%
1958	113,855	13,006	11.42%
1959	121,559	63,011	51.84%
1960	126,839	68,760	54.21%
1961	140,476	29,044	20.68%
1962	148,763	32,361	21.75%
1963	160,611	31,725	19.75%

- - - - - - - - - - -

Source: Derived from Conley (1964: Tables 4-1 and 4-3, pp. 54, 57).

altered the time period in which earnings before acceptance could be measured in hope of obtaining more information for use in evaluating earnings improvements. More specifically, the RSA thought that by lengthening this time period, they might capture work histories of otherwise nonreporting clients.

The danger of this approach is that too long a period might include earnings by rehabilitants before onset of their disabling condition. Too brief a time period would fail to take into account a client's work history if the client were unemployed at acceptance owing to a disabling condition. As Conley observes, "presumably there is an optimal period where the errors would just offset each other, but we have no way of knowing what this optimal period is" (1964, p. 69).

In 1959 and 1960, VR clients were asked to report their total earnings for twelve months before acceptance. In addition, "cases for whom no earnings were reported were assumed to have the same proportion with earnings and the same average earnings as all other rehabilitants before and after services"

(Conley 1964, p. 57).[1] The combined effects of these two measures would help to explain the over four-fold increase in the percentage of the accepted clients reporting earnings at acceptance (see Table 6.1).

During the years 1961–1963 the RSA again changed the time period for reporting earnings at acceptance. For these three years, clients were asked to report their earnings for the three months before acceptance. The percentage of clients reporting earnings at acceptance dropped by over 50 percent. In 1961, the RSA officially adopted the practice of imputing an earnings value for all clients reporting no earnings at acceptance, based on the average earnings of all other clients (Conley 1964, p. 59). Conley reports that "the effect of this practice on the estimated annual rise in earnings was insignificant in 1961. In 1962 it depressed the estimated annual rise in earnings by about $2 million, because of the greater numbers for whom data were not reported at acceptance" (1964, p. 59).

Since 1964 the RSA has been asking clients to report earnings for one week before the date of acceptance.

A FURTHER EXPLORATION OF THE PROBLEM

A change in the earnings of rehabilitants between the time of referral and closure is an acceptable, if less than perfect, method of evaluating the economic impact of the VR program. However, analysts of the program will hesitate to proceed with this measure of the program's impact when dealing with VR clients who report no weekly earnings at referral.

First, there is uncertainty about the role of the VR program in improving the earnings of these clients. How much of a positive impact on earnings can be attributed to VR participation when a client reports zero earnings at acceptance into the program and positive earnings at closure? If analysts use 100 percent of the difference between weekly earnings at referral and at closure to evaluate the economic impact of the VR program, they are assuming that: (1) the earnings of these clients actually represent all of the benefit of their participation in the VR program; (2) the clients' preprogram earnings would have remained unchanged in the absence of VR participation; (3) clients designated as nonsuccessful rehabilitants experience no significant impact on their earnings as a result of being in the VR program; and (4) the level of the rehabilitants' earnings at closure will be constant over the remaining measurement period (Conley 1964). If these assumptions are unacceptable, then analysts must decide how to separate the improvement in earnings attributable to VR participation from the improvement due to previously obtained skills or knowledge.

Second, certain human capital considerations may make it difficult to apply the change in earnings measure in a simple fashion. If clients report zero weekly earnings at referral, should that value be accepted as representative of the actual market value of their stock of human capital? If the market value of the clients' stock of human capital (in the form of weekly earnings) represents the value of their marginal product, can it truly be the case that rehabilitants have so little human capital to offer in the market to warrant zero earnings? Should a minimum value of human capital be assumed for each client reporting zero earnings at acceptance?

If we decide that it is necessary to impute an earnings figure to clients reporting zero earnings at acceptance in order to arrive at a more realistic assessment of the program's economic impact, then we face a new set of problems, econometric in nature. What method should be used to predict earnings for this group of clients? One solution is to estimate the expected earnings of these clients (if working) based on the information given by clients who are reported as working at referral. However, in general, it is unacceptable simply to run a regression on a sample of clients working at referral and then apply the resulting coefficients to clients not working at referral to impute an earnings figure for them. There are likely to be unmeasurable characteristics that influence both the work/not work decision and the measured earnings for working clients. If we do not account for these characteristics, we are likely to obtain biased estimates.

The presence (or absence) of a client's reported weekly earnings at acceptance can be modeled by a jointly determined decision criterion. This decision criterion simultaneously optimizes a labor force participation choice and a labor supply decision.

The labor force participation choice is specified as

(1) $\qquad P_i = Pr(D_i = 1) = f(X_{4i}, U_{4i})$

where P_i = probability of labor force participation
X_{4i} = a matrix of exogenous variables
U_{4i} = a normally distributed random variable that captures the effects of unmeasurable variables
D_i = 1 if participating in the labor force
D_i = 0 if not participating in the labor force

The probability that client i is in the labor force, P_i, is a function of various exogenous variables, X_{4i}, such as education, sex, age, family income, and a random variable, U_{4i}.

The labor supply decision is modeled in an earnings equation form. A client's earnings equation is specified as

(2) $\qquad Y_i = f(X_{2i}, U_{2i})$

where Y_i = client's weekly earnings
X_{2i} = a matrix of exogenous variables
U_{2i} = a normally distributed random variable that captures the effects of unmeasurable variables

The presence of earnings at acceptance is also a function of various exogenous variables, X_{2i}, not necessarily mutually exclusive from the exogenous variables in the participation model X_{4i}, and a random variable, U_{2i}. The random variables U_{2i} and U_{4i} are generally modeled to be correlated. Correlated exogenous variables pose no problems in estimation. However, correlated unmeasurable variables pose serious problems. If the correlation between U_{2i} and U_{4i} is not accounted for, ordinary least squares estimation of equation (2) will produce biased coefficients and lead to biased estimates of benefits in further analysis.

THE THEORETICAL MODEL

One solution to correct the zero weekly earnings at referral problem is to treat earnings within a censored sample framework. James Heckman (1976) introduced a method to generate consistent estimators using a two-stage technique for censored samples.

The sample is censored because nearly complete information is available for each client with the exception of those individuals who report zero weekly earnings at acceptance. Since the dependent variable is weekly earnings at acceptance, these clients are defined as having "censored" weekly earnings at acceptance. Heckman posits a method to impute earnings to these clients that revolves around unmeasurables, represented by the error term in regression equations. If the errors in the earnings function and the participation equation are correlated, then a sample selection-bias problem exists. Regressions estimated using a sample of clients with positive earnings at referral will not constitute a random sample. Regression equations based on a nonrandom sample will bias the estimated coefficients and therefore will lead to biased estimates of the imputed earnings of nonreporting clients.

To alleviate these problems—the influence of an error term on work status and subsequently on the availability of the earnings data and the selection-bias problem—the model can be recharacterized within a specification error framework.

By using a subset of data from clients reporting positive earnings at referral, we are selecting a nonrandom sample. We can identify observations for inclusion in the sample by the sample selection rule. Using this subset of data from clients reporting positive earnings data, we can specify a function including a sample selection rule such as:

(3) $\quad E[\ Y_i^{ref}\ |\ X_{2i},$ sample selection rule]
$= X_{2i}B_2 + E[\ U_{2i}\ |$ sample selection rule]

where Y_i^{ref} = the weekly earnings at referral of client i as determined by the market
X_{2i} = a k x i matrix of all observable exogenous variables
B_2 = a k x 1 vector of generated coefficients
U_{2i} = the earnings error term for client i

If the expectation of U_{2i} conditional upon the sample selection rule is zero, then the selected sample will meet all the requirements for consistent ordinary least squares estimates. However, this is generally not the case.

Let the client's weekly earnings reported at referral, Y_i^{ref}, be a function of a vector of exogenous (measurable) variables, X_{2i}, and an unmeasurable variable, U_{2i}. And let the client's reservation earnings, Y_i^{res}, also be a function of a vector of exogenous (measurable) variables, X_{3i}, and an unmeasurable variable, U_{3i}.

(4a) $\quad Y_i^{ref} = X_{2i}B_2 + U_{2i}$

(b) $\quad Y_i^{res} = X_{3i}B_3 + U_{3i}$

where B_n is a vector of parameters, $n = 2, 3$.

If a client is reported as working, then $Y_i^{ref} > 0$ and $Y_i^{ref} > Y_i^{res}$ and $Y_i^{ref} - Y_i^{res} > 0$. The market earnings Y_i^{ref} will be observed but Y_i^{res} will not be observed. For VR clients at referral, we propose a sample selection rule as follows.

If we assume that every client recorded as working at program acceptance will also report positive earnings at acceptance, then the Pr(working at referral) $= Pr(D_i = 1)$

$$= Pr(Y_i^{ref} > Y_i^{res})$$
$$= Pr(Y_i^{ref} - Y_i^{res} > 0)$$

and conversely,

Pr(not working at referral) $= 1 - Pr(D_i = 1)$
$$= 1 - Pr(Y_i^{ref} > Y_i^{res})$$

where Y_i^{res} represents the client reservation earnings.

The client will be drawn into the labor force if the offered market earnings exceed the client's reservation earnings. Let the probability that Y_i^{ref} is greater than Y_i^{res} be denoted as

(5) $\quad P_i = Pr(D_i = 1) = Pr(Y_i^{ref} > Y_i^{res})$
$$= Pr(Y_i^{ref} - Y_i^{res} > 0)$$
$$= Pr[(X_{2i}B_2 + U_{2i}) - (X_{3i}B_3 + U_{3i}) > 0]$$
$$= Pr[(X_{2i}B_2 - X_{3i}B_3) > (U_{3i} - U_{2i})]$$
$$= Pr[X_{4i}B_4 > U_{4i}] = Pr[U_{4i} > - X_{4i}B_4]$$

(6) $\quad$ and $1 - P_i = 1 - Pr(D_i = 1)$ otherwise.

where $\quad P_i \quad$ represents the labor force participation choice

$\qquad D_i = 1$ indicates a client is participating in the labor force

$\qquad D_i = 0$ otherwise

$\qquad X_{4i} =$ the union of X_{3i} and X_{2i}

$\qquad U_{3i} - U_{2i} = U_{4i}$

$\qquad B_n =$ a vector of parameters, $n = 2, 3, 4$

$$\begin{bmatrix} U_{2i} \\ U_{4i} \end{bmatrix} \sim N \left[\begin{pmatrix} 0 \\ 0 \end{pmatrix} \begin{pmatrix} \sigma_{22} & \sigma_{24} \\ \sigma_{42} & \sigma_{44} \end{pmatrix} \right]$$

If equation (4a) were estimated using ordinary least squares on a sample of clients reporting positive earnings at referral, we would be likely to obtain biased results. One of the primary assumptions under which the method of least squares yields consistent estimates is that the expectation of the error term, U_{2i}, conditional on the exogenous variables must be zero for each client; $E[U_{2i}|X_{2i}] = 0$.

Let P_i be a function of a vector of exogenous variables, X_{4i} and an unmeasurable variable, U_{4i}.

(7) $\quad P_i = f(X_{4i}, U_{4i})$

Using (3) and (4a,b), we can respecify our equations as:

(8) $\quad \begin{aligned} E[Y_i^{ref}|X_{2i},D_i = 1] &= E[X_{2i}B_2 + U_{2i}|D_i = 1] \\ &= X_{2i}B_2 + E[U_{2i}|D_i = 1] \\ &= X_{2i}B_2 + E[U_{2i}|U_{4i} > -X_{4i}B_4] \end{aligned}$

If we are to continue to use the method of least squares to estimate unbiased parameters for equation (4a), the expectation of the error term, U_{2i}, conditional upon the measurable variables (X_{4i}) and unmeasurable variable (U_{4i}) in equation (8) must be equal to zero;

(9a) $\quad E[U_{2i}| U_{4i} > -X_{4i}B_4] = 0.$

In general, it is not the case that the expected value of U_{4i} in (7) will be zero. It is not unreasonable to expect that U_{2i} and U_{4i} will be correlated. In fact, Gronau (1974) and Killingsworth (1983) have shown that

(b) $\quad E[U_{2i}| U_{4i} > -X_{4i}B_4] = \dfrac{\sigma_{24}}{(\sigma_{44})^{\frac{1}{2}}} \lambda_i$

(c) $\quad E[U_{4i}| U_{4i} > -X_{4i}B_4] = \dfrac{\sigma_{44}}{(\sigma_{44})^{\frac{1}{2}}} \lambda_i$

where

$$\lambda_i = \frac{\Phi(Z_i)}{1 - \Phi(Z_i)} \quad ; \quad Z_i = \frac{-X_{4i}B_4}{(\sigma_{44})^{\frac{1}{2}}}$$

Continuing on with the stated objective of estimating equation (4a), we can now rewrite the equation as follows:

(10) $\quad Y_i^{ref} = X_{2i}B_2 + \dfrac{\sigma_{24}}{(\sigma_{44})^{\frac{1}{2}}} \lambda_i + V_{2i}$

from

$$E[Y_i^{ref}|X_{2i}, V_{2i}, D_i = 1]$$

$$= X_{2i}B_2 + E[U_{2i}|U_{4i} > - X_{2i}B_4] + E[V_{2i}|X_{2i}, \lambda_i, U_{4i} > - X_{4i}B_4]$$

$$= X_{2i}B_2 + \frac{\sigma_{24}}{(\sigma_{44})^{\frac{1}{2}}} \lambda_i$$

If ordinary least squares are to be used on equation (10), it must be shown that the expected value of the new error term, V_{2i}, conditional upon the other variables is equal to zero;

(11)   Let $V_{2i} = U_{2i} - \dfrac{\sigma_{24}}{(\ddot{\sigma}_{44})^{\frac{1}{2}}} \lambda_i$

Using (11), we can respecify equation (10) as:

(12) $E[(U_{2i} - \dfrac{\sigma_{24}}{(\sigma_{44})^{\frac{1}{2}}} \lambda_i)|X_{2i}, \lambda_i, U_{4i} > - X_{4i}B_4]$

$$= E[U_{2i}|X_{2i}, \lambda_i, U_{4i} > - X_{4i}B_4]$$

$$- E[\frac{\sigma_{24}}{(\sigma_{44})^{\frac{1}{2}}} \lambda_i|X_{2i}, \lambda_i, U_{4i} > - X_{4i}B_4]$$

$$- \frac{\sigma_{24}}{(\sigma_{44})^{\frac{1}{2}}} \lambda_i - \frac{\sigma_{24}}{(\sigma_{44})^{\frac{1}{2}}} \lambda_i = 0$$

where the expectation of the left hand side was previously given and the expectation of the right hand side, a constant, is a constant.

Equation (10) demonstrates that the missing data problem in the dependent variable can be respecified within a specification error framework with respect to the explanatory variables and the error term. A likely specification of the earnings equation in the style of equation (4a), for our estimation problem, fails to take into account the correlation of U_{2i} and U_{4i} by omitting

$$\frac{\sigma_{24}}{(\sigma_{44})^{\frac{1}{2}}} \lambda_i$$

as a regressor and would therefore provide biased coefficients if equation (4a) were estimated by ordinary least squares. Equation (10) is purged of any sample selection bias for the subset of clients having positive earnings at referral if the λ_i term is included as a regressor, and if the new error term V_{2i} has a conditional expected value equal to zero.

The previous exposition of equation (10) and (11) is of no value unless λ_i and Z_i can be explicitly estimated. Heckman (1976) has shown that for censored samples one can estimate the probability that an observation has missing data; therefore, it is possible to estimate Z_i and λ_i.

In order to estimate the λ_i (via the Z_i's), we must begin with the labor force participation equation. The dependent variable in equation (1), D_i, is set as a $0 - 1$ variable and regressed on a vector of exogenous variables, X_{4i}, and an unmeasurable variable, U_{4i}. After the regression, the predicted values of the dependent variable, $\hat{P}_i$, are constrained to fall inside the interval from 0 to 1.

These predicted values are interpreted as the probability that an individual is or is not participating in the labor force, given a vector of exogeneous variables and an unmeasurable variable; hence the 0 to 1 interval constraint.

Recall that for clients participating in the labor force, we know

(13a) $P_i = Pr(D_i = 1) = Pr[Y_i^{ref} - Y_i^{res} > 0]$
$= Pr[U_{4i} > Z_i]$
$= Pr[U_{4i} > -X_{4i}B_4]$

and conversely for clients not participating in the labor force:

(b) $1 - P_i = 1 - Pr(D_i = 1) = 1 - Pr[Y_i^{ref} - Y_i^{res} > 0]$
$1 - Pr[U_{4i} > -X_{4i}B_4]$

The maximum likelihood estimation of the probit model determines the labor force status of clients—that is, whether clients are in or out of the labor force—by comparing their individual values ($Y_i^{ref} = X_{4i}B_4 + U_{4i}$) relative to a threshold level ($Y_T = X_TB_T + U_T$).

Since the probability of participating in the labor force must fall between 0 and 1, P_i must assume the form of a cumulative distribution function, Φ. Further, by the central limit theorem and by standardizing with respect to the participation equation, Φ is assumed to have a standard normal distribution.

More formally, the distribution for clients who are determined to be in the labor force is:

(14) $P_i = Pr(D_i = 1)$
$= Pr[U_{4i} > - X_{4i}B_4]$
$= Pr\ U_{4i} > - X_{4i}B_4$
$= Pr \left[\dfrac{U_{4i}}{\sigma_{4i}} > \dfrac{-X_{4i}B_4}{\sigma_{4i}} \right]$
$= \displaystyle\int_{\frac{-X_TB_T}{\sigma_T}}^{\infty} \dfrac{1}{\sqrt{2\pi}\ \sigma_{4i}}\ e^{\left\{ \frac{-U_{4i}-\overline{U}_{4i}}{2\sigma_{4i}} \right\}^2}$
$= 1 - \Phi(-X_TB_T/\sigma_T)$

where $\overline{U}_{4i} = 0$

and the distribution for those who are determined to be out of the labor force:

(15) $1 - P_i = 1 - Pr(D_i = 1)$
$= 1 - Pr\ U_{4i} > -X_{4i}B_4$
$= \displaystyle\int_{-\infty}^{\frac{-X_TB_T}{\sigma_T}} \dfrac{1}{\sqrt{2\pi}\ \sigma_{4i}}\ e^{\frac{-U_{4i}-\overline{U}_{4i}}{2\sigma_{4i}}}{}^2$
$= \Phi\ (-X_TB_T/\sigma_T)$

The likelihood function for the sample is:

$$(16) \quad = \prod_{i\epsilon K} \{ 1 - \Phi (-X_T B_T/\sigma_T\} \prod_{i\epsilon \overline{K}} \{ \Phi(-X_T B_T/\sigma_T) \}$$

where $i\epsilon K$ represents clients determined to be in the labor force with positive weekly earnings at referral

$i\epsilon \overline{K}$ otherwise.

The conditional probability that a client, j, is working can be estimated by

$$(17) \quad \hat{\lambda}_j = \frac{\phi(-X_{4j}\hat{B}_{4j}/\hat{\sigma}_{4j})}{1 - \Phi(-X_T\hat{B}_T/\hat{\sigma}_T)}$$

Alternatively, a client j' who is not working at referral will have an estimated lambda value of

$$(18) \quad \hat{\lambda}_j' = \frac{\phi(-X_{4j}\hat{B}_{4j}/\hat{\sigma}_{4j})}{\Phi(-X_T\hat{B}_T/\hat{\sigma}_T)}$$

Therefore, by means of probit analysis, it is possible to estimate λ for every working and nonworking client in the sample, and to estimate equation (10) directly.

THE DATA

We used a 10 percent random sample ($N = 71,930$) of clients drawn from the fiscal 1982 national R-300 data set ($N = 720,612$) in this analysis (U.S. Dept. of Education 1983). Key variables were tested for representativeness relative to the data set from which they were drawn. As expected for randomly generated samples, no significant differences were found between the population and sample statistics. Table 6.2 gives the key variables used in our analysis, along with the procedure we used to categorize the variables into 0-1 dummy variables. Table 6.3 gives the percentage of clients who fall into each category.

We divided the variable for age at referral into four groups: 14 to 24 years, 25 to 34 years, 35 to 44 years, and greater than 45 years. Education was also divided into four categories: 0 to 8 years, 9 to 11 years, 12 years, and greater than 12 years. We created two cohorts for race—whites and nonwhites—and three cohorts for marital status—"married," "never married," and "not married" (widowed or divorced). We used three classifications for the number of dependents—none, 1 or 2, and 3 or more dependents—and six classifications for the disabling condition at referral—physical, severe physical, emotional, severe emotional, mental and severe mental.[2]

TABLE 6.2

DEFINITIONS OF VARIABLES USED IN THE
EARNINGS AND PARTICIPATION EQUATIONS

Variable Name	Code	Value
Age at Referral	AGE00	= 1 if 14 - 24 years, 0 otherwise
	AGE25	= 1 if 25 - 34 years, 0 otherwise
	AGE35	= 1 if 35 - 44 years, 0 otherwise
	AGE45	= 1 if 45+ years, 0 otherwise
Education	EDUC8	= 1 if 0 - 8 years, 0 otherwise
	EDUC11	= 1 if 9 - 11 years, 0 otherwise
	EDUC12	= 1 if 12 years, 0 otherwise
	EDUC13	= 1 if 13+ years, 0 otherwise
Race	RACEW	= 1 if white, 0 otherwise
	RACENW	= 1 if nonwhite, 0 otherwise
Disabling Condition	PHYSICAL	= 1 if physical, 0 otherwise(1)
	SEVPHY	= 1 if severe physical, 0 otherwise(2)
	EMOTIONAL	= 1 if emotional, 0 otherwise(3)
	SEVEMOT	= 1 if severe emotional, 0 otherwise(4)
	MENTAL	= 1 if mental, 0 otherwise(5)
	SEVMENT	= 1 if mental, 0 otherwise(6)
Number of Dependents	NODEP	= 1 if no dependents, 0 otherwise
	DEP1OR2	= 1 if 1 or 2 dependents, 0 otherwise
	DEP3	= 1 if 3 or more dependents, 0 otherwise
Marital Status	MARRIED	= 1 if married, 0 otherwise
	NVMARRIED	= 1 if never married, 0 otherwise
	NTMARRIED	= 1 if presently not married, 0 otherwise

----

(1) PHYSICAL includes disability codes 100 to 449 or codes greater than 600 with the special federal program identifier less than 400
(2) SEVPHY includes disability codes 100 to 449 or codes greater than 600 with the special federal program identifier greater than or equal to 400
(3) EMOTIONAL includes disability codes 500 to 529 with the special federal program identifier less than 400
(4) SEVEMOT includes disability codes 500 to 529 with the special federal program identifier greater than or equal to 400
(5) MENTAL includes disability codes 530 to 534 with the special federal program identifier less than 400
(6) SEVMENT includes disability codes 530 to 534 with the special federal program identifier greater than or equal to 400

TABLE 6.3

VARIABLE PERCENTAGES FOR WORKING
AND NONWORKING CLIENTS, BY SEX

Variable	Male		Female	
	Working (N=2,331)	Nonworking (N=16,052)	Working (N=1,918)	Nonworking (N=9,075)
AGE00	28.6	28.8	22.5	32.1
AGE25	32.9	29.7	31.1	25.5
AGE35	18.1	18.6	21.2	18.5
AGE45	20.4	19.5	25.2	23.9
EDUC8	15.2	16.1	13.5	13.1
EDUC11	21.1	28.6	20.7	28.2
EDUC12	42.9	39.6	44.7	42.2
EDUC13	20.8	15.7	21.1	16.5
RACEW	87.4	80.0	82.5	82.2
RACENW	12.6	20.0	17.5	17.8
PHYSICAL	41.2	28.9	49.1	32.5
SEVPHY	33.3	34.0	25.0	31.3
EMOTIONAL	4.7	4.6	7.9	8.1
SEVEMOT	5.1	10.3	6.5	13.9
MENTAL	12.4	14.7	9.0	9.5
SEVMENT	3.3	7.5	2.5	4.7
NODEP	44.3	58.0	55.7	69.3
DEP1OR2	31.6	24.4	32.5	23.1
DEP3	24.1	17.6	11.8	7.6
MARRIED	35.4	34.8	27.0	29.8
NVMARRIED	47.8	44.3	28.2	35.2
NTMARRIED	16.8	20.9	44.8	35.0

THE EMPIRICAL MODEL

Before proceeding to apply the theory outlined in this chapter, we will set forth and examine the economic specifications of the empirical model.

The dependent variable in the earnings equation, weekly earnings of a client, is expected to be positively related to years of schooling and job experience and inversely related to health status (see Bartel 1979, Luft 1975, and Mincer 1974). The more severe the disabling condition reported at referral, the greater the likelihood of a negative impact on earnings capacity.

Other personal characteristics accounted for in the model include race, age, and experience. Since no explicit earnings history is available for each client, we have used age at program acceptance as an experience proxy. In traditional human capital theory, the expected effect of lifetime experience on lifetime earnings is for earnings over time to rise, reach a peak, and then begin to fall (Mincer 1974). Since this is also the typical relationship between age and earnings, we would expect that the coefficients on the age dummies would be positive, but the size of the coefficient would be smaller in the older age group.

Other variables, such as the number of dependents and the marital status of the client, may influence earnings through the number of hours worked per week. However, since our data give us only a weekly earnings figure, we exclude those variables that influence the number of hours worked. The choice of hours worked probably influences annual earnings more than weekly earnings; hence this exclusion should not affect our findings to a great extent.

The probability that a client will be in the paid labor force will be a function of the same variables used in the previously specified earnings equation, together with the variables that influence hours worked. This is based on the assumption that the labor participation decision—whether a person will enter the labor market or not—depends upon receiving a wage offer greater than the individual's reservation wage. Therefore, all variables that influence wage will affect the work/no work decision. Also, it is assumed that all variables that determine an individual's reservation wage will also determine the number of hours worked per week. For this reason, in the labor force participation equation (unlike the earnings equation), we include all variables that affect the number of hours worked.

The probability of client i being in the paid labor force at the time of program acceptance is also expected to be positively related to age at program acceptance and years of schooling and inversely related to health status and the number of dependents.

APPLICATION

The 10 percent sample was divided by sex into two subsamples. Cleaning the data set of missing data in the primary variables resulted in data sets of 18,383 males and 10,993 females.[3] Further, we identified clients who reported positive earnings at acceptance and those who indicated they were working during the week of acceptance into the VR program.[4] The identification of these individuals was based on the assumption that every client working at acceptance will also report positive earnings at acceptance. This was generally found to be true. Of the male clients, 2,331 were working at referral; of the female clients, 1,918 were working.

We used Heckman's two-step technique, described above, to compute an adjusted weekly earnings estimate for clients not reporting earnings. In the first step, we used probit analysis to obtain the probability that the value of time in the paid labor force is greater than the value of time out of the paid labor force. By means of probit analysis, lambda, λ, was calculated for each client. This variable eliminates the possible correlation between the unobservables that might influence both the participation decision and the earnings of an individual. In the second step of the technique, we estimated an ordinary least squares earnings equation that included lambda as an explanatory variable for all clients reported as working with positive weekly earnings at referral. The coefficients from the adjusted earnings regression were used to compute unbiased predicted weekly earnings for all other clients in their respective subsamples.

EMPIRICAL RESULTS

Table 6.4 gives the result of the probit analysis of the labor force participation decision. We see that, in general, years of schooling is positively related to the probability of working for both males and females. For both men and women, white clients are more likely to be employed than black ones. Age of the client is inversely related to labor force participation for men but positively related for women. As one would expect, the effect of marital status on the decision to work depends upon the sex of the client. Married men are more likely to work than men who are not married; women who are not married are more likely to work than married women. An interesting finding is the negative coefficients on the dummy variables for the number of dependents in the female probit. This finding suggests that those with three or more dependents are more likely to work than those with two or less dependents. Thus it seems that family obligations weigh as heavily on females as they do on males. The motivation to work would be especially felt by women who are single heads of households. In all but one group, clients who are classified as having a severe disability are less likely to work than clients not diagnosed as severely disabled. Those with a physical disability are more likely to work than those with either an emotional or a mental disability.

In Table 6.5, we present the results of the adjusted and unadjusted earnings equations. It should be noted that the Heckman two-step method should correct for any possible selection-bias so that the expected value of the error term in the earnings equation would be zero. However, this error term might not have a constant variance. This means that, while the parameter estimates will be unbiased, the standard error of the estimates and thus the t-statistics are incorrect (see Heckman 1976).

As we would expect, the coefficients on the years of education dummies are positive and highly significant for both men and women, implying that more education is positively correlated with earnings. The coefficients on the age dummies are also positive in both equations. The largest coefficient is on the age 34 to 44 cohort; the coefficient for the over 45 age group is smaller than that for the age 34 to 44 group, but larger than the coefficients for the other age cohorts. These results give us the expected relationship between age and earnings: earnings increase with age but at a decreasing rate. A surprising finding is the negative sign on the coefficient of the race dummy (significant

TABLE 6.4

PROBIT ANALYSIS FOR
LABOR FORCE PARTICIPATION CHOICE

Variable	Male Probit Coefficient	t-statistic	Female Probit Coefficient	t-statistic
INTERCEPT	-1.2952	-14.50 ***	-0.9713	-10.25 ***
AGE00 (basis)				
AGE25	0.0035	0.10	0.2468	5.58 ***
AGE35	-0.1152	-2.69 **	0.1827	3.61 ***
AGE45	-0.7987	-4.54 ***	0.1953	3.91 ***
EDUC8 (basis)				
EDUC11	-0.9665	-2.37 **	-0.1301	-2.56 **
EDUC12	0.8289	2.23 **	0.8606	1.82 *
EDUC13	0.2199	5.16 ***	0.2273	4.23 ***
RACENW (basis)				
RACEW	0.2493	7.33 ***	0.0766	1.99 **
EMOTIONAL (basis)				
PHYSICAL	0.1738	2.91 **	0.3252	5.79 ***
SEVPHY	-0.0490	-0.81	-0.5868	-1.01
SEVEMOT	-0.3329	-4.59 ***	-0.3924	-5.59 ***
MENTAL	-0.4014	-0.62	0.4017	0.57
SEVMENT	-0.3610	-4.54 ***	-0.2864	-3.04 **
DEP3 (basis)				
NODEP	-0.1929	-4.11 ***	-0.3000	-5.72 ***
DEP1OR2	-0.0114	-0.32	-0.6592	-1.22
NTMARRIED (basis)				
NVMARRIED	0.0021	0.05	-0.7093	-1.62
MARRIED	0.1081	2.59 **	-0.2181	-5.99 ***
-2 x log likelihood	499.7 ***		503.1 ***	

----

* statistically significant at the 0.10 level or better
** statistically significant at the 0.05 level or better
*** statistically significant at the 0.01 level or better

Dependent variable is working at referral

only in the male equation), which implies that, all else being equal, white male clients would earn $16 less per week than nonwhite male clients. This result could be partly explained if those disabled individuals who apply to the VR program are not a random sample of all disabled persons. It may be that the VR agencies are seeing only those white clients whose average earnings are well below the average earnings of all disabled persons who are white. Disabled whites who are more affluent may decide to seek private rehabilitation services instead of applying to the federal-state program. On the other hand, because these same private services may not be as readily available for disabled nonwhites, the average earnings of nonwhite clients who apply to VR might be closer to the average of all disabled nonwhite persons.

TABLE 6.5

EARNINGS EQUATIONS FOR CLIENTS WITH
WEEKLY EARNINGS AT REFERRAL, BY SEX

Male

Variable	Adjusted Model		Unadjusted Model	
	Coefficient	t-statistic	Coefficient	t-statistic
INTERCEPT	393.80	9.69 ***	38.88	3.04 **
AGE00 (basis)				
AGE25	28.80	5.22 ***	43.76	8.15 ***
AGE35	58.52	9.44 ***	60.37	9.57 ***
AGE45	52.60	8.33 ***	60.89	9.57 ***
EDUC8 (basis)				
EDUC11	36.43	4.98 ***	20.72	2.86 **
EDUC12	34.31	5.27 ***	44.09	6.74 ***
EDUC13	33.07	4.20 ***	62.23	8.49 ***
RACENW (basis)				
RACEW	-16.49	-2.16 **	25.05	3.99 ***
EMOTIONAL (basis)				
PHYSICAL	-15.73	-1.47	18.98	1.85 *
SEVPHY	23.23	2.28 **	21.57	2.08 **
SEVEMOT	42.06	2.92 **	-14.99	-1.13
MENTAL	29.18	2.63 **	24.21	2.14 **
SEVMENT	55.79	3.53 ***	-0.52	-0.03
LAMBDA	-187.21	-9.18 ***	----	----
R-square	.1347		.1033	

Of special interest is the sign of the coefficient of the lambda variable, which is large, negative, and highly significant for both men and women. This result implies that the unobservable characteristics that increase the probability that a client will enter the labor force are negatively related to the unmeasurable characteristics associated with higher earnings potential.

The result of this negative correlation between the unobservables in the labor force participation equation and the earnings equation is that the expected earnings of clients who are not working at referral will be higher than those working at referral. Using the coefficients from the selection-bias corrected earnings equation, we estimate the average earnings for all (working and nonworking) male and female clients. For males, we estimate that the mean weekly earnings for a nonworking client at referral will be approximately $470, much higher than the estimated $152 for a working client at referral. For women, we estimate that the mean wage for those not working at referral is approximately $168, as opposed to an average wage of $115 for those working at referral. These predictions represent earnings that are purged of any unmeasurable characteristics found to be unique to clients working and reporting positive earnings at referral.

TABLE 6.5--Continued

	Female			
	Adjusted Model		Unadjusted Model	
Variable	Coefficient	t-statistic	Coefficient	t-statistic
INTERCEPT	127.62	4.84 ***	76.48	7.98 ***
AGE00 (basis)				
AGE25	8.14	1.37	15.81	3.37 ***
AGE35	14.84	2.43 **	21.74	4.22 ***
AGE45	2.26	0.36	8.14	1.56
EDUC8 (basis)				
EDUC11	17.67	2.88 ***	15.60	2.58 **
EDUC12	26.29	4.52 ***	29.28	5.18 ***
EDUC13	45.69	6.75 ***	51.14	8.19 ***
RACENW (basis)				
RACEW	-2.17	-0.48	-1.26	-0.28
EMOTIONAL (basis)				
PHYSICAL	-6.52	-0.90	0.01	0.01
SEVPHY	12.83	1.82 *	10.27	1.48
SEVEMOT	-3.11	-0.30	-13.50	-1.50
MENTAL	-5.11	-0.62	-4.95	-0.60
SEVMENT	-8.13	-0.64	-15.94	-1.30
LAMBDA	-29.45	-2.08 **	--	--
R-square	.0653		.0632	

----

* statistically significant at the 0.10 level or better
** statistically significant at the 0.05 level or better
*** statistically significant at the 0.01 level or better

Dependent variable is weekly earnings at referral

The prediction that nonworking VR clients will have earnings at referral higher than the earnings of clients reported as working at referral may run counter to intuition, but it is theoretically and statistically possible. As we suggested earlier in this chapter, clients who are not working at referral may have chosen to remain outside the labor force because the value of their time in the home (the reservation wage) is greater than the value of their time in the labor force (the market offer wage). The value of time for clients who participate in the labor force is observed to be the market offer wage. The value of time for clients outside the labor force is a function of disability transfers and all other transfer payments.

Burkhauser and Haveman (1982, p. 54) provide a good explanation of the negative effects of a generous income replacement program on the work efforts of the disabled. Consider the example of a female client whose guaranteed level of disability insurance (such as SSDI) is $400 per month. Suppose that this client can earn up to $350 per month without forfeiting any part of the allotted $400 per month payment; but once she earns more than $350 per month, she becomes ineligible for the disability-related transfers. If this client's health condition improves over time to the point that she could find full-time employment at wages of $750 per month, she is likely to forego such employment rather than to give up the income from transfers. Because leisure is usually a "normal" good, a utility-maximizing client would choose to work part-time for a wage of $350 while remaining eligible for $400 in disability transfer payments, rather than work full-time for an identical amount of total income, $750.

Burkhauser and Haveman also report that the disincentive effects of transfer payments on labor force participation increase with decreases in health status (p. 53). Therefore, the notion that VR nonworking clients are typically the most severely disabled with the fewest skills to offer in the labor market does not invalidate our findings.

Again, the value of time spent in the home (out of the labor force) is increased by the clients' disability transfer payment income. The value of time spent out of the home (in the labor force) must be greater than the disability transfer income to draw these clients fully into the labor force. Therefore, we can state that nonworking clients have higher reservation earnings than clients already in the labor force whose reservation earnings have been exceeded by the market offer (accepted) wage. The higher reservation wages of the nonworking clients in turn account for the higher predicted earnings of this group.

CONCLUSIONS

The usual method of estimating benefits attributable to the VR program is to compare client earnings before and after program participation. We encounter two problems, however, when attempting to measure the change in earnings capacity attributable to the VR program for clients with zero earnings at referral and positive earnings at program closure. The first is sample selection bias. The second is a data set problem.

This chapter addressed the need for a technique to correct sample selection bias. It may be unrealistic to assume that a client who reports zero earnings at the time of referral has no earnings capacity. As an alternative, we can impute a value for earnings capacity to these clients and, in doing so, ensure that the effect of VR participation upon earnings will not be overstated. Obviously, the differences in earnings attributable to VR will be enormous when we compare methods imputing earnings to clients reporting zero earnings against methods leaving zero reported earnings unchanged.

One way of predicting earnings for clients reporting zero wages at referral is the method of ordinary least squares. However, it is generally unacceptable to run a regression on a sample of clients working at referral and then apply the resulting coefficients to clients not working at referral in order to impute an earnings figure for them. This chapter presents an improved method of imputing earnings to clients reporting zero earnings at referral to the VR program. Both of these methods for imputing earnings values at referral make use of earnings information from workers who enter the program and report positive earnings at referral. They are also dependent upon many other characteristics of workers such as education, the number of dependents, age, race, and sex.

The technique proposed in this chapter for predicting weekly earnings is best suited to measure the benefit received by the individual client from participation in the VR program. Benefits accruing to the client are not necessarily the same as benefits received by society as a whole or the VR agency itself. We have discussed the relationship that exists between predicted weekly earnings and the opportunity cost of forfeiting disability transfer payments for paid labor market activities. From the client's perspective, if $400 in guaranteed disability benefits at referral are forfeited for full-time employment of $750 at closure, the benefit attributable to VR participation would be $750 − 400 = $350. However, if this same client had worked part-time and earned $350 in addition to the guaranteed benefit of $400 for total earnings of $750, the client might question whether participation in the program had brought any benefits. On the other hand, in this same situation, society would very clearly benefit. The individual would be freed from dependence on government funds; society would no longer bear the cost of disability transfers in the amount of $400 per month.

The model we have developed, then, is limited in that it measures benefits from the perspective of the client. It does not enable us to measure the benefits that would be realized by society. Nor does it enable us to assess the contribution of the VR agency. The two-step technique cannot produce predicted earnings for individual clients solely as a function of their labor market skills (human capital) and personal characteristics. The technique instead predicts earnings in the context of what clients would have to earn in order to be drawn into the labor market, not what clients could earn in one week in return for their labor. The VR agency ideally strives to improve the human capital of its clients. Measuring improvements in human capital achieved through VR participation requires a different model, one that would control for the reduced work effort induced by disability transfer payments.

The second problem that confronts the analyst working with R-300 data is a missing information problem. The R-300 data are reported by counselors who draw their information from case records and interviews with clients. Checking and editing of the data appear to be casual. Two percent of the clients in the sample do not have a reported sex and 6 percent do not have a reported race. While these omissions do not constitute a large missing information problem, they do represent deficiencies in the editing process. The significance of the nonreported data grows as the nature of the information to be collected becomes less straightforward. Better data on client earnings, characteristics, and disabling condition could add significantly to the robustness of our findings.

NOTES

1. We understand this to mean that clients who have reported no earnings have this value imputed to them, but clients who report zero earnings remain as zero values.

2. The severity of the primary work disabling condition is identified by a counselor check item. See the RSA Manual (U.S. Dept. of Education 1974, pp. 56-64.)

3. Variables cleaned of missing data are: Weekly Earnings at Referral, Age at Referral, Work Status at Referral, Years of Schooling, Number of Dependents, Major Disabling Condition, Sex, and Race.

4. According to the RSA Manual (U.S. Dept. of Education 1974, p. 44), a person who did any work at all during the preceding week is to be classified as working in one of the first six categories.

WORKS CITED

Bartel, Ann, and Paul Taubman. 1979. "Health and Labor Market Success: The Role of Various Diseases." *Review of Economics and Statistics* 61:1-8.

Becker, G. 1964. *Human Capital.* New York: National Bureau of Economic Research.

Bellante, Donald M. 1972. "A Multivariate Analysis of a Vocational Rehabilitation Program." *Journal of Human Resources* 7:226-41.

Berkowitz, M., and M. Anderson. 1974. *PADEC: An Evaluation of an Experimental Rehabilitation Project.* Final Report. New Brunswick, N.J.: Rutgers University, Bureau of Economic Research.

Bloom, D. E., and M. K. Killingsworth. 1982. "Pay Discrimination Research and Litigation: The Use of Regression." *Industrial Relations* 21:318-39.

Burkhauser, Richard V., and Robert V. Haveman. 1982. *Disability and Work: The Economics of American Policy.* Baltimore: Johns Hopkins University Press.

Conley, Ronald W. 1964. *The Economics of Vocational Rehabilitation.* Baltimore: Johns Hopkins University Press.

———. 1969. "A Benefit-Cost Analysis of the Vocational Rehabilitation Program." *The Journal of Human Resources* 4:226-52.

———. 1973. *The Economics of Mental Retardation.* Baltimore: Johns Hopkins University Press.

Dean, David H., and Robert C. Dolan. 1984. "Toward an Improved Methodology for Estimating Benefits of the Vocational Rehabilitation Program." Paper presented at the Fifty-Fourth Annual Conference of the Southern Economics Association.

Ferber, Marianne A., and Carole A. Green. 1985. "Homemakers' Imputed Wages: Results of the Heckman Technique Compared with Women's Own Estimates." *Journal of Human Resource* 20:90-99.

Gronau, Reuben. 1974. "Wage Comparisons—a Selectivity Bias." *Journal of Political Economy* 82:1119-44.

Heckman, J. J. 1976. "The Common Structure of Statistical Models of Truncation, Sample Selection, and Limited Dependent Variables, and a Simple Estimator for Such Models." *Annals of Economic and Social Measurement* 5:475-92.

———. 1979. "Sample Selection Bias as a Specification Error." *Econometrica* 47:153-62.

———. 1980. "Sample Selection Bias as a Specification Error," in *Female Labor Supply: Theory and Estimation.* Ed. James P. Smith. Princeton: Princeton University Press.

Hill, Anne. 1985. "Economic Analysis of the Labor Market Placements of the New Jersey Commission for the Blind and Visually Impaired." Final Report. New Brunswick, N.J.: Rutgers University, Bureau of Economic Research.

Judge, G. G., W. E. Griffiths, R. C. Hill, and T. C. Lee. 1982. *Introduction to The Theory and Practice of Econometrics.* New York: John Wiley & Sons.

Kennedy, Peter. 1979. *A Guide to Econometrics.* Cambridge: MIT Press.

Killingsworth, M. R. 1983. *Labor Supply.* New York: Cambridge University Press.

Lewis, H. Gregg. 1974. "Comments of Selectivity Biases in Wage Comparisons." *Journal of Political Economy* 82:1145-55.

Luft, Harold S. 1975. "The Impact of Poor Health on Earnings." *Review of Economics and Statistics* 57:43-57.

Mincer, Jacob. 1974. *Schooling, Experience, and Earnings.* New York: National Bureau of Economic Research.

United States Dept. of Education. Office of Special Education and Rehabilitative Services, Rehabilitation Services Administration. 1974. *Rehabilitation Services Manual.*

———. 1983. *State Vocational Rehabilitation Agency Program Data, Fiscal Year 1982.* Washington, D.C.: GPO.

Worrall, John D. 1976. "Some Economic Aspects of the Vocational Rehabilitation Program." Ph.D. Diss. Rutgers University.

———. 1978. "A Benefit-Cost Analysis for the Vocational Rehabilitation Program." *Journal of Human Resources* 13:285-98.

7   *David H. Dean and Robert C. Dolan*

IMPUTING BENEFITS TO PERSONS CLOSED NOT REHABILITATED

One possible source of the bias in benefit-cost calculations is the assignment of zero benefits to clients who are closed not rehabilitated in status 28, even though the total cost of services received by this cohort is fully weighed in the denominator. Of course, the reason for this approach is also clear. By definition, status 28 case files do not contain earnings data. Even so, the presumption of zero benefits for status 28 clients in the conventional benefit-cost model seems unjustified on both conceptual and factual grounds.

First, from a conceptual standpoint, economic evaluation should not lose sight of the broad intent of the program—to reduce the extent to which functional limitations restrict work. The earning gains reported for rehabil- itated clients are merely the best empirical proxies available to assess the extent to which a functional limitation has been mitigated. While earnings are a legitimate measure of program benefits for status 26 closures, it may be inappropriate to presume the converse is true—that a lack of earnings as indicated by a 28 closure necessarily implies an absence of benefits. This emphasis on the existence or absence of earnings has thus led evaluators to take a binary view of program performance.

However, functional capability, though admittedly difficult to measure, is a continuous variable in that any changes that occur are incremental. So too is the nature of service receipts. Logically, it seems unduly conservative to conclude that clients who receive substantial amounts of services realize no benefits because they are judged not rehabilitated after a rather arbitrary sixty-day vigil.

Furthermore, as a purely factual matter, evidence exists that many clients closed in status 28 do ultimately get jobs (see Chapter 12). Re- cent studies of the long-term impact of vocational rehabilitation services have found that several persons closed unsuccessfully in the traditional VR nomenclature did indeed have postclosure earnings. For example, of those persons treated and closed by VR in 1975, Social Security data link records for 1977 reveal that the "unsuccessful" status 28 population had average earnings of $3,662. Moreover, these earnings were not dramatically lower than the $4,041 averaged among VR's successful status 26 clients.

Finally, these actual earnings need not be greatly surprising when one recognizes the important respects in which the status 28 cohort is similar to its "successful" status 26 counterpart. The data in Table 7.1 illustrate this point. Observe that the status 28 clients exhibit characteristics that are strong predictors of earnings in traditional labor market analysis. For example, note that the two cohorts are virtually the same mean age, have comparable educational backgrounds, and are of nearly the same average marital status and racial composition. Table 7.1 also reveals that the status 28 cohort receives a substantial level of VR services. Compare, for example, the duration and value of specific services received across cohorts. The average status 28 client in Virginia received a total of $1178 of services.

In sum, there is adequate reason to believe that many status 28 clients derive significant benefit from their VR experience, even though researchers lack the convenient sixty-day earnings datum to measure it. While it is true that the earnings gains of this group are probably less than those of successful clients and that many clients closed status 28 are in fact "too severely disabled" to be placed, it is also true that many clients are deemed not rehabilitated for reasons quite unrelated to either function capabilities or the VR program. Clients who move out of state, for example, are classified as

TABLE 7.1

COMPARING STATUS 26 AND 28 POPULATIONS

Description	Status 26 Mean (n=2969)	Status 28 Mean (n=1722)
Client Demographics:		
Age at referral	30.72	30.62
Mean years of school completed	9.46	9.29
*Gender (% male)	57.0	60.0
*Race (% white)	70.0	64.0
*Marital status (% married)	26.0	20.0
Service Duration:		
*Time in restoration (months)	3.57	6.57
*Time in training and/or education (months)	12.59	10.14
Service Expenditure:		
Value of restorative services	1080.59	1198.33
*Value of educational services	1968.82	1339.71
*Value of training services	254.88	584.85
*Value of total services	1654.18	1178.34

* Denotes that the difference in means is significant at the .05 level
Source: Virginia Department of Rehabilitative Services, FY 1982, Richmond, Virg.

status 28 closures. Hence we contend that it is inappropriate for benefit-cost analysis to assign zero benefits to these clients while fully accounting for their service costs.

IMPUTING STATUS 28 EARNINGS

A growing body of literature within labor economics treats the issue of missing data that we have encountered in one form here (Gronau 1973; Lewis 1974; Heckman 1976, 1979; Heckman, Killingsworth, and MaCurdy 1981; Bloom and Killingsworth 1982; and Killingsworth 1983). In a generic sense, our attempt to estimate earnings for the status 28 population falls within a censored sample framework. The status 28 client represents a "censored" observation because the case service file, although complete in every other respect, lacks the earnings datum necessary to measure benefits.

One way to adjust for a censored sample is to fit an earnings datum to each censored observation from the closure earnings reported in the status 26 case files. These earnings may be assigned based on similarities in demographic characteristics, education, impairment, and service receipts across clients in the two cohorts. This procedure, however, is not entirely appropriate for our purposes, although it is defensible in many research settings. Drawing such cross-inferences presumes that the two populations are "identical on average," which is probably not true. Although we have argued that the status 28 cohort certainly receives something greater than the zero benefits traditionally assigned them, we are not suggesting that their success is equal to that of their status 26 counterpart. In short, such an assumption would press the thesis of this chapter a bit too far.

Indeed, we would argue that there is very likely an important element of unobservable difference between successful and unsuccessful clients. This unobservable attribute in the status 26 cohort might be characterized as an attitudinal variable across clients—call it "a preference for work," "perseverance," or "a need to succeed." We are not suggesting that this type of attitude, which clearly influences the likelihood of successful closure, is unobservable to the counselor; rather, it is an attribute not reflected in the R-300 data. In other words, a subtle yet systematic difference exists between status 26 and 28 clients that may be quite evident to the counselor but not apparent to the analyst examining the data profile. Unless we can control for the part played by perseverance in explaining the earnings of a status 26 client, the earnings imputed to status 28 clients from the status 26 case files would tend to overstate the future earnings capability of unsuccessful, yet otherwise similar, VR clients.

As shown in Chapter 6, a statistical method of adjusting for this problem has been developed by Heckman (1976, 1979). This solution incorporates a two-stage, selection-bias-corrected regression technique. The core of the estimation is an earnings equation. The purpose of this equation is to identify how closely earnings gains by VR clients are associated with a broad array of client and program characteristics. The earnings equation is written:

(1) $EARN_c = f(MST, SEXM, RACEW, AGE_r, EDUC_r, EARN_r,$
$RTIME, TTIME, \$REST, \$TRAIN, \$EDUC, DCOND)$

$EARN_c$ is earnings at closure, the outcome variable of the program. The top row variables are in general nonprogrammatic characteristics that exist within the VR clientele. MST, SEXM, and RACEW are "either/or" binary variables distinguishing clients who are married, male, and white. AGE_r, $EDUC_r$, and $EARN_r$ denote clients' circumstances at program referral regarding age, last year of education completed, and earnings if any. The second row variables reflect programmatic dimensions: time in restoration (RTIME) and/or training (TTIME); dollars of services in restoration ($REST), training ($TRAIN), and/or education ($EDUC); and the nature of disabling conditions (DCOND). This specification of the earnings equation departs from convention in two respects. First, because earnings vary widely in most labor market analyses, it is common to rescale the dependent variable as the natural log of earnings. This was not done here in order to be consistent with the more recent manpower training evaluations and to retain the most intuitive possible interpretation of the regression coefficients. Second, it is more common to control for the influence of sex and race by subsampling on these attributes rather than including them as independent regressors. This partitioning was done, but the results were consistent with those reported here. In the interest of economy, we do not present results for the four individual race/sex subsamples. A summary of the variables appears in Table 7.2.

Equation (1) represents a multivariate regression model (ordinary least squares). The appeal of the ordinary least squares technique is that it approximates a randomized laboratory experiment that controls for the contribution to closure earnings that may be more correctly attributable to nonservice variables. These would include such specific preservice client characteristics as education, age, earnings history, and the like. Estimation of this equation based on case service data yields an estimated coefficient for each of the variables listed on the right-hand side of the equation. The interpretation of the estimated coefficients is straightforward and intuitively appealing. Generally, a coefficient reflects the predicted change-in-earnings that may be associated with a "unit" change in the level of the right-hand variable, holding all other variables constant. Of course, the particular interpretation of a unit change in each case depends on how the variable is measured—either continuously, as in the case of years of education, or as a binary condition, reflecting whether a client is male/female, white/nonwhite, or married/nonmarried.

If one were comfortable with the assumption that the status 26 and 28 cohorts are roughly identical on average, benefits could be imputed to status 28 clients from the coefficients obtained by estimating Equation (1) with the complete status 26 case data. However, if, as we have argued, a systematic difference exists, a strict earnings extrapolation would impute benefits to the 28 cohort that are biased. Thus we employ the Heckman bias-correction technique.

The Heckman adjustment generates a new variable, lambda (λ), which may be broadly interpreted as controlling for the possibly unobservable impact of perseverance on both the likelihood of successful closure and the level of earnings. The inclusion of lambda renders an augmented earnings specification differentiating the two cohorts. The significance of this variable indicates latent differences that may exist between status 26 and 28

TABLE 7.2

SUMMARY OF VARIABLES USED IN EARNINGS REGRESSION

Independent Variables	Description	Mean 26 & 28 Cohorts (n=3691)
AGE	Client age entering VR	30.7
EDUC	Average number of years of schooling	9.4
MST	Marital status (% married)	23.8
SEXM	Sex (% male)	58.1
RACEW	Race (% white)	67.5
EARNR	Weekly earnings prior to VR	7.23
RTIME	Time in restoration (months)	1.3
TTIME	Time in education &/or training (months)	6.3
$TRAIN	Value of training services received ($)	232.13
$EDUC	Value of education services received ($)	340.39
$RESTOR	Value of restorative services received ($)	407.02
SENSORY	Visual or hearing impairment	5.7
PHYSIC	Amputee or orthopedic impairment	22.2
MENTILL	Emotional disorders	20.0
RETARD	Mental retardation	29.7
INTERN	Internal disorders	22.4

Dependent Variable = Weekly Earnings

clients. In other words, the addition of the variable allows for a possible redistribution of the explanatory power across the variables in the earning equation and purges the right-hand side regressors of any correlation with the unobservable component of the error term. If the anticipated bias exists, this adjustment may affect the magnitude, although not necessarily the significance, of the coefficients on the variables in the earnings equation. Hence, these bias-corrected estimates become valid parameters upon which to impute earnings to the status 28 population.

The results for the ordinary least squares bias-corrected estimates appear in Table 7.3. Recall that the general interpretation of any coefficient is the amount that the dependent variable ($EARN_c$) correlates with a change in a given independent variable, when other variables are held constant. For example, observe that a client is predicted to enjoy $5.75 higher earnings at closure for each additional year of education at referral, other attributes being the same. Similarly, the coefficient on SEXM indicates that a male client closes with $31.36 greater earnings than an otherwise identical female.

For our purposes, the results may be discussed in the context of two composite clients, one each from the status 26 and 28 cohorts. These two clients are composite constructions in that they take on the mean value of each demographic, service, and disability variable for their respective cohorts. Although the clients are fictitious, our procedure is an appropriate heuristic method by which to identify the likely source of earnings differences that exist between the status 26 and 28 cohorts.

The bottom row of Table 7.3 indicates that the estimated weekly earnings for our hypothetical status 26 and 28 clients are $148.73 and $138.81 respectively. These figures are obtained by multiplying the bias-corrected ordinary least squares coefficients by the corresponding mean characteristic values and summing, along with the intercept, across characteristics. Recall that the bias-correction technique now permits the use of the ordinary least squares parameters since any unobservable differences between the two cohorts that may contribute to status 26 closure are captured in the coefficient on lambda.

It is important to note that, under our revised methodology, there appear to be two broad sources of difference between the status 26 and 28 cohorts that contribute to differential earnings. First, concerning observable factors, it is clear that the status 26 cohort, although similar, is not identical to the status 28 counterpart. Status 26 clients are on average slightly more educated, more married, and more white; they have a slightly better earnings record when they enter the program. Accordingly, the status 26 cohort is predicted to close with modestly higher earnings. Collectively, these observable attributes account for $5.58 of the $9.92 weekly earnings difference previously cited. The remaining difference of $4.34 in status 26 earnings is systematically related to successful closure as traditionally defined. Although unobservable, this is the effect gleaned from the construction and insertion of lambda in the earnings equation. In sum, however, our results suggest that the status 28 clients achieve substantial earnings following their VR experience.

CONCLUSION

The statistical inference that the average status 28 client may actually enjoy earnings of $138.81 is rather startling when juxtaposed with the traditional assumption that these clients received no measurable benefits

TABLE 7.3

STATUS 26 AND IMPUTED STATUS 28 EARNINGS

	Bias-Corrected Coefficients	Status 26		Status 28	
		Mean	Earnings Impact	Mean	Earnings Impact
SOCIO/DEMOGRAPHICS					
AGE	-0.06	30.72	($1.84)	30.62	($1.84)
EDUC	5.75	9.46	$54.40	9.29	$53.42
MST	0.17	7.73	$1.31	6.37	$1.08
SEXM	17.43	0.26	$4.53	0.2	$3.49
RACE	31.36	0.57	$17.88	0.6	$18.82
EARNR	10.81	0.7	$7.57	0.64	$6.92
SERVICE DURATION					
RTIME	0.64	3.57	$2.28	6.57	$4.20
TTIME	0.69	12.59	$8.69	10.14	$7.00

TABLE 7.3--Continued

SOCIO/DEMOGRAPHICS	Bias-Corrected Coefficients	Status 26		Status 28	
		Mean	Earnings Impact	Mean	Earnings Impact
SERVICE EXPENDITURE					
$REST	-0.0002	344.47	($0.07)	443.3	($0.09)
$EDUC	-0.00005	245.85	($0.01)	395.22	($0.02)
$TRAIN	-0.019	192.91	($3.67)	254.88	($4.84)
DISABLING CONDITION *					
SENSORY	8.97	0.07	$0.63	0.03	$0.27
PHYSIC	-0.18	0.22	($0.04)	0.22	($0.04)
MENTILL	-20.25	0.16	($3.24)	0.26	($5.27)
RETARD	-13.45	0.29	($3.90)	0.31	($4.17)
SELECTION BIAS CONTROL					
LAMBDA	7.75	0.56	$4.34	—	—
INTERCEPT	59.88	1.00	$59.88	1.00	$59.88
ESTIMATED WEEKLY EARNINGS			$148.73		$138.81

----
* Reference group is internal disorders

from participation in the VR program. Obviously, our methodology will have a marked impact on benefit-cost analysis of the program because it entails adding status 28 benefits to a calculation that typically has considered only the service cost of this cohort. For example, in the Virginia VR program to which these data pertain, our model implies additional closure earnings of almost $11.9 million. Moreover, this figure represents a 54 percent increase in closure earnings as conventionally measured. In the context of these inferences, we might reflect on our earlier observation that the 1975 status 28 population had actual annual earnings in 1977 that were only $379 less than those of the status 26 clients. It is interesting to note that when the weekly earnings estimates cited in Table 7.3 are annualized, they suggest a roughly similar difference of $496.

We recommend that our extrapolations be greeted cautiously. Indeed, these figures are presented largely to underscore our basic premise and should be appreciated more for their conceptual significance than for their quantitative precision. Our point is simply that program evaluation ought to account for the earnings prospects of status 28 clients. As a minimum, this might involve a further refinement of the selection-bias correction technique applied here.

WORKS CITED

Bloom, David, and Mark Killingsworth. 1982. "Pay Discrimination Research and Litigation: The Use of Regression." *Industrial Relations* 21.3:319–31.

Gronau, Reuben. 1973. "The Effect of Children on the Housewife's Value of Time." *Journal of Political Economy* 81:S168–99.

Heckman, James. 1976. "The Common Structure of Statistical Models of Truncation, Sample Selection and Limited Dependent Variables and a Simple Estimator for Such Models: A Survey of Recent Developments." *Annals of Economic and Social Measurement* 5.4:475–93.

———. 1979. "Sample Selection Bias as a Specification Error." *Econometrica* 47:153–61.

Heckman, James, Mark Killingsworth, and Thomas MaCurdy. 1981. "Empirical Evidence on Static Labour Supply Models: A Survey of Recent Developments," in *The Economics of the Labour Market.* Ed. Horstein, Grice, and Webb. London.

Killingsworth, Mark. 1983. "Second-Generation Studies of Static Labor Supply Models: Methodology and Empirical Results," in *Labor Supply.* Cambridge: Cambridge University Press.

Lewis, H. Gregg. 1974. "Comments on Selectivity Biases in Wage Comparisons." *Journal of Political Economy* 82:1145–55.

III

Activity at the State Level

In Part II of this volume, the authors demonstrated what could be learned from conducting benefit-cost analysis using the national data source, the R-300 set. Although the authors in general adhered to "before and after" comparison of earnings as a measure of program benefits, they experimented with a number of methods adjusting the earnings figures. While they did reach conclusions that have a direct bearing on program analysis, their manipulations of the existing data still did not produce a benefit-cost ratio for the program that invites complete confidence. All of the econometric corrections that can be applied to the R-300 data will fall short of this goal. In part, the problem can be traced to the data base. Better longitudinal data is needed; data on the postclosure earnings of clients would enable researchers to apply their corrections for earnings of nonrehabilitants more confidently and to back up their assumptions about the job retention of rehabilitants. Deficiencies in the data base are not the only problem, however. Firm conclusions about the economic benefits of the VR program can be drawn only if a control group is studied.

With Part III, we move from program evaluation at the federal level to evaluation at the state level. The authors in the following two chapters examine the kinds of benefit-cost analyses currently being conducted by the states. Have individual states adopted a more sophisticated methodology than that used by the RSA over the years? Have they obtained more precise measures of costs and benefits by introducing the kinds of adjustments carried out by the authors in Part II? Part III also investigates whether the states have at their disposal more client information than they actually use in program evaluation. Does the information maintained by some states remedy certain of the deficiencies of the R-300 data set?

In Chapter 8 below, Frederick Collignon offers an overview of the states' experience with benefit-cost analysis. He observes that wide variations exist in the ratios obtained by the states in evaluating their programs, but he contends that these variations reflect differences in methodology as well as differences in performance. He singles out for discussion those states that employ more advanced methods of benefit-cost analysis, and he describes the California model at some length.

Collignon also reports on certain trends in the evaluation of state VR programs that are unfavorable to benefit-cost analysis. He suggests that the federal government is not providing effective guidance concerning evaluation. The government has relaxed its demands on the states for benefit-cost accounting, and it has not come forward with appropriate models and better data for state use.

In Chapter 9, Stanley Portny surveys the information-gathering and evaluation activities of fifteen state agencies. In presenting his findings for each state, he focuses on certain key practices: the maintenance of comprehensive client statistical and financial data, the recording of "similar benefits," the use of follow-up studies, and the application of some kind of functional assessment test. Each of these practices is in some sense a measure of the *capacity* of the state to perform benefit-cost analysis of a meaningful kind.

Portny's survey suggests that some states have in fact collected data that would enable them to reach a truer assessment of the costs of service delivery and the benefits of program participation. The survey also indicates, however, that these states have not taken advantage of the information available to them. How such information could be put to use in the evaluation of the program will be the chief concern in Part IV of this volume.

Portny's findings on the practices of state agencies bear out some of the conclusions reached in the preceding chapter. Like Frederick Collignon, Portny perceives a decline in state commitment to benefit-cost analysis and he relates this development to the slackening of federal leadership and federal expectations in program evaluation.

8 *Frederick C. Collignon*

BENEFIT-COST ANALYSES CONDUCTED BY STATE AGENCIES

This chapter considers state practices in benefit-cost analysis. My intention was to investigate the models and methods of analysis currently in use by the states. Because the practices of the states have changed since the late 1970s, I have also sought to identify and explain some of the broad trends in program evaluation.

By now, most states at some time have used benefit-cost analyses to justify their programs to their state legislatures. When such analyses are undertaken, the principal data base used is the R-300. The states will often use national studies issued by the RSA to indicate the worth of their program or will use what economists would term fairly crude calculations emphasizing changes in earnings projected over a lifetime for clients in that state compared to average client costs. A number of states, however, have done more sophisticated analyses.

The basic model for these studies, whether explicitly recognized by the states or not, has been the model developed by Ronald W. Conley and set forth in his work, *The Economics of Vocational Rehabilitation.* (See John Worrall's commentary on the model in Chapter 3 of this volume.) The four generations of models developed by Berkeley Planning Associates (BPA) derive from Conley's model. Even when states cite sources other than BPA or Conley, the models prove on close examination to be quite similar. Essentially, these models recognize a number of the problems detailed in Part II above. They attempt to solve such problems as zero earnings at referral or the uncertain duration of earnings at closure by adjusting the earnings figures in accordance with information derived from independent studies. The discussion of the California model in the next section will illustrate how the states have attempted to modify and correct the traditional methods of analysis employed at the federal level.

Although the state models have structural similarities, there is high variability across states in analytic findings. These differences can be traced to the types of benefits and costs included in the model as well as to variations in state program performance. Those states that use more comprehensive lists of benefits do *not* have higher benefit-cost returns because they tend also to use a more comprehensive list of costs and to be more rigorous in their measurement.

Invariably, states report favorable benefit-cost ratios. Only the more sophisticated models occasionally offer an unfavorable finding for a particular disability group. This could be seen simply as a logical agency response—if a finding is negative, don't present it. But in fact, I could identify no example of a state that had not found generally positive findings, even with extended adjustments to R-300 data.

Major differences did exist in the relative performance of the states. State studies tend to compare results to national studies if they are favorable. They are silent on such comparisons if the state performance falls below the national average.

States generally consider only VR program costs in their analyses. With the exception of California, they do not attempt to measure the costs borne by clients or other agency programs within the state, or the indirect costs (such as expenditures for training, research and demonstration, administration) incurred by the federal government.

When subgroup analyses are done, states are willing to consider change in earnings and direct program costs as recorded on the R-300. The worries among researchers concerning the lack of data for a subpopulation (such as disability-specific mortality rates or follow-up data) are ignored by state programs. Since such data do not exist, and perhaps could be gathered only at great cost, the state agency practices are not unreasonable.

"BEST PRACTICE" MODELS

Regional offices and other observers of the VR program have praised the benefit-cost models used by a number of states, including Alaska, Arizona, Delaware, Michigan, California, Nevada, Oregon, Virginia, and Washington. Although all of these states provided some information when contacted about their evaluation practices, Delaware and Nevada indicated that they were no longer doing benefit-cost analysis other than simple comparisons of earnings changes with costs, and Virginia indicated that it was working on a new model. Information on benefit-cost studies in the other six states is summarized in Table 8.1. Of these six studies, the most frequently cited by other states in recent years is the Oregon model, developed by Ross Moran as part of an RSA program in which six states were made "model states" for evaluation. Also singled out for commendation was the Arizona state study. Interestingly, however, the authors of the Arizona study acknowledge that their methodology derives from the Oregon model, and the authors of the Oregon study in turn indicate their indebtedness to the BPA models.

Despite the attention given to these models of more recent origin, the California state benefit-cost study remains the state-of-the-art study. The California model represents the fourth and last generation of the Berkeley model, and no subsequent models have proved to be more comprehensive or more data-based in their structure.

I review the California model here as an illustration of state efforts to reach plausible estimates of the costs and benefits of the VR program. The model is based on aggregate data of all costs occurring within a year and information on all closures during that year. The model adjusts the reported costs in a number of ways in order to capture the full range of service costs. Added to the case service costs and overhead costs routinely reported on the R-300 are estimates of the service costs borne by the clients themselves and by other agencies. "Similar benefits"—services prescribed by the VR agency but paid for by another state or federal agency—are factored in as 25 percent of the case service costs. The model has parameters to adjust other costs such as research and training and demonstration expenditures.

The model's measure of benefits is based on a comparison of earnings the week before referral and earnings at closure, but adjustments are made in both figures. Prerehabilitation earnings are adjusted by comparing referral average earnings with average earnings three months before referral; other adjustments to prerehabilitation earnings are based on data from BPA studies and RSA audits. The model rejects the assumption that the higher earnings of rehabilitants at closure will continue indefinitely. The worklife is assumed to end at age sixty-five, and an adjustment is made for mortality using data drawn from two sources—the Railroad Retirement Board for data on the life expectancy of the severely disabled and the Society of Actuaries for data on the life expectancy of the nonseverely disabled. The model's assumptions about employment retention are based on follow-up surveys carried out by the state rehabilitation program showing that 63.5 percent of clients closed in competitive employment were still employed a year later. The model also recognizes that earnings of rehabilitants will vary according to educational attainment, age, and change in wage levels in the economy as a whole.

Homemaking is valued as a benefit; the source for this valuation is the replacement cost by taxes, and in California this was computed as $7,772 per year. The model also takes fringe benefits into account, valuing such benefits as about 25 percent of total earnings. The data are adjusted, however, to reflect the fact that not all disabled persons are employed in positions providing fringe benefits.

One final modification deserves mention. The change in earnings from referral to closure is reduced by 20 percent to account for increases not attributable to the VR program. The 20 percent adjustment was based on a state review of case files and the clinical judgments contained therein.

The California model corrects a number of the deficiencies in the traditional method of benefit-cost analysis; it aims at a comprehensive assessment of costs and benefits, and its assumptions are supported by data derived from the experience of the agency and from independent studies.

TRENDS IN STATE AGENCY EVALUATION

Recent discussions with state agency personnel shed light on the kinds of program evaluation that the states are now conducting. When benefit-cost analysis is used, its form is not one of societal return for the resources being invested but rather taxpayer payback for the specific VR program expenditure of funds. Economists have long questioned such an approach, but it appears to be the approach that the majority of the state agencies currently find most responsive to the concerns of state legislatures. Such analyses permit separate calculations for the return to state as well as federal taxpayers. State calculations do not include, however, analysis of the state's contributions to the federal costs. Rather, they treat the federal contribution as implicitly matched by tax payments by state residents to the federal

TABLE 8.1
REVIEW OF MAJOR STATE BENEFIT-COST MODELS

State	Alaska	California	Michigan
Source of Model			
BPA	Like BPA's	X	
RSA			
Other	State		State
Type of Analysis			
Taxpayer			
Payback		Used	
Benefit-Cost	X	Not used regularly	X
Frequency of Use	Annual	Monthly report to DR	Has not run in 2-3 years
Special Groups			
Major			
Disabilities		X	
Other	Severe disability	Business Enterprise Program; severe disability/ nonsevere disability	Local level
Assumptions Concerning Job Retention	70% of 26's	63.5%	Yes
Source	Follow-up survey (one year)	State survey	Two-year follow-up survey
Earnings Increase	Do not know	Yes	
Source		State survey 14.8% first Year	
Homemaker Valuation	No	Yes	Yes, early on--but not in later years
Source		Replacement costs by taxes- $7772/year	RSA study
Recidivism	No	Yes	Yes
Basis		R-300	R-300--10%

TABLE 8.1--Continued

Washington	Arizona	Oregon
	X (indirect)	X
State	State/Ore	State
X	X	X
	X	Break-even rate of return
Monthly	Annual--used once, but not for last 3 years	Annual
	Severe/nonsevere disability	13-severe/nonsevere agency referral source (11) deaf, mental illness--but by source, not as disability group
Variety of options considered	76.5% approx.	92%
	Other studies; Arizona RSA annual reviews	State unemployment rate--8%
	7.4%--rate of change in general state population income	No--assumption that wage increases are offset by retention changes
	Source not given	
No	No--Arizona discourages all homemaker closures	No
No	No	No

TABLE 8.1--Continued

State	Alaska	California	Michigan
Control Group Adjustment	Pre-post earnings comparison	20% reduction on top of earnings change	Pre-post earnings comparison
Basis		State review of cases--clinical judgment	
R-300 Basis	R-300 (service)	R-300	
Other Data Source	Budget to state	Accounting Department	Follow-up survey
Costs Included			
Services	X	X	X
Similar Benifits	No	X--25% of case service costs	No
Salaries/Admin.	X	X	X
Adjustment to Earnings Prior to Referral	No	Yes	Average earnings in
			preceding year
Amount Source		RSA audits/BPA	From intake interview
Mortality			Did not know
Expectation Age	65--average age = worklife	65	
Source		Society of Actuaries, for nonseverely disabled; Railroad Retirement Board, for severely disabled	
Adjustment for Young Clients	No	Yes	No
Basis		1975 U.S. Census age/earnings profile	
Public Assistance Reductions--Types Included	SSI/DI, GA, AFDC (from R-300)	SSI/DI, GA, AFDC (from R-300) Medicare	SSI/DI, GA, AFDC (from R-300)
How Far Projected?	Worklife	Until payback occurs	One year
Basis	R-300	R-300	R-300

TABLE 8.1--Continued

Washington	Arizona	Oregon
Pre-post earnings comparison	Pre-post earnings comparison	Yes--20% reduction
		Source: BPA
R-300, RSA2, and RSA113	R-300	R-300
	External (nonstate)	State surveys
	Total state VR budget	
X	No	X
No	No	No
X	No	X
No	Yes	Yes
	+39%	+39%
No	Moran/Oregon	State survey (+29%) with adjustments
Yes	3.5%/year	3.5%/year
Did not know	Retirement age of 62	62
	Moran/Oregon	Bureau of Census, 1976 (adjusted for sex/age)
No	No	No
R-300 source	Total state public assistance; social security	SSI/DI minimum benefit; public assistance as reported on R-300
Over payback period	Worklife	Break-even %
		calculated
Constant	R-300	R-300

government. Sometimes (as in Arizona) they treat the federal payment as a windfall and do the taxpayer analysis solely with reference to the return to the state treasury.

Even those states that were among the first to do extensive benefit-cost studies and follow-up surveys of clients on an ongoing basis have since cut back on such efforts. Michigan was the lead state in such analyses in the earlier 1970s. It initiated routine annual extensive follow-up surveys in the late 1960s, long before the federal government encouraged states to do such studies. But Michigan no longer conducts follow-up surveys. Its model is now quite simple. Similarly, California, which for a number of years gave the state legislature both a benefit-cost model and a payback model, now gives only a payback analysis on a regular basis.

Federal leadership in providing forms, models, and exhortations to do benefit-cost studies has always been a principal factor in inducing states to undertake such studies. In recent years, the federal government has not been providing such strong directives. States now carry out their own program as long as basic accountability is ensured. In that environment, many states have cut back on doing follow-up studies.

The current focus of the states has shifted from benefit-cost analysis to cost-effectiveness analysis. States routinely compare the costs of achieving 26 closure with the costs of achieving other kinds of closure. Such data will be reported to legislatures and used internally for resource allocation. Dollar appraisals of the worth of such rehabilitation are given to legislatures, when at all, in the context of the overall state program—often using national memoranda issued by RSA rather than individual state studies.

The Program Standards suggested by RSA have been more influential than benefit-cost studies in shaping the kinds of analyses done by states internally. In recent years, state and RSA evaluation units have directed their efforts to helping states understand how to improve their performance in numbers of rehabilitants and the reduction of costs, not in overall benefit-cost analysis.

A good example in many states has been state agency reaction to supporting college education for disabled clients. Although such support is often justified by benefit-cost analysis for disabled clients (albeit in the absence of control groups for clients having that capacity), most states now discourage such services. The costs per rehabilitant are high and the gain in earnings is ignored.

Interestingly, in states that have done benefit-cost studies, agency personnel often contend that such studies are not influential in persuading legislatures to allocate more money. This may be because all agencies in these states are skilled at analytic data-based justifications of programs, so that all those programs which have survived with extensive funding over the years have at some time been justified by benefit-cost analysis. In such an arena of program competition, and given the inevitable uncertainty in projection of future benefits, success in getting resource allocations goes to those programs that can exercise political clout and demonstrate efficiency by keeping the costs per rehabilitant low.

State agencies rarely use benefit-cost analysis for internal resource allocation among clients. Rather, benefit-cost analysis is principally used to justify the overall program in competition with other programs for legislative resource allocation.

States do use cost-effectiveness analysis for internal allocation, however. It is used somewhat for setting priorities among types of clients but more often for setting priorities among sources of referrals and among types of closures (for example, giving low priority to homemaker closures).

The politics within programs make it difficult for any state program to rule out services to a particular disability group. Most importantly, the mandate of the federal legislation—which is strongly backed by public opinion and state politics in most states—is to serve the most severely disabled. This mandate may be directly adverse to the usual prescription of benefit-cost analysis to serve those clients who can produce the most benefits for resources expended. To be sure, with proper control groups, it might emerge that the severely disabled yield the highest benefit-cost returns. Obviously only rigorous benefit-cost studies could answer such questions.

CONCLUSIONS

Reviewing the overall situation among states, I offer the following conclusions.

1. The California benefit-cost model still represents the most complete model yet used among the states.

2. Federal leadership in providing easy models for state use and, most importantly, in providing better data on key assumptions (such as control group adjustments and other indirect benefits and costs) can be very influential. States will adopt practices that are urged on them by RSA and models that can be implemented without difficulty. The influence of the Berkeley model and, more recently, the Oregon model, is largely attributable to the presentation of these models in such a way that they could be readily programmed by state agencies. With the advent of microcomputers and their use in most states, it should be much easier in the future for states to do benefit-cost analysis, especially if the software is directly provided. Nonetheless, in a federal-state environment where states are not required to issue benefit-cost returns as part of federal reports, state agencies with performance problems or limited resources will resist investing in such analyses. A comparative analysis across states issued by a federal agency would be highly controversial, but it would be very effective in forcing state atten-

tion to benefit-cost analysis. If Social Security data links were forged, such analysis would be feasible. A comparative taxpayer payback analysis would be difficult because it would require separate analyses using different states' tax schedules. Still, such data are obtainable.

3. Much could be learned from a comparison of state benefit-cost studies. Unfortunately, such comparisons would be difficult to carry out at the present time because the states vary in their definitions of benefits and costs and in the assumptions they use in their models. Those components of benefit-cost analysis that differ from state to state include mortality rates, discount rates, follow-up data or assumptions concerning job retention, earnings increase, the valuation of similar benefits, and the valuation of homemaker closures.

9 Stanley E. Portny

COLLECTION OF DATA BY STATE AGENCIES

Having seen how some states are constructing benefit-cost models, we now turn our attention to the capacity of states to conduct this kind of analysis. A prerequisite is a data base, the foundation on which program evaluation must be built. It is important to look not only at the data that states collect but also at the form in which the data are collected and stored.

DESCRIPTION OF AGENCY DATA

My group consulted with fifteen state vocational rehabilitation (VR) agencies to assess their interest in benefit-cost analysis and to determine what types of information they collected that might be useful in conducting benefit-cost studies. The inquiries were made in January 1985, and the data collection procedures reported in this chapter for each agency are those in operation at that time. Table 9.1 gives some basic statistics on each of the agencies surveyed, including the region in which each agency is located, its combined federal and state obligations for basic support services, the number of cases served (statuses 10–30), and the number of successful rehabilitations (status 26) in fiscal year 1982.

Although the states were not selected by a strictly random or a structured sampling process, they tend to represent a cross section of the state VR agencies throughout the country. All but two of the ten federal regions are represented. The fifteen agencies include six general agencies, six special-

TABLE 9.1

SELECTED CHARACTERISTICS OF AGENCIES SURVEYED

Agency	Region	Federal and State Sec.-110 Obligations FY 1982	Total Cases Served (Active Statuses) FY 1982	Successful Rehabilitations FY 1982
New Jersey General	II	$21,263,491	22,933	5,722
New Jersey Blind	II	$5,191,791	1,653	348
Pennsylvania General	III	$50,597,268	56,609	14,431
Pennsylvania Blind	III	$7,588,035	3,326	569
Virginia General	III	$25,908,052	20,563	5,087
Virginia Blind	III	$3,212,006	1,566	404
Delaware Blind	III	$562,061	105	24
Florida General	IV	$34,646,919	31,565	7,931
South Carolina Blind	IV	$2,533,084	871	221
Illinois Combined	V	$38,959,743	29,735	7,051
Louisiana General	VI	$29,950,517	30,190	6,045
Texas General	VI	$56,512,001	46,466	13,908
Iowa Blind	VII	$2,518,046	542	90
Wyoming Combined	VIII	$4,069,336	2,444	747
Nevada Combined	IX	$4,755,514	2,599	1,030

ized agencies for the blind, and three agencies providing combined services. The agencies include some of the largest in the country in both obligations and clients served (Pennsylvania General and Texas General), as well as some of minimum activity (Wyoming Combined and Nevada Combined).

Through consultation with these agencies, I hoped to learn what kinds of program evaluation the states had undertaken and what kinds of evaluation they were equipped to undertake, given the available data. I therefore asked each agency to provide background documentation on its evaluation activities and information systems. My associates and I reviewed these materials and, in addition, queried key staff about the agency's commitment to benefit-cost studies. Was benefit-cost analysis an agency priority? If benefit-cost studies were carried out, how were the results put to use? Staff members were also asked to describe agency procedures for gathering and maintaining client data. What kinds of information were routinely collected in the agency's client statistical system and its financial information system? I was particularly interested in identifying data maintained by the agencies that could be used by analysts to evaluate the benefits of program participation and the costs of service delivery. I was also interested in identifying data in state agency information systems not recorded in the national data source, the R-300 set.

One line of inquiry focused on the recording of similar benefits. As other authors in this volume have noted, similar benefits—services authorized by the VR agencies but paid for by other agencies—are not recorded in the R-300 set, and they have generally been disregarded in the calculation of benefit-cost ratios for the VR program. If the states maintained information about similar benefits, and if they took these expenditures into account in their studies of the program, they could arrive at a truer estimate of the cost of services and hence a truer assessment of the program's economic performance.

In interviews with staff members, I also asked whether follow-up studies had been conducted. Those agencies that had looked into the work experience of clients closed from the program were asked to describe the substance of their studies and the specific procedures they had adopted. The reason for investigating state follow-up practices again relates to my interest in the capacity of the states to carry out benefit-cost analysis. Postclosure data should figure importantly in the estimation of program benefits. A fair measure of the impact of VR services on client earnings, for example, would take job retention into consideration.

Another set of questions focused on agency use of functional assessment tools or indicators to describe client capabilities. The use of such tools bears on program evaluation in two ways. Most obviously, improvements in functional ability constitute one measure of the benefits of VR services. Beyond this, however, the analyst who wishes to obtain an accurate estimate of the increase in earnings attributable to participation in the VR program would control for health or level of functioning (see Chapter 11, "Using Better Measures of Disability Status," for a more thorough investigation of this issue). The R-300 data set contains only a crude measure of client functioning at referral. The RSA-911, the data collection instrument devised to replace the R-300, included a brief set of Functional Gain Indicators at an earlier stage in its design, but its final form also lacks a means of assessing changes in the functional ability of clients. In discussions with state agency personnel, I wished to learn whether individual states had recorded information on client functioning at referral and at closure, and if so, what type of assessment tool they had used to obtain the information.

Finally, I asked the staff of agencies that had conducted benefit-cost studies of their services to discuss the focus and methodology of the studies in detail. I expected that their responses would reveal whether the states were making the best use of the information available to them for the purposes of benefit-cost analysis.

The results of these inquiries are presented in Table 9.2. The information for each state agency is broken down in accordance with the issues just outlined. In the following section, the findings are discussed in more general terms.

A DISCUSSION OF BENEFIT-COST DATA MAINTAINED BY SELECTED STATE VR AGENCIES

Overview

The principal objective of this investigation was to explore the information available to state VR agencies that could be used to support benefit-cost analyses of their programs. In speaking with staff from fifteen selected state rehabilitation agencies, I found that, while most indicated a general interest in ascertaining the costs and the benefits of program services, none had declared the performance of a benefit-cost analysis to be a true agency priority.

The majority of the agencies interviewed have developed or are in the process of developing automated systems for recording and maintaining client statistical and financial data. The principal objective of these systems is to provide accountability and compliance with federal and state program guidelines; in addition, the systems are used to support efficient service delivery and agency program and financial management. Because the agency objectives in using the systems are consistent from state to state, the core data maintained in the different systems tend also to be similar. However, a number of unique and innovative approaches are being taken by different agencies to use these systems to gain insight into some aspects of the true costs of service delivery and the benefits realized from program participation.

TABLE 9.2

BENEFIT COST INFORMATION

State Agency	New Jersey Division of Vocational Rehabilitation Services (NJDVRS)	New Jersey Commission for the Blind and Visually Impaired (NJCBVI)
Information Systems		
Principal Objectives	Management information system, now in final stage of development, will make it possible to monitor individual and agencywide case service delivery and financial transactions	Accountability and compliance with federal and state requirements; provision of accurate data in support of service delivery, financial transactions, and overall agency management
Client Statistical Information Systems	Will contain essentially the same data as the R-300 set	New computerized system has been operational for over one year. Contains essentially the same data as the R-300 set
Financial Information Systems	Will include complete records of all financial transactions related to purchased case services. Date and amount of obligations, cancellations and expenditures will be noted, as well as type, amount and provider of services. It will be possible to determine total expenditures to date for each client, caseload and entire agency; and cumulative expenditures to date for the life of the case (total and by individual service category)	New system will be operational within 5 months. Will include detailed records of all commitments, cancellations, invoices and payments; records of staff time devoted to individual clients; records of total expenditures for life of given case, specified types of services in a given fiscal year, and total expenditures for particular vendors in a given fiscal year
Similar Benefit Information	Will have capability to maintain similar benefits information: type, source and cost of service; client outcomes	Financial information system has capability to maintain records of similar benefits. This capability may be used at future date

TABLE 9.2--Continued

State Agency	NJDVRS	NJCBVI
Integration of Client and Financial Information Systems	New system will integrate client information and financial data	Complete integration of client statistical and financial information systems is not planned at present
Capacity to Support Special Studies of the Data	New system will support a variety of B-C analyses if appropriate software is developed	Considerable data will be available to support B-C analyses; however, built-in capacity of statistical and financial systems to support special studies is limited
Use of Functional Assessment Instruments	No instruments used	NJCBVI has not yet found a satisfactory instrument
Conduct of Follow-up Studies	Two follow-up surveys conducted. Most questions focus on client satisfaction with program; other questions concern client's employment situation at time of survey, earnings, job retention, and principal source of financial support. Response rates to surveys were low, and no attempt was made to link patterns of response to client characteristics	NJCBVI plans to conduct follow-up studies of all clients closed from the program one year after date of closure. Questionnaire has been developed and piloted
Interest in, and Conduct of, Benefit-Costs Studies	1982 study, "A Program Cost/Benefit Model for N.J. DVR," described benefits realized by the client, by the government, and by society in general, and compared them to costs of providing services. Study was based on questionable assumptions: 1) difference in client income at referral and at closure can be attributed to VR services; 2) costs for VR services borne by clients and other parties are negligible; 3) an appropriate proxy for the cost of a successful rehabilitation is the total basic support program expenditures for the year divided by the number of rehabilitated clients	B-C analysis not a priority to date. No studies to assess relative benefits and costs of program have been undertaken

TABLE 9.2--Continued

State Agency	Louisiana Division of Vocational Rehabilitation (LDVR)	Texas Rehabilitation Commission (TRC)
Information Systems		
Principal Objectives	Redesigned and updated information systems will insure accountability, facilitate transaction processing, and provide a responsive database to support management oversight of agency operations	Support of efficient service delivery; provision of database for the estimation of program costs and benefits
Client Statistical Information Systems	Contains essentially the same data as the R-300 set	Contains essentially the same data as the R-300 set, with the addition of functional gain indicators
Financial Information Systems	New system will maintain detailed records of all authorizations and expenditures for purchased services	Contains detailed records of all authorizations and expenditures for purchased services. Each entry includes a record of vendor, and the service type and amount
Similar Benefit Information	Comprehensive information on the type and amount of similar benefits is not maintained in a central data base at present	Information on similar benefits use is not maintained in a central data base
Integration of Client and Information Systems	Extent to which new systems will be integrated is not known	While certain data are maintained in both the client statistical and financial information systems, the systems are not fully integrated

TABLE 9.2--Continued

State Agency	LDVR	TRC
Capacity to Support Special Studies of the Data	Capacity of redesigned systems to support ad hoc analyses of selected service costs or the analysis of service costs for clients with specified characteristics is not yet known	Both financial and client statistical information systems will support a variety of B-C analyses
Use of Functional Assessment Instruments	No instruments used at present. Agency staff may consider them in future	The following functional gain indicators, originally incorporated in the RSA-911, are completed for each client at acceptance and closure: education, self-care supervision, self-care assistance, type of residence, mobility, expressive communication, receptive communication, adjustment. TRC has found these measures to be of limited value, however, and plans to drop them after the current fiscal year
Conduct of Follow-up Studies	LDVR has conducted follow-up studies of clients closed from the program, as required by VR Standards. Questionnaire elicited information about client's present work situation, total income received by the client and by family dependents the preceding month, and total wages earned the preceding week	TRC conducted a follow-up survey of a sample of status 26, 28, and 30 closures in 1983. Survey posed questions about client satisfaction with program, client's current work status, pay, and number of hours worked per week. Response rate was low
Interest in, and Conduct of, Benefit-Costs Studies	LDVR has not conducted any studies specifically designed to develop B-C ratios for agency VR programs. Agency administrators are interested, however, in identifying more effective ways of estimating the costs and describing the benefits of program participation	TRC conducted analyses of program benefits and costs in 1982 and 1983

TABLE 9.2--Continued

State Agency	Delaware Division of the Visually Impaired (DDVI)	Florida Office of Vocational Rehabilitation (FOVR)
Information Systems		
Principal Objectives	Compliance with federal and state requirements; monitoring of agency's financial status	Computerized system, now under development, will maintain a wide variety of data related to service costs and benefits to support agency decision making and service delivery
Client Statistical Information System	Manually maintained. Contains essentially the same data as the R-300 set	Will maintain client data similar to the R-300 set, but with significant additions. Will identify other agencies within the Dept. of Health and Rehabilitative Services that provide services to FOVR clients or their families, and the sources and monthly amounts of public assistance provided to FOVR clients. Will also record the number of hours the client worked the week before application and at closure, the client's principal source of support at application and closure, and the monthly amount the client received
Financial Information System	Existing system, manually maintained, includes records of all revenues and expenditures. New automated system will be operational by April 1985 and will record all authorizations, commitments and expenditures	Will include detailed records by client of authorizations, cancellations and payments for purchased care services. Name of vendor and type and amount of service will be entered for each transaction. System will have built-in capability to generate the following information for clients identified by 1 or more criteria (e.g. district, status, disability, referral agency): number of cases, year-to-date average cost, life of case average cost

TABLE 9.2--Continued

State Agency	DDVI	FOVR
Similar Benifits Information	Not maintained	The following similar benefits data will be entered for each client: type, date, and approximate value of benefit
Integration of Client and Financial Information Systems	Systems not integrated	New system will integrate client information and financial data
Capacity to Support Special Studies of the Data	Systems will have little capacity to support special studies	System will support a variety of analyses of agency B-C relationships
Use of Functional Assessment Instruments	No instruments used at present. DDVI has not found an instrument that adequately addresses the special situation of blind clients	The following functional gain indicators, originally incorporated in the RSA-911, are completed for each client at acceptance and closure: education, self-care supervision, self-care assistance, type of residence, mobility, expressive communication, receptive communication, adjustment
Conduct of Follow-Up Studies	No studies conducted currently	FOVR has conducted studies in the past and plans to conduct them in the future. A 1983 survey assessed client satisfaction with program, but did not elicit information on client's economic situation
Interest in, and Conduct of, Bendfit-Costs Studies	No studies conducted to date. While DDVI recognizes that B-C information would be useful to support agency planning decisions, data constraints and limitations on staff time would narrow the range of possible B-C methodologies	FOVR has not conducted any B-C analyses of the program within the past 5-6 years

TABLE 9.2--Continued

State Agency	Iowa Commission for the Blind (ICB)	Wyoming Division of Vocational Rehabilitation (WDVR)
Information Systems		
Principal Objectives	Provision of information on program performance to the public; support for budget requests	Integrated information system, now in early stages of development, will enable WDVR to improve its assessment of costs and benefits of program
Client Statistical Information Systems	Manually maintained. Contains essentially the same data as the R-300 set	Existing system contains essentially the same data as the R-300 set
Financial Information Systems	Manually maintained. Includes a detailed record of authorizations, invoices, and expenditures for purchased services	Existing system contains detailed records of authorizations and expenditures for purchased services
Similar Benefits Information	Not routinely collected	Now maintained in clients' case folders. WDVR will maintain this information centrally when the new integrated system is developed
Integration of Client and Financial Information Systems	Systems not integrated	Client data and financial data files are not integrated at present. Integrated information systems will be completed in 2 years

TABLE 9.2--Continued

State Agency	ICB	WDVR
Capacity to Support Special Studies of the Data	Manual information services can provide only limited support for special analyses. Summaries of cost data by service type or client characteristic would be extremely time-consuming to develop	Existing systems will not support specialized analyses of data
Use of Functional Assessment Instruments	No instruments used at present. Instruments examined by ICB did not adequately address the special situation of blind clients	WDVR has reviewed different instruments, but has not found one that suits its needs. Agency plans to develop its own instrument in the future
Conduct of Follow-Up Studies	ICB conducted follow-up studies on clients closed from the program when required to do so by the VR Standards. While the agency has not conducted such studies for the past several years, it is contemplating conducting one in the future	WDVR conducts follow-up studies of clients who have been out of the VR program for 5 years
Interest in, and Conduct of, Benefit-Costs Studies	ICB has not undertaken a full-scale B-C analysis of its program. It has, however, adapted existing methodologies to develop rough estimates of program benefits and costs. Benefits are estimated in public assistance payments saved, and additional income and social security tax payments made by rehabilitated clients who earn salaries	WDVR has adapted existing methodologies to develop approximate B-C ratios for the program, and has also investigated alternative approaches for measuring nonvocational gains, retention of program benefits, and program costs

TABLE 9.2--Continued

State Agency	Nevada Rehabilitation Division (NRD)
Information Systems	
Principal Objectives	Desire to provide improved information regarding program benefits and costs
Client Statistical Information System	Contains essentially the same data as the R-300 set
Financial Information System	Contains detailed records of authorizations and expenditures for purchased services
Similar Benefits Information	Information on amount of similar benefits used is not centrally maintained
Integration of Client and Financial Information Systems	No information provided
Capacity to Support Special Studies of the Data	Difficult to perform special or ad hoc analyses of data
Use of Functional Assessment Instruments	No information provided
Conduct of Follow-Up Studies	No information provided
Interest in, and Conduct of, Benefit-Cost Studies	NRD has conducted B-C studies in the past

TABLE 9.2--Continued

State Agency	Pennsylvania Office of Vocational Rehabilitation (POVR)	Pennsylvania Bureau of Blindness and Visual Services (PBBVS)
Information Systems		
Principal Objectives	Support of service delivery and financial transactions, and overall agency monitoring of budget and program operations	Agency seeks to improve existing information systems so that they are capable of supporting efficient service delivery and program management. Although current systems are automated, agency staff often rely on backup records manually maintained in the field
Client Statistical Information Systems	Contains essentially the same data as the R-300 set	Contains essentially the same data as the R-300 set
Financial Information Systems	POVR is introducing computerized system. Will record authorizations, cancellations and expenditures; 3rd party reimbursements; client contributions to cost of VR services. Will make detailed cost breakouts (cumulative cost per client, cumulative cost by service category, etc.) possible	Records individual financial transactions, but does not provide for the ready analysis of costs on a client, service or vendor basis
Similar Benefit Information	Source, service type, and amount of similar benefits are recorded; cumulative total of cost savings for each case is also recorded	Information on similar benefits use is not maintained in the centralized system. Plans to use similar benefits are noted in IWRPS, but the dollar value of benefits actually used is not recorded
Integration of Client and Financial Information Systems	Systems essentially not integrated	Systems not integrated

TABLE 9.2--Continued

State Agency	POVR	PBBVS
Capacity to Support Special Studies of the Data	Special programming will be required to extract data in the appropriate format to support B-C analysis	Capacity of information systems to support accurate assessments of program benefits and costs is questionable
Use of Functional Assessment Instruments	POVR has experimented with different instruments, but uses none at present. Counselors indicate that questionnaires require too much time to complete	No instruments used
Conduct of Follow-up Studies	Annual follow-up study of 5% sample of cases closed. Survey assesses client satisfaction with program and current employment situation. Includes questions concerning hours worked per week, present earnings, and external sources of support. Respondents also asked to assess improvements in ability to perform self-care functions; rehabilitants closed as homemakers asked to assess improvement in homemaking skills	No follow-up studies conducted
Interest in, and Conduct of, Benefit-Costs Studies	B-C studies not a priority to date, largely because of insufficient data. Measures have been taken to improve scope and quality of data	PBBVS undertook analysis of program benefits and costs in 1982. B-C measures included the ratio of discounted expected future earnings of client to the one-time cost of rehabilitation, and ratio of expected tax payback to agency expenditures. Primary measure of client economic benefit was difference in weekly earnings at referral and closure. At present, B-C analysis per se is not a priority, but interest does exist in obtaining realistic estimates of program benefits and costs

TABLE 9.2--Continued

State Agency Information Systems	South Carolina Commission for the Blind (SCCB)	Illinois Department of Rehabilitation Services (IDORS)
Principal Objectives	SCCB is seeking to improve its client and financial information systems in order to obtain better data on case costs and the benefits of program participation	Support of service delivery, overall management of financial and administrative transactions, and the monitoring of similar benefits use and other activities designed to reduce agency costs
Client Statistical Information Systems	Existing system contains essentially the same data as the R-300 set	Contains essentially the same data as the R-300 set
Financial Information System	Existing system maintains records of receipts, expenditures and balance of funds. It cannot be used to develop reports in different formats or expenditure summaries by type of service. What information will be recorded in the new financial system is not clear	Includes detailed records of all authorizations, cancellations and expenditures for purchased care services
Similar Benefit Information	New client information system will record the source and value of similar benefits used	The following information on similar benefit use is recorded and maintained: source, service code, service description, client status at time of service, amount IDORS would have authorized for the service if similar benefits had not been received. IDORS also produces summaries, by service type and geographic location, of the amount of savings realized as a result of similar benefit usage
Integration of Client and Financial Information Systems	The extent to which the new financial information system will be integrated with the client information system is not known at present	Systems not integrated

TABLE 9.2--Continued

State Agency	SCCB	IDORS
Capacity to Support Special Studies of the Data	Capacity of new information systems to support ad hoc analyses is not known at present	It would be difficult to obtain accurate tallies of expenditures for particular types of services for clients with specified personal or closure characteristics
Use of Functional Assessment Instruments	No instruments used	No instruments used
Conduct of Follow-up Studies	SCCB does not regularly conduct follow-up studies of clients. Those surveys that have been conducted focus on client satisfaction with the program	IDORS staff are planning to survey status 26 closures (and possibly status 28 closures). Questions will focus on client's employment situation
Interest in, and Conduct of, Benefit-Costs Studies	SCCB has not conducted any studies specifically designed to assess the B-C ratio of program services, although it has sought to establish certain broad measures of operating efficiency (e.g. total program budget divided by total number of successful rehabilitations)	IDORS conducted a B-C analysis of the program in 1981. The B-C ratio derived only reflects total program costs and projected earnings of rehabilitated clients; it does not take into account savings due to reductions in public assistance or social security payments, or additional revenues generated by increased income tax payments

TABLE 9.2--Continued

State Agency	Virginia Department of Rehabilitative Services (VDRS)	Virginia Department for the Visually Handicapped (VDVH)
Information Systems		
Principal Objectives	New systems, now under development, will be designed to facilitate service delivery, financial transactions, and financial monitoring	Systems designed to meet minimum requirements for financial accountability and program compliance
Client Statistical Information Systems	Current system contains essentially the same data as the R-300 set	Automated data file. Contains essentially the same data as the R-300 set
Financial Information Systems	Existing system includes data on authorizations, cancellations and expenditures. Service type, amount and provider are recorded for each transaction	Case cost records are maintained manually. Automated records of all agency expenditures are maintained as part of state's general accounting system. No uniform procedures exist for maintaining ongoing records of counselor budgets, authorizations and cancellations
Similar Benefit Information	Not maintained in the existing information system. Counselors' field books do contain some similar benefits data, but format of the data varies greatly	Not maintained in central information system. Source and amount of similar benefits noted in IWRPs only
Integration of Client and Financial Information Systems	Not possible with current system to combine financial data with caseload and client data	VDVH may develop integrated information systems during next two years

TABLE 9.2--Continued

State Agency	VDRS	VDVH
Capacity to Support Special Studies of the Data	Not possible with current system to develop special analyses of the data, e.g. amount of expenditures by provider, or average expenditure for a certain type of service provided by a particular vendor. New system may have this capability	Difficult to extract special tabulations of the data. Since service codes used in case cost records and automated financial systems are not the same, it would be difficult to develop breakouts of total expenditures by type of service, by client or by vendor
Use of Functional Assessment Instruments	VDRS has investigated the use of functional indicators to describe nonmonetary benefits of program, but is awaiting federal lead before acting to adopt one or more instruments	No instruments used
Conduct of Follow-up Studies	VDRS conducts follow-up survey of sample of clients closed in status 26 and status 28 twelve months after they leave program. Questions concern client's employment situation--hours worked, average gross pay at present and at time of closure--and client's principal source of support	Annual follow-up studies were conducted when required by VR standards, but no plans to resume them exist at present
Interest in, and Conduct of, Benefit-Costs Studies	B-C analysis not a specific agency objective at present, but VDRS actively explores alternative approaches for assessing the effects of VR services and the overall costs of services. Most recent B-C analysis of program was undertaken in 1978. Agency is now required to give the governor progress reports containing information on average weekly earnings of rehabilitants, estimated increase in earned income of rehabilitants, and estimated payment of taxes to government	B-C analysis not an agency priority

Client statistical data

All fifteen of the agencies in the survey routinely collect and maintain client statistical data similar to those required in the R-300; thirteen of the fifteen agencies have or are in the process of developing automated information systems to maintain these data. However, only two agencies, Texas General and Florida General, collect additional client data that would be particularly useful for a benefit-cost analysis. Both agencies are currently using the Functional Gain Indicators originally included in the RSA-911 to describe the client's situation at acceptance and at closure; and both are storing the results of these assessments for all clients in their centralized client information systems. However, Texas plans to discontinue this practice at the end of the current fiscal year because agency staff have found the information to be of little use.

In its new information system, Florida is planning to include several data elements and procedures in addition to the Functional Gain Indicators. First, all VR clients will automatically be entered into the Department of Health and Rehabilitative Services Client Information System, so that it will be possible to determine whether the client or any family member is receiving services from other DHRS programs. Second, the sources and dollar amounts received will be separately maintained for up to three sources of public assistance. Third, in addition to earnings one week before application and upon closure, the number of hours worked per week in each case will be recorded. Fourth, the monthly amount received from workers' compensation at application and at closure will be maintained. Fifth, the client's principal source of support at application and at closure will be recorded. And finally, it will be noted whether the client's counselor had direct or indirect involvement in the client's placement.

Financial data

Each of the fifteen agencies in the survey maintained detailed records of all expenditures for purchased case services; apparently this information is required to satisfy program accountability requirements. Most of the agencies also noted in these records information about the type and amount of service provided and the identity of the vendor. In almost all cases, information was also maintained about authorizations for services.

However, although thirteen of the fifteen agencies had automated at least some portion of their financial systems, the extent to which special groupings of this information could be obtained varied greatly, as did the possibility of obtaining integrated descriptions of the costs of services for clients with particular characteristics. Less than one-third of the agencies had developed or were in the process of developing automated financial information systems that would be fully integrated with their client statistical data bases. Further, at least half of the agencies indicated that it would be difficult to run special analyses of the financial records to obtain totals of the amounts of funds expended by service category, vendor, or other grouping. Several agencies noted that it would be difficult or impossible to determine accurate estimates of the cost of purchased services over the life of a particular case.

Similar benefits

All of the agencies in the survey indicated that agency policy encouraged the use of similar benefits whenever possible to support services included in the individualized written rehabilitation program. However, only five of the agencies had developed or were developing procedures for the routine collection and central maintenance of information about the magnitude of similar benefits used.

Pennsylvania General, Florida General, and Illinois General have counselors record and submit for each client the source, service type, amount, and approximate value of similar benefits used. In a new financial information system currently being developed, Pennsylvania will record the dollar value of third party reimbursement to the agency for all purchased services paid for by the agency and one or more external funding sources (including the clients themselves). In addition, each of these agencies has developed detailed guidelines and procedures and has conducted extensive training of agency staff in the use and reporting of similar benefits. In their new financial information system, the New Jersey General agency will record the dollar value of similar benefits used. The New Jersey Blind agency will also have the capability in their new financial information system to record this information, but there are no present plans to require field staff to do so.

Follow-up studies

Each of the agencies interviewed had conducted follow-up studies of clients closed from the VR program in the past when required to do so by the VR Standards. However, only Pennsylvania General and Virginia General regularly conduct such studies at present. In addition to asking questions regarding the client's satisfaction with services received, both agencies solicit information about the client's employment situation and earnings at the time of the follow-up. Pennsylvania surveys 5 percent of selected groups of status 26, 28, and 30 closures and most recently has obtained about a 50 percent response rate. Virginia surveys 20 to 25 percent of status 26 and 28 closures and obtains between a 25 to 35 percent response.

Of the remaining agencies, six indicated that they were planning to conduct follow-up surveys in the future and were in various phases of questionnaire design and pilot testing; each of the six indicated that the survey would seek information regarding the client's current employment situation, the number of hours per week worked, and the client's gross salary. The remainder had no plans for follow-up studies at the present time.

Functional assessment indicators

Only two of the fifteen agencies in the survey are regularly using functional assessment indicators at present. Both Florida General and Texas General currently are having counselors complete the Functional Gain Indicators from the original RSA-911 for each client at acceptance and at closure; Texas, however, will be stopping this practice at the end of the current fiscal year.

Six of the fifteen agencies have studied one or more existing instruments but have not chosen to adopt them. (The instruments most frequently examined were the Preliminary Diagnostic Questionnaire from the West Virginia Research and Training Center, the Functional Assessment Inventory from the University of Minnesota, the Life Status Indicators from New York University, and the Functional Gain Indicators from the original RSA-911.) Several of the agencies for the blind examined one or more of these instruments but felt that they did not adequately address special situations of blind people.

Agency studies

Six of the fifteen agencies in the survey have conducted one or more benefit-cost studies during the past six years. For their study methodology, each agency used an approach described in available literature in the VR field. Three of the agencies used the approach proposed by the West Virginia Research and Training Center, two cited the RSA approach discussed in a 1980 information memorandum, and one adapted the methodology employed by the Oregon Vocational Rehabilitation Division.

Each of the studies conducted relied on benefit and cost data currently existing in agency files. Consequently, cost of services was approximated by either the cost of *purchased* services or the total agency budget divided by the total number of successful rehabilitations for the year. Increase in client earnings was approximated by the difference between the client's earnings at closure and the week before application.

CONCLUSION

Much of the data now being collected at the state level could be used to obtain more precise measures of VR costs and benefits than those currently in use. Despite the availability of this information, however, the states have generally failed to incorporate it in their evaluation of the program. The interest in benefit-cost analysis has declined, and agencies that do conduct benefit-cost studies tend to define costs narrowly and to compute benefits in the traditional fashion—that is, as the difference between client earnings at referral and at closure.

A second problem concerns the form in which the states maintain their data. A number of the states have information systems that would not allow for special investigations of statistical and financial data. In many states, the statistical and financial systems are not integrated, making it difficult for program analysts to explore the relationships between service costs and selected client characteristics and outcomes.

My interviews with agency personnel suggested that the states will follow the federal lead in matters of program evaluation. If the federal government were to support the collection of data and to provide demonstrations of its usefulness for the analysis of program performance, there would no doubt be a change in state practices.

IV

Using Augmented Data Bases

A look back at the ground we have covered may be useful at this point. The initial chapters in this volume stressed the unreliability of benefit-cost analysis as it has traditionally been conducted in the vocational rehabilitation program. The costs of services have often been interpreted very narrowly and questionable assumptions have been made about the earnings increases and job tenure of rehabilitants. The weaknesses of the analysis can be traced in large part to the inadequacy of the national data base—a theme here taken up in many variations.

In Parts II and III of the volume, we saw that techniques exist that allow the program analyst to compensate for the deficiencies of the data. Statistical and econometric methods of correction can be applied to the existing data on costs and benefits to obtain more reliable estimates. The authors of Chapters 6 and 7, for example, used such techniques to impute wages to those clients who report zero earnings at referral and to those who are closed out unsuccessfully from the program. A second method of adjusting the reported figures on costs and benefits is in use in a number of the state agencies. This method is exemplified by the California model of program analysis described in some detail in Chapter 8. The model employs data from independent studies carried out in the state to adjust the prerehabilitation and postclosure earnings of clients. Thus, a state survey finding that the job retention rate among one group of California rehabilitants was 63.5 percent is used to correct the reported earnings increases of subsequent rehabilitants. In essence, the California model uses the experience of one cohort to predict the experience of another; a correction factor is derived from the results of independent inquiries and applied across the board. In Part IV, this procedure is called a cookbook method because it assumes that the same recipe holds for the group under examination as for the group that was the subject of the earlier study.

There is no question that such methods of adjusting the existing data do lead to more realistic estimates of the costs and benefits of vocational rehabilitation. Nevertheless, a clearly superior approach to program analysis involves the generation of comprehensive data and the use of such *actual* data in benefit-cost studies. Part III demonstrated that some states do in fact collect data for fiscal and management purposes that goes beyond what is available in the national R-300 set and that is of considerable potential value to the benefit-cost analyst. As the authors in Part III indicate, however, the states have failed to take advantage of this data for the purposes of evaluation.

Having considered what the state VR agencies are capable of doing with the information they have at their disposal, we move on in Part IV to an actual demonstration of what can be done with the state data. In Chapter 10, David Dean and Robert Dolan examine the augmented Virginia data base to obtain figures on the true costs of services received by individual clients of the state VR program. The authors make use of information in the Virginia files on the actual costs of services provided—as opposed to the R-300 estimates of the value of services prescribed—to present a more accurate account of the costs of the state program. In addition, they are able to draw on the state agency's records detailing the type, frequency, date, and duration of services in order to explore the ways in which particular patterns of service affect the earnings outcomes of rehabilitants. A third class of information available in the state files, albeit in limited form, concerns counselor caseloads; the authors adapt this information to study the relationship of counselor services and client outcomes.

Chapter 10 demonstrates that economic analysis supported by comprehensive data can yield more than a simple assessment of the overall performance of the VR program. It can be used by program personnel for "internal evaluation"—for example, to learn more about the cost effectiveness of particular services and the cost effectiveness of counselor time. The genius of the VR program has been its ability to bring to bear a wide variety of services from physical restoration to retraining to solve an individual's problems. The analyst can assist in this effort to respond in a flexible way to the needs of a very diverse population by identifying effective and efficient programs of service for particular classes of clients.

Chapter 11 focuses on another feature of the enhanced state data base that is useful in program analysis. Will Milberg and David Dean discuss the significance of a measure of health or functioning in the calculation of benefits. As they point out, the analyst must control for the level of health that clients bring to the program in order to isolate the impact of VR treatment on their earnings. In addition, an improvement in the level of a client's functioning represents another kind of benefit that may be realized through participation in the VR program.

Early in the chapter, the authors consider the problem of conceptualizing health and survey some of the diagnostic tools that have been applied by counselors and physicians to assess the health status or functional ability of clients. They contrast the condition classification codes used by the Rehabilitation Services Administration, which fail to measure the severity of the impairment, with instruments like the Functional Assessment Inventory (FAI) used by the Wisconsin VR agency and other state VR agencies, which do record information on the degree of impairment.

The claims for the importance of a health measure are borne out by the analysis of the earnings outcomes of a group of clients served by the Wisconsin VR agency. The sample data set includes an account of the services delivered to the clients, as well as the FAI measures of health. The authors set out to estimate the impact of specific services on earnings, while experimenting with the use of a health variable in the earnings equation. Their results show clearly that a health variable sensitive to differences in the level of severity can help to explain differences in the earnings levels of rehabilitants.

The last chapter in Part IV, "Establishing a Mini-Data Link," again underscores the value of additional data in calculating VR program benefits. A number of authors in the volume have called attention to the problem of tracking the time path of wages when the national data set records information on client earnings at only two points in time—referral and closure. The change in client earnings from referral to closure is the customary measure of benefits, but how can the analyst be sure that the earnings increase recorded for a particular rehabilitant will continue over time? The analyst can adjust the earnings figures with reference to certain assumptions about the relationship of age and earnings, the results of independent surveys on the job retention rate of other groups of rehabilitants, or published data on the life expectancy rates of the disabled, but the best solution to the problem is to maintain longitudinal data on the actual postclosure earnings of the VR clients under examination.

In Chapter 12, David Dean and Robert Dolan match the records of the Virginia Department of Rehabilitative Services with records maintained by the Virginia Employment Commission to find data on the earnings of clients fifteen to twenty-seven months after they had been closed from the state program. This minidata link provides a number of insights into the relative level of labor market success achieved by clients in different closure statuses. It also sheds light on the issue of job retention and the pattern of labor force participation for different cohorts within the client population.

The data link at the state level suggests what could be accomplished at the federal level if RSA records were matched with Social Security earnings data. If actual data on earnings for some period of time before referral and after closure were available to program analysts, then it would be possible to compute the overall benefits of the VR program much more realistically. The corrections for zero earnings at acceptance discussed in Chapter 6 and the corrections for earnings of those clients closed as nonrehabilitants could be applied with greater assurance. No data link will ever match all records, but the number of omissions should be relatively few and more amenable to econometric correction.

10 *David H. Dean and Robert C. Dolan*

USING A BETTER MEASURE FOR SERVICES

The information on service costs available in the R-300 data set falls far short of the needs of the economic analyst. Current R-300 data reveal only the value of total services prescribed to a client along with a checklist for each client indicating receipt or nonreceipt of particular services. The lack of comprehensive data restricts the analyst to a view of the rehabilitation process as a "black box": the client enters the box, receives certain services, and reemerges, but the exact nature of the rehabilitation experience and the elements of that experience that contribute most to the client's success or lack of success are not open to examination.

From the standpoint of economic evaluation, the R-300 data are deficient in a number of respects. First, they provide no information regarding the intensity or duration of specific services. Evaluation based on specific service data would further our understanding of the relationship between earnings outcomes and particular service patterns. This evaluative focus would yield information on the cost-effectiveness of specific services and lead to recommendations for allocating resources throughout the program.

Second, the accuracy of the total cost data now available is open to question. The costs reported in the R-300 are the value of services as estimated by a counselor from the case records. Much more reliable for the purposes of economic evaluation would be a record of *actual* service expenditures. In the analysis that follows, we take advantage of the enhanced data set for the Virginia VR program, which records "vouchered services"— that is, services actually paid out. Significantly, this procedure revealed actual total service costs that were different from the Virginia R-300 figures.

A third problem with the service data is that they do not capture fully the range of services that a client can receive. Because VR is the service provider of last resort, one duty of counselors is to identify whether clients are eligible for services under other programs such as the Veterans Administration, Aid to Families with Dependent Children, or Supplemental Security Income. In such cases, clients receive "similar benefits"—services prescribed by VR but paid for by another federal, state, or private agency. Even though these services can contribute to a client's success in the program, the value of similar benefits is not included in the total service cost figure reported on the R-300. Efforts to remedy this deficiency are presented in the second section.

Finally, there is no specific accounting for counselor services. Under present cost reporting, counselor input must be treated as a component of overhead. This treatment is defensible only if the quantity of counselor time spent per client is uniform across clients regardless of the nature of their impairment. An attempt to incorporate counselor time on an individual client basis is presented in the third section.

Our overall aim in this chapter is to reach an accurate assessment of the cost of services received by clients in one state VR program. Our analysis of the Virginia data illustrates an improved method of calculating costs and should make it possible to arrive at more exact estimates of benefit-cost ratios. The procedure we follow in the chapter is to take the direct costs of services provided (see Table 10.1) and to allocate them on an individual client basis. The procedure does not include the allocation of any indirect or governance and administrative costs. The allocation of this overhead component is a separate issue beyond the scope of this paper.

TABLE 10.1

ALLOCATION OF VIRGINIA DEPARTMENT OF REHABILITATIVE SERVICES
FISCAL YEAR 1982

Direct costs

Case services	$12,997,650	
Similar Benefits	$5,183,219	
Counselors	$3,728,250	
	============	
		$21,909,119

Indirect costs

Evaluators	$571,665	
Supervisors	$1,168,650	
Field support	$7,234,815	
	============	
		$8,975,130

Administrative		$1,920,675
		============
Total		$32,804,924

ENHANCED SERVICE COST DATA

The data analyzed in this study reflect all closed cases for the Virginia Department of Rehabilitative Services (VDRS) in 1982. This data set is more comprehensive than those typically available under the Federal R-300 reporting system because it contains matching demographic and service-specific cost files for each client closure. This accounting renders two significant improvements to the R-300 data. The data on service costs are more accurate because they are compiled from records of vouchered services. In addition, client records containing individual voucher services have the advantage of permitting analysis of the pattern of services received. Researchers who work with records indicating only the total service cost per client must ignore the variations in services' nature and intensity. Even broadly defined, the services to a client represent a mix of diagnostic, restorative, educational, vocational, and direct financial assistance. Studies that relate total service expenditures to earnings cannot reveal how the service pattern itself may influence outcomes. Yet when government or program personnel set out to formulate rehabilitation policy, they will want to know how dollars are spent in a successful rehabilitation program as well as how much is spent.

Figure 10.1 depicts the criteria applied in defining the target sample. While VDRS recorded 17,622 closed cases in 1982, only 9,465 persons were accepted for either VR services (status 10) or extended evaluation. The sample was further restricted by the condition that clients report earnings at closure. This condition eliminated two broad categories of closed cases. First, clients who are "unsuccessfully" closed usually will not report earnings. Second, even a "successful" closure does not necessarily imply remunerative employment. For example, a status 26 closure will apply to those individuals who are placed as homemakers or unpaid family workers. Together, these categories eliminated 5,098 clients—4,376 and 722, respectively. For most of the remaining 4,367 closures, service-specific cost files were available for all expenses incurred during a four-year period before closure in 1982.

These fiscal files contained information on the specific types of service provided to individual clients, as well as the frequency, date, and duration of those services. Consistency checks of the data revealed that 797 clients did not have the matching fiscal records necessary for our analysis. Two factors accounted for the absence of records: (1) 348 cases closed in 1982 had costs incurred more than four years earlier, beyond the longitudinal scope of our data; and (2) 449 did not receive any contracted service. The individuals in the latter group most likely received only counseling or job placement services, which are provided in-house; such services do not show up as a specific vouchered expenditure. These clients may also have received

Figure 10.1
DEFINING THE TARGET SAMPLE

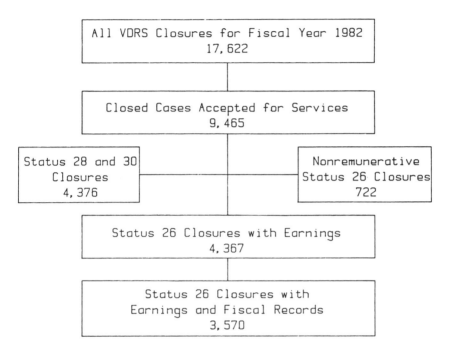

similar benefits. Once these clients were discounted, 3,570 clients remained in the sample.

In summary, the sample contained clients closed from the program with earnings and complete records of specific VR services provided. Since VDRS provides a total of sixty-two different contracted services, these services were grouped within five broader categories: (1) diagnostic, (2) restorative, (3) training, (4) education, and (5) maintenance, transportation, and other. The client sample was also stratified according to the following modified RSA disability classifications: (1) physical impairment, (2) mental retardation, and (3) emotional impairment.

DISTRIBUTION AND VALUE OF SERVICE RECEIPTS

Table 10.2 provides a descriptive overview of service-specific receipts. This table shows the number of persons receiving each service, the mean value of services, and the receipt rate within each disability category. The far

TABLE 10.2

SPECIFIC VR SERVICES RECEIVED BY IMPAIRMENT COHORT

Service / Variable Description	Impairment			
	Physical (n=2180)	Mentally Retarded (n=876)	Emotional (n=514)	All Impairments (n=3570)
Restorative				
Average Receipt (in $)	$1,206	$389	$517	$1,061
# of Clients Receiving	1471	212	128	1811
% of Total Receiving	67%	24%	25%	51%
Training				
Average Receipt (in $)	$541	$1,076	$751	$825
# of Clients Receiving	301	406	229	936
% of Total Receiving	14%	46%	45%	26%
Education				
Average Receipt (in $)	$1,586	$2,918	$1,732	$2,024
# of Clients Receiving	291	191	148	630
% of Total Receiving	13%	22%	29%	18%
All Services				
Average Receipt (in $)	$1,462	$2,112	$1,547	$1,633

right-hand column presents all-impairment figures for each service category and the bottom row reports the mean value of total service receipts across each disability group. For example, education is the most expensive service category, $2,024, and mentally retarded clients receive the highest average value of services, $2,122.

The distribution of the remaining three service categories across clients varies predictably with disability type. For example, average restorative services of more than $1,200 were provided to physically impaired clients and at the relatively high receipt rate of 67 percent. In comparison, only 25 percent of emotionally impaired or mentally retarded clients received restorative services, with a mean benefit value of $389 and $517, respectively. On the other hand, mentally impaired clients received the bulk of training services. Note that 635 of the 936 training service recipients were either mentally retarded (406) or emotionally impaired (229), with a mean service value of $1,076 and $751, respectively. The receipt rate for training among mentally impaired persons was almost 50 percent. Generally, these results reflect this cohort's need for personal or work adjustment training. In contrast, the average training service received by physically impaired persons was less than $541, with a receipt rate of only 14 percent.

The design of Table 10.2 has omitted two of the specific-service categories mentioned earlier—diagnostic services and maintenance, transportation, and other (MTO). The omission of MTO reflects our judgment that these expenditures tend to be supportive rather than rehabilitative. Diagnostic services are omitted because they are received by the vast majority of clients in our sample (71.7 percent) and in relatively equal amounts. Consequently, diagnostic services are unlikely to surface as a differentiating variable in the rehabilitative process. However, our decision to omit these service categories leaves one important fact undisclosed: 588 of the successful closures in the sample (16.5 percent) reported diagnosis as the only form of contracted VR services received.

ACCOUNTING FOR SIMILAR BENEFITS

Another deficiency in the traditional cost-benefit analysis of the VR program is the failure to account for similar benefits in the cost of the service package received by clients. Recall that these are services that have been provided to a client of the VR agency but funded by another federal, state, or private agency. Although the VR agency itself is relieved of those expenses, similar benefits still constitute an important service cost from the standpoint of social accounting. Moreover, the provision of similar benefits will still involve time and effort on the part of VR counselors; in fact, counselors may work just as hard to procure these services as they do for those purchased by the agency or provided "in-house."

To get some estimate of the magnitude of the problem, consider that for 1982 the amount of services purchased by the VR agency totaled just under $13 million (see Table 10.1). The estimated cost of the similar benefits provided during the same period was over $5 million. Some 30 percent of services received by clients are overlooked in a cost framework that examines only services purchased by the VR agency.

Neglecting to include these similar benefits in an estimation of the impact of services on outcomes results in an omitted variable bias. This will present two different types of problems. If these benefits are distributed equally among the clients, then the resulting analysis will overestimate the impact of the purchased services. If these services are not evenly distributed, then the omitted variable will bias the impact of the reported services. To avoid these problems, we must aggregate both VR-purchased and similar benefits on an individual client basis.

In order to incorporate data on similar benefits, we had to make the data compatible with existing cost of service data. The R-300 data set classifies the services received by a client into twelve different categories. Each service received is designated as being provided with cost to the agency, without cost, or shared cost. The latter two classifications represent similar benefit provision. "Without cost" means that an outside agency paid for the entire cost of the service; "shared cost" implies some cost-sharing between the VR agency and an external funding source. If the outside agency funded the entire cost of the service, then no record of this service cost would appear on the R-300 file. If the VR agency bore some portion of the cost, only that portion would be recorded; the actual cost of the service would not appear.

The breakdown of the services received in this schema is presented in Table 10.3. In only two service groups—maintenance and business school—were external funding sources used to provide services for less than one-third of the clients receiving such services. For six of the twelve categories more than half of the services received were funded at least in part by similar benefits. For instance, the two services most frequently provided, diagnostic and other, were funded by other agencies for 62.3 and 95.6 percent of the clients.

The omission of similar benefits in cost accounting clearly represents an oversight of considerable magnitude. How, then, can the analyst correct for this deficiency? Many states keep at least cursory records on the dollar amount of similar benefits provided to their clientele. In Virginia, the counselors record the estimated costs of the services that are *supposed* to be delivered when they draw up the individal written rehabilitation plan for clients. While similar benefits are not vouchered services, the value assigned by counselors to such services is based on cost estimates provided in the counselors' *Medical Services Manual.* The counselors' records contain, in addition to the estimated dollar amount, the type of service provided and an

TABLE 10.3

VR-PURCHASED SERVICES AND SIMILAR BENEFITS

Service	Number of Clients Receiving	Number Receiving Paid by VR	Number Receiving Similar Benefits	Percent Receiving Similar Benefits
Diagnostic	9118	3436	5682	62.3
Restorative	3444	2264	1180	34.3
College	561	348	213	38.0
Other academic	331	49	282	85.2
Business school	168	116	52	31.0
Vocational school	1005	525	480	47.8
On-job-training	262	96	166	63.4
Work adjustment	1698	976	722	42.5
Miscellaneous	575	207	368	64.0
Maintenance	841	667	174	20.7
Other services	4567	203	4364	95.6
Services to family	65	24	41	63.1

indication whether the service was funded by a governmental or by a non-governmental agency. These records are cumulated in a file that tracks all such services prescribed for clients in a particular fiscal year regardless of the clients' closure status.

The cost data for our sample should include all similar benefits provided to the 9,465 clients closed during 1982. Unfortunately, the only file that the VDRS maintained covered expenditures for 1982. Thus if clients received any similar benefits before the fiscal year in which they were closed out, there would be no record of such service provision. Nonetheless, we were able to obtain the file for the year in which the clients were closed.

A total of 5,882 records showing service expenditures of $5,183,182 were reported for this period. The average value of a similar benefit was over $880. While one-sixth of these services were under $50, more than 20 percent of the individual services were valued at over $1,000. In and of itself, this information underscores the importance of taking similar benefits into account. The usefulness of these records to the analyst, however, goes beyond simple demonstrations of this kind. Since these service records were not tied to individual recipients, we sought to combine these files with the existing augmented R-300 data base.

In merging this data with the file of VR-purchased services, we encountered numerous obstacles. The similar benefit file contained records for clients who were still active in the program. These records could not be used. A significant portion of the closed cases received no similar benefits. Many clients received more than one similar benefit and thus multiple records were generated for them. These files had to be combined into a single file in order to match the VR-purchased data.

After these problems were resolved, a merged file was created that contained the similar benefit information for the clients closed in 1982 who had received any services. A total of 3,174 clients received some similar benefits in 1982, roughly one-third of the entire sample. Since there are over fifty different services purchased by external funding sources, these were grouped into the diagnostic, training, education, restoration, and maintenance, transportation, and other categories to make them comparable to the VR-purchased services. The amounts of each category received by the sample are reported in Tables 10.4 and 10.5.

The results of this procedure can be examined in two ways. First, we could investigate the impact of incorporating similar benefits into the

TABLE 10.4

AVERAGE VALUE OF THE SIMILAR BENEFITS RECEIVED
IF A CLIENT RECEIVED ANY SUCH SERVICES
(N=3174)

Service Received	Average Amount Received
Diagnostic	$204.00
Restorative	$461.00
Educational	$254.00
Training	$406.00
Maintenance, Transportation & Other	$210.00
Total	$1,535.00

TABLE 10.5

VALUE OF SIMILAR BENEFITS RECEIVED

Service Received	Number of Clients Receiving	Average Amount Received	Total Amount Received	Average Services as a Percent of Total Services
Diagnostic	138	$4,707	$649,610	52.60%
Restorative	1468	$996	$1,462,580	11.13%
Educational	686	$1,174	$805,310	13.12%
Training	1051	$1,227	$1,289,600	13.71%
Maintenance, Transportation, & Other	787	$845	$665,330	9.44%
Total		$8,949	$4,872,430	100.00%

accounting of services for the average client who received *any* similar benefits. Note that the average value of restorative and training services was over $400. Diagnostic, education, and maintenance, transportation, and others were each more than $200. The sum of these services, again for the average client, was in excess of $1,500.

The other way to look at the impact of similar benefits is to concentrate on those clients who received a particular service. Only 138 clients received diagnostic services that were at least partially funded by an external agency. However, the average amount received was quite high—some $4,700. These clients received one-eighth of the total estimated expenditure for external agencies during 1982.

The most frequently received service was that categorized as restorative. Almost 1,500 clients, just under one-sixth of the entire sample, received some $1.5 million of restorative services that had previously been overlooked. This turns out to be just under $1,000 worth of services for each of these clients that does not show up in an R-300 cost accounting. To put this underreporting in a proper perspective, we note that the entire VR-purchased expenditure for restorative services was $4,108,417. Over one-third of the restorative services received by clients in dollar terms are not reported.

The most expensive service is training, and thus we might conclude that the omission of similar benefit accounting in this area would cause the greatest distortion in the analysis of VR costs. More than 1,000 clients received almost $1,300 of training services. Finally, the impact of externally funded education and maintenance services should not go unnoticed. The value of externally funded educational services was almost $1,200, and maintenance and other support services valued at almost $850 were provided to clients.

COUNSELOR SERVICES

The third component of the VR menu of services disregarded in cost accounting concerns the value of counselor services. Since this service dimension is customarily treated as a component of overhead, the analyst cannot easily assess the cost-effectiveness of counselor time spent with the client. Although one should be cautious in interpreting a single datum, it is remarkable that roughly one in every six clients closed from the program with improved earnings received only VR-purchased diagnostic services. This finding suggests that, for purposes of program evaluation, current accounting procedures obscure the conceivably major role of counselor services in the VR process.

Our intent in this section is to find a way to analyze counselor time and to monetize the value of such services on a per client basis. It will then be possible to compare the marginal impacts of counselor services on client outcomes in the same fashion that we examine purchased services. We will investigate various ways of allocating counselor time and suggest one possible formulation using our enhanced state data base.

Researchers have suggested numerous cookbook methods to allocate counselor costs in the absence of individual counselor caseloads. By "cookbook" methods, we mean procedures applied universally on the basis of a selected sample. As Frederick Collignon has noted,

> The alternative allocation procedures are in terms of the percent of such clients in the total case mix (which assumes each client generates the same time requirements for counselors), the ratio of the average case service costs for the client group to the cost for the average rehabilitant (assuming that counselor time is most heavily influenced by the complexity of the service plan required by the client), and the ratio of the average time in process for the client group compared to the average rehabilitant (assuming that counselors spend the same time per client each month). (Collignon, Dodson, and Root 1977)

The problem with these methods is that they provide no indication of the intensity or actual duration of the counselor time provided. All that can be gleaned from the R-300 file is the total cost of purchased services and the elapsed time spent in various service statuses. Incorporating the aforementioned methods will lead to serious biases in the estimates of counselor impacts. Given existing national data, there is no way of determining whether the counselor is merely serving as a broker of purchased services for the client or instead is actively providing guidance, job placement, and the like to the individual client. Moreover, the fact that a client receives many purchased services or is in a particular status for many months does *not* indicate that the counselor is providing a concomitant amount of time.

The augmented Virginia R-300 data base has some additional information that gives some insight into counselor time per client. On each client record is the identification number of the counselor coordinating the service provision. This marker enables us to determine the size of the individual counselor caseload. If we make use of this information and assume that each counselor provides the same amount of time to each client in the caseload, we can get a crude proxy of counselor costs per client. Of course such an estimate cannot discern the amount of client contact time, which is the true measure of intensity.

We found that the average counselor served sixty closed cases during 1982. On an average annual salary of roughly $20,000, an hour of counselor time is valued at $10 per hour for a 2,000 hour work-year. Dividing the salary by the number of clients served yields $330 of counselor services for the average counselor. If the counselor has larger caseloads, the cost per client will decline. Thus for the clients in the counselor caseload of 211, the average amount of counselor time received would be valued at less than $100.

Because this procedure is based only on closed cases and cannot distinguish among time differentials for individual clients, it produces an estimate only marginally better than previous estimates. However, it is an important first step in deriving the total cost of services provided to the individual client.

CONCLUSION

Vocational rehabilitation programs provide a variety of different services, funded by numerous agencies, to a group of clients with vastly dissimilar capabilities. Given the host of services and their disparate nature, it is reasonable to think that the provision of these services will have different impacts. The current federal reporting system does not examine the individual components of the program, nor does it provide estimates of the level of externally funded services or of counselor services provided within the agency.

This chapter has explored methods of obtaining the true costs of services provided to individual clients of the vocational rehabilitation program. Such an undertaking involves the development and use of augmented state data bases. Using data from Virginia, we were able to construct an enhanced data set that included specific services, estimates of similar benefits, and a proxy for counselor services.

From these three sources, we determined that the average client received over $1,600 in services purchased by the VR agency, over $1,500 in externally funded services (if the client was eligible), and over $300 in counselor services. By adding the components, we can obtain the actual costs of the services provided within the VR framework. Calculations of this kind will enable the analyst to get a clearer picture of the costs and benefits associated with this program.

WORK CITED

Collignon, Frederick, Richard B. Dodson, and Gloria Root. 1977. *Benefit Cost Analysis of Vocational Rehabilitation Services Provided by the California Department of Rehabilitation.* Berkeley: Berkeley Planning Associates.

11 *David H. Dean and William Milberg*

USING BETTER MEASURES OF DISABILITY STATUS

The purpose of this chapter is to demonstrate the additional precision that can be obtained when the analyst uses an augmented state VR data base as opposed to the standard federal R-300 reporting system. The federal R-300 data base includes information on client demographics, a condition classification of client impairment, and a record of the types of services received and the interval of time during which services were received. The numerous shortcomings of such a data base have been noted in detail by other authors in this volume.

Our analysis employs the augmented data base of the Wisconsin State VR Agency. This data base includes all the information from the federal reporting system and valuable information on the dollar amount of services received by each client as well. In addition, the Wisconsin VR Agency sample contains a measure of health or functioning, called the Functional Assessment Inventory (FAI).

The new state data base enhances our ability to perform cost-benefit analysis of the VR program. Specifically, the information on dollars expended on particular services enables us to draw conclusions about the differential impact of service utilization patterns. In addition, the FAI data permit a specification of functioning superior to that used in other studies. This allows us to control statistically for health or functioning in our estimate of the impact of VR services on client outcomes.

In this chapter, the first section presents the standard earnings equation specification and examines its enhancement with the inclusion of a health variable. We then discuss alternative methods of conceptualizing health, including the FAI. The second section provides a full description of the Wisconsin VR Agency data set and a description of the variables used in our specification of the earnings equation. The third section presents results of estimation of the earnings equation using alternative formulations of the health variable. Our results show conclusively that the factor analytic transformation of the FAI data gives the greatest explanatory power in determining the impact of services on client outcomes. In the concluding section, we suggest ways to refine research on the measurement of functional ability in the future.

EARNINGS EQUATION DEVELOPMENT

Numerous benefits can be ascribed to the vocational rehabilitation program. Using a formal cost-benefit framework, the analyst can measure these benefits in the form of changes in health status, job adaptability, and earnings capabilities. These models incorporate measures such as the change in functioning or the change in earnings as outcome measures, which can then be used to compare the efficacy of the menu of services provided by the rehabilitation process. Such a framework entails a longitudinal study requiring measures of preprogram earnings and functioning levels, services received during the course of the program, and postprogram earnings and functioning levels.

Currently, few VR agencies employ data collection methods that will support these research endeavors. Elsewhere in this volume, the deficiencies in the earnings data are referral (Chapter 6) and closure from the program (Chapter 7) have been investigated. A much more serious shortcoming is the lack of a measure of the change in client functioning after completion of the prescribed program. With only a measure of client functioning at program referral, and that a crude one, it becomes all but impossible to reach a meaningful estimate of the impact of a regimen of services on the individual client.

For instance, consider two individuals with identical observed characteristics and initial functioning levels who undergo the same program treatment. After they have completed the program, one client has a markedly higher functioning capability and goes on to earn $250 per week, but the other client earns only $150 per week. Without a measure of postprogram functioning, the use of standard econometric techniques could not account for the difference and it would be assigned to the random error term and any other variables correlated with functioning.

Nonetheless, these potentially fatal variable omissions have not daunted economic inquiries into the vocational rehabilitation program. The typical economic treatment (Bellante 1972, Conley 1965, Worrall 1978) has proceeded with the implicit assumption that the change in functioning is proxied by the change in client earnings. These studies have then attempted to control statistically for the initial level of functioning by incorporating the R-300 condition classifications (such as heart condition, arthritis, mental retardation, and so forth). While this measure was very rough and from our point of view wholly unsatisfactory, it was for many years the customary means of controlling for the level of client impairment.

Our purpose here is to find a better method of controlling for health in an earnings equation framework. This will enable us to reach a more concrete understanding of the impact of the specific services provided by the VR agency. As one group of researchers has noted,

Since functional assessment attempts to measure the actual performance of an individual while giving consideration to his or her environment, some program evaluators believe that functional assessment data may contribute to the demonstration of rehabilitation service outcome through the measurement of small gains as opposed to the absolute fact of employment. (Habeck et al. 1985)

In recent years, health researchers have made numerous attempts to operationalize the concept of health or functioning into a meaningful construct (Jette 1980b). One such construct has been the Functional Assessment Inventory (FAI). The remainder of this section will examine the necessity of controlling for health in an earnings equation, develop a taxonomy of health indices suitable for such purposes, assess the deficiencies of previous attempts by economists to incorporate these measures, and look at the merits and shortcomings of the FAI.

Vocational rehabilitation can be viewed as a manpower training program designed for persons who meet a specified disability criterion. The eligible client must have a medically determined disability that is a vocational handicap but can be remediated through the provision of VR services. The method typically used by economists to quantify the impact of the category "poor health" for such persons has been to append the Mincer-Becker human capital framework. This consists of modifying the standard earnings equation to incorporate the services provided and to control for the level of health in some fashion. Hence:

(1) $\text{Ln } Y = a + bK + cX + dH + e$

where Y is the individual's earnings, Ln is the natural log function, K is a vector of human capital variables including schooling and work experience as well as vocational rehabilitation services, X is a vector of demographic and family background variables, H is the measure of the client's health or functioning status, and e is the random error incorporating unobserved variation and measurement error. Note that a, b, c, and d are the intercept and parameter estimates for the respective variables. In the absence of a control for health, this model clearly suffers from omitted variables bias. This bias will increase the magnitude of e, rendering all parameter estimates less efficient, and will also alter the magnitude of any parameter estimates whose variable is correlated with health. Our interest here, then, is in the proper specification of the client's health variable, not in a respecification of labor supply models.

Economists estimate labor force participation models (does a person work or not?), labor supply models (how many hours per period does the client work?), or earnings equations (what was the client's hourly wage rate?). Earnings, as measured with VR data, consist of the client gross pay for the week ending two months after placement into employment. Given this measure, one cannot tell whether an increase in earnings represents a higher wage, more hours worked, or a combination of both. The R-300 data set provides information only on weekly client earnings, which is an amalgam of hours worked and the hourly wage rate. Because of the paucity of data about client earnings, one should interpret any results with proper skepticism. Thus we shall proceed to examine the various methods employed in previous studies to estimate health.

Recent economic inquiries into the impact of manpower training have utilized a fixed-effects framework to estimate program benefits (Ashenfelter 1978, Bassi 1983 and 1984; see also the discussion in Chapter 3 of this volume). Programmatic impacts of an undifferentiated treatment variable are isolated by examining the difference in earnings before and after program intervention. The prior earnings figure incorporates many demographic variables that are independent of the treatment variable. With the dearth of information about preprogram earnings for most clients, it becomes impossible to operationalize such models in a VR setting using existing data.

Such models assume a generic treatment effect constant across program participants. Given the breadth of services provided to persons with dramatically differing disabilities, such an approach appears inappropriate for the VR program. Since different services will have varying impacts on earnings, it is at least necessary to account for several types of treatment effects. A further problem is the correlation and possible endogeneity between the client's disability and the service regimen. Such simultaneity problems are not addressed in this chapter.

Recognition of the need to include a health measure in the earnings equation raises the question of the exact form this variable should take. Health is an amorphous concept and has received many different representations in the literature. In the following subsection, we discuss the ideal health/functioning measure and review past attempts to develop an appropriate measure for health. We will conclude the section by discussing the merits and drawbacks of the Functional Assessment Inventory, the variable incorporated in our augmented state data base model.

Past attempts to operationalize health

We turn now to the problem of creating a conceptually appropriate and administratively feasible health/functioning variable. The first difficulty faced by researchers has been in defining health. Two kinds of definition are possible: health can be seen as an assessment of medical condition or an assessment of functioning. Each of these conceptions may, in turn, be interpreted or applied in many different ways. For example, medical diagnostic measures could vary from the dichotomous mortality indexes often used in economics studies (see Parsons 1982) to the hundred-plus condition classifications used by the RSA to categorize the disabled. Similarly, functioning may be interpreted in relation to the level of independence at home (ability to dress, toileting, and the like) or the ability to interact well with others in the workplace. Defining health, then, is not a trivial issue and is the first step in creating a health variable.

To reach a clearer notion of health, we might liken it to a chain with many links. The first link in the chain of health is a *condition classification,* a medical diagnosis of a physical, mental, or emotional ailment. Such a condition may result from what Whitten refers to as a "pathology": "Pathology . . . may be the result of infection, metabolic imbalances, degenerative disease processes, trauma, or other etiology" (in Lambrinos 1982, p. 207). A diagnosed condition may lead to an *impairment,* depending on the severity of the condition. Impairment is the second link in the chain; the term indicates "a physiological, anatomical or mental loss or other abnormalities." An impairment may then lead to a *functional limitation,* defined as an inability to perform physical, mental, or emotional activities. A. L. Stewart et al. (1981) has analyzed the concept of functional limitation in a way that can be usefully adapted to our metaphor of the chain of health. They define functional status as "the performance of (or the capacity to perform) a variety of activities that are normal for people in good physical health," and they identify five categories of functioning: self-care activities, mobility, physical activities, role activities (work, school, or household), and leisure activities (p. 473). We would simplify Stewart et al.'s taxonomy by grouping together self-care, mobility, physical, and leisure activities; limitations in these areas constitute basic *activity limitations,* the third link in our chain. The fourth link is based on the notion of role activities; we designate it as *job activity limitations.*

Link five in the chain of health is *disability or handicap.* Disability is not an absolute category. It depends on social norms and economic factors as well as an individual's job activity limitations. We cannot draw a one-to-one correspondence between a functional limitation and a disability. For example, the same back problem endured by President Kennedy while in office might render a dockworker completely disabled (Berkowitz 1978, Nagi 1982, Lambrinos 1982). The chain of health in society is summarized in Figure 11.1.

Operationalizing health via a functioning scale

The question of how to create a conceptually appropriate health variable can be rephrased as: At what point in the chain do we seek to measure health? Deciding on this point narrows considerably the field of appropriate health variables. For the analysis of the impact of VR services on client

FIGURE 11.1
THE CHAIN OF HEALTH IN SOCIETY

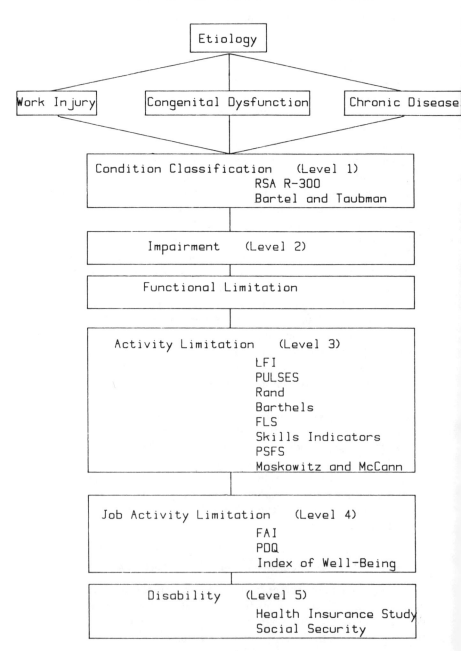

earnings, we seek a measure of health that assesses job activity limitations, or, in other words, a measure that assesses health at level four in Figure 11.1.

Health measured at levels one, two, or three would probably not be relevant to an assessment of vocational capability and thus earnings. No necessary relationship exists between medical illness and employability or earnings. For example, according to Crewe and Athelstan,

> identifying a person as having a closed head injury does not tell a counselor whether the individual can speak, walk, handle perceptual tasks, or remember events from one hour to the next. Furthermore, such a medical diagnosis says nothing about the ability to relate to other people, vocational skills, or the environmental system. Functional assessment, on the other hand, can pinpoint such problems and can also call attention to the similarities among some clients with different diagnoses. (1981, p. 299)

Health measured at level five would assess too narrowly a client's vocational status. That is, the step from level four to level five involves imposing very specific sociological and technological requirements closely associated with particular jobs. It is only at the fifth level that President Kennedy and the dockworker would be assessed differently; the dockworker would be defined as disabled and Kennedy would not. In our analysis of VR services, we seek to isolate and remove the sociological element in assessing the influence of functioning on earnings. Such an assessment would provide the most appropriate health measure for determining employability and earnings potential.

Most existing health indexes assess health at our assigned levels one, two, or three. One type of index that fits in at level one is the mortality index (Parsons 1982). While this measure has the virtue of being exogenously determined (that is, determined by a physician, an outside and presumably objective party), it has numerous drawbacks that make it unsuitable for our purposes. Mortality indexes are crude and binary, ignoring all nonfatal dysfunctions. Moreover, we have a cross-sectional rather than a longitudinal data set, making it necessary to examine differences across individuals and effectively eliminating mortality measures from consideration.

Another example of a level one health index is the RSA condition classification scheme. This system classifies each client according to over a hundred medical conditions as defined by the RSA. That the variable is not the most appropriate for our analysis is evidenced by the earnings equation estimates presented below using alternative health variables.

The condition classification scheme used by the RSA to determine client impairments has numerous other deficiencies. Some of these deficiencies stem from the narrow scope of medical diagnosis. Bartel and Taubman (1979) discuss this problem in an analysis of their index of health, another "level one" measure:

> Our measure of health differs from the ideal one in several ways. First, we have no indication of severity other than the passing of some threshhold, and we do not know if there have been any cures or remissions. Second, a person can be ill without being so diagnosed. Third, a diagnosis can be wrong. As is well known, random measurement error, if uncorrelated with the true independent variables, will bias coefficients towards zero. (p. 2)

Another difficulty with the RSA measure is that it cannot assess the vocational limitation caused by the condition. We are concerned with an inability to perform work-related skills. Different clients may have the same functional limitation, such as restricted use of an arm, with varying causes of the limitation. This limitation could be due to arthritis, an amputation, or a musculo-skeletal injury. The existing index does not permit us to identify the type of functional limitation.

One further problem with this system is that it cannot account for multiple causes or outcomes, except through the presence of a secondary condition. This mutual exclusivity effectively rules out interacting multiple impairments, which are what typically cause the client's vocational limitation. A final shortcoming of such a specification is the binary nature of the condition classification.

Many of the indexes that attempt to assess functioning do so at level three, the level of activity limitations, as opposed to level four, job activity limitations. The list of such indexes is long. Many of these—including PULSES, Barthels, the Functional Life Scale, the Programmed Summary of Functional Status, the Moskowitz and McCann index, and Skill Indicators—measure functioning in relation to the so-called "activities of daily living" (ADL) (Halpern and Fuhrer 1984). A brief description of several of these indexes is helpful.

The main functions assessed by ADL measures are physical mobility, home chores, kitchen chores, and personal care (Jette 1980a). For example, the PULSES scale measures six categories of functional status, where P stands for *physical* condition (including diseases of the viscera and neurological disorders), U stands for self-care activities dependent mainly upon *upper* limb function, L stands for mobility activities dependent mainly upon *lower* limb function, S stands for *sensory* functions relating to communication and vision, E stands for *excretory* functions, and S stands for intellectual and emotional *stability,* support from family unit and financial ability.

The Rand Health Insurance Study functional status index goes slightly beyond the simple ADL scales, combining a functional limitations battery (mobility, physical activities, role activities, self-care) and a physical capacities battery (Stewart, Ware, Brook 1981).

The Sickness Impact Profile also goes beyond the standard ADL measure, but this instrument has been criticized for its imprecision. As A. M. Jette

(1980b) argues, the Sickness Impact Profile "uses multiple functional activities within the same question which may be performed at different levels of function" (p. 571).

Crewe, Athelstan, and Meadows' (1975) Functional Life Scale essentially assesses level three functioning. They offer the following description of the instrument:

> It can be used to provide a quantitative measure of an individual's ability to participate in all of the basic daily activities which are customary for the majority of human beings. The areas assessed include cognition, activities of daily living, home activities, outside activities and social interaction. The scale appears to be very promising as a means of assessing the overall effectiveness of a rehabilitation program in returning an individual to everyday life. It does not deal with many of the factors which would be most relevant for determining employment potential, however. For example, a diabetic might score well on this scale and still face great problems in finding work. (p. 514)

Utilizing these daily living activities scales as a health construct in an earnings equation specification poses several problems for the analyst. One major shortcoming is their emphasis on physical functioning and mobility—an emphasis that neglects many of the mental and emotional aspects of vocational functioning. Given the high percentage of vocational rehabilitation clients who experience mental or emotional dysfunctioning, this oversight would render ADL scales inappropriate for our purposes. Moreover, as Berkowitz (1978) has noted, there is not necessarily a correlation between the ability to perform such ADL skills and the ability to hold a full-time job.

Level four is the level at which we would define our ideal health variable. Such a measure would assess the VR client's functioning in regard to vocational limitations and would be consonant with our larger purpose—the estimation of the impact of VR services on labor market outcomes. Several measures have been constructed to assess this type of health or functioning. These include the Functional Assessment Inventory (FAI), the Index of Well-Being, and the West Virginia Preliminary Diagnostic Questionnaire (PDQ). Our study employs the FAI. A brief review of these level-four scales will be helpful.

The FAI was designed to aid vocational rehabilitation counselors who must work with clients exhibiting a broad range of disabilities. Since counselors may not be aware of the consequences of various disabling conditions, the FAI seeks to identify the pertinent vocational aspect of a disability. Thus, while it is largely diagnostic, it is concerned with vocationally related functions. Crewe and Athelstan (1981), the originators of this instrument, describe its purpose as follows: "The FAI was developed to provide an accurate description of client potential for vocational planning. . . . It identifies strengths and limitations that may or may not be modifiable but which need to be taken into account in developing a rehabilitation plan" (p. 299).

The two strengths of the FAI in comparison with the other measures we have examined are that it is counselor-assessed and that it examines emotional and mental functioning. As a counselor-assessed measure of vocational limitations, the FAI avoids the endogeneity problem that arises with self-assessed measures and the problem of the exceedingly narrow focus of physician-assessed measures.

The FAI also has disadvantages. First, administration of the FAI requires the counselor to have extensive knowledge of the client. This limits the general applicability of the inventory. Second, its virtue as a diagnostic tool to assess a variety of disabling conditions also leads to occasional lack of specificity. For example, the FAI contains only one question about vision, whereas other measures include a battery of questions relating to many different aspects of visual acuity. Third, the scaling of responses is limited to four discrete values (zero to three) that may lack the desired sensitivity to the degree of functioning.

The Index of Well-Being is more sophisticated but for our purpose is less useful than other indexes that assess health at level four. This instrument assesses the level of physical dysfunction in physical activity, mobility, and social activity. It also assesses expected future functioning. According to Jette (1980b), the creators of the index "define health as the product of (expected values) of the social preferences assigned to levels of function and the probabilities of transition among the levels over the life expectancy of the individal or group" (p. 572). The speculative element in this instrument distinguishes it from others while making it inappropriate as the basis of an explanatory variable in an earnings equation.

The Preliminary Diagnostic Questionnaire attempts to assess the functional capacities of a person in relation to employment, that is, level four functioning. In general, it covers cognitive functioning, physical limitations, emotional functioning, motivation, and social, economic, and personal conditions (Moriarty 1981). It covers essentially the same areas as the FAI. The two instruments differ, however, in that the PDQ relies heavily on self-reported evaluation while the FAI is strictly counselor-assessed. The problems inherent in a self-assessed measure are discussed below.

The final level (level five) in our chain of health and functioning is disability. The problem with incorporating measures of disability in our scheme is that what is observed is the complex interaction of socioeconomic, demographic, and functional limitation variables. The most prevalent health measures used in early economic analyses were those gleaned from available surveys such as the Health Insurance Study and the Social Security Survey of Disabled and Nondisabled Adults. These health measures rely on criteria such as the "number of bed-disability days" or "restricted days," as well as self-rated work limitations and declarations of health as "excellent," "good," "fair," or "bad." As Lambrinos (1982) notes, exogenous health indexes can be created from any of the five levels we have defined, *except* for disability (p. 207). Such disability measures do not reflect an individual's level of well-being but rather an individual's occupational status or taste for work.

One of the major flaws with such measures is that they cannot objectively distinguish differences in health levels. Two individuals with vastly different functional capabilities may declare themselves equally work-disabled because they face differing economic opportunities and constraints. Thus, the measures provide no indication of the actual severity of the impairment underlying the perception of health. In specifying the earnings equation with such a health measure, the analyst will find a great deal of heterogeneity and, as a consequence, large amounts of uncontrolled variation.

In the same vein, the fact that two persons with the same health level may view themselves as experiencing different levels of well-being or different degrees of limitation in their ability to work makes self-assessed measurement inappropriate as a control for health in the estimation of an earnings equation. Moreover, as Chirikos and Nestel (1981) observe:

> A more significant flaw is that behavioral measures of health are not necessarily independent of the labor force behavior that they are supposed to explain. . . . Thus the behavioral evidence used to document poor health or classify the population under study as "disabled" may be identical to the behavior to be explained, namely, reductions in labor supply. (p. 94-95)

As other economic studies concerned with the labor force participation decision of disabled persons have shown (Lambrinos 1982, Parsons 1982), socioeconomic conditions may induce individuals to declare themselves in poor health. The problem with incorporating such measures into an earnings equation specification is that they result in simultaneity bias. Inclusion of such health measures alters the magnitude and significance of the desired parameter estimates being investigated.

Other criteria for a health variable

Earlier in the chapter, we mentioned two criteria that should be used to evaluate health indexes. We have just discussed the first criterion, that the instrument should measure health at the appropriate level. We turn now to the second, that it be administratively feasible, in time, money, and assessor training. We seek a measure that can provide empirical data for large samples at a low cost. The instrument should not take too much time to administer. The skill level required of the assessor is also important. Self-assessed instruments create potential endogeneity problems. Physician-assessed instruments tend to be aimed at medical diagnosis. Counselor-assessed measures are thus most appropriate for labor market studies. It is also important that training of the assessor (whether physician or counselor) not be too time-consuming or costly. Of course, the instrument should also exhibit significant inter-rater reliability.

DATA AND VARIABLE DESCRIPTION

The sample data set, forwarded to us by Abt Associates, was collected by counselors from the Wisconsin Division of Vocational Rehabilitation Services for clients entering the program from March through July 1981. During this interval, 1,670 program participants were surveyed. The data set includes the dollar amount of specific services delivered to each client (as in Chapter 10) and the counselor-administered Functional Assessment Inventory, in addition to the usual client demographic and programmatic characteristics.

This data set differs from the standard R-300 reporting system in another significant aspect. The R-300 data contain information on all clients terminated from the VR program sometime during the fiscal year. For this customized Wisconsin sample, the data gathering process was stopped at the end of September 1983, regardless of closure status. As a consequence, the sample included clients of different status in the program.

Specifically, some of the clients surveyed were still receiving services and were designated as still active in the VR program. Those clients no longer active in the program were designated as having successfully completed the program by being suitably employed for a minimum of sixty days after receiving rehabilitation services, or as having unsuccessfully completed the program. Of the 1,670 clients sampled, 524 (31.4 percent) were still active in the program, 782 (46.8 percent) were successfully rehabilitated, and 364 (21.8 percent) were not rehabilitated.

The decomposition of the data set by VR program status is important because analysis of the impact of services on earnings requires client earnings data upon completion of the program. Clients who were still active in the program obviously cannot be included for the purpose of such an analysis. Also, earnings at closure were not reported for clients who unsuccessfully completed the VR program. Unfortunately, they must also be excluded from analysis of the beneficial effects of program services on earnings, even though these clients may have achieved demonstrable gains from the program.

While we must exclude the active clients and the nonsuccesses from the earnings equation estimation, we have no reason to exclude them from estimation of a health/functioning variable. There is ample evidence that nonsuccesses eventually report earnings (see Chapter 7). Furthermore, those clients who were still receiving services at the time of the survey would at some point be closed out of the program, either successfully or unsuccessfully, and therefore might eventually report earnings. Using the information on the health status of *all* clients should therefore not bias the estimation of the impact of the health variable on the reported earnings at closure of successful clients.

On the other hand, nonsuccessful clients and those still active in the program may differ in socioeconomic and demographic variables from those successfully rehabilitated. Significant differences in these variables may indicate both systematic and unobservable variation. Each of these variations present problems in estimating service impacts on earnings.

If there is unobservable variation among subsamples, such as motivation to work, perseverance, and the like, then the estimated impacts of the explanatory variables on earnings may be significantly biased. The fact that a client was still active may mean that the duration of services received was greater than for a client in the other subsamples. A client receiving a service over a long period of time—as, for example, education—may differ unobservably as well as systematically from a client receiving surgery or training.

For instance, the education of the father of the client is an unobserved variable (to the researcher) that may have some bearing on the earnings level of the client. It is not unreasonable to think that clients receiving a college education may differ in this unmeasured element from clients receiving work adjustment training. To estimate earning impacts of services while accounting for the difference in unobservables among the cohorts requires the use of a Heckit-type procedure that is beyond the scope of this study.

The demographic and socioeconomic characteristics, RSA and FAI disability classifications, and services received for the sample of 1,670 are presented below. We will also briefly discuss the expected impact of each variable on client earnings.

Demographic variables

The demographic variables include client age at referral, race, and sex. Traditional earnings equations based on human capital theory have posited that the impact of age on earnings should be quadratic (Mincer 1974). This implies that as persons get older, they can expect increased earnings; the increase, however, will occur at a decreasing rate. In other words, the *rate* of increase in earnings declines as one ages and the accumulated stock of human capital depreciates. For a clientele that is predominantly mentally impaired, the impact of age on earnings is less certain.

The impact of race on earnings has been the subject of countless economic inquiries. Because of factors such as lower investment in human capital, discrimination, and the like, the earnings of nonwhites are lower than those of whites, other things being equal. The expected effect of being nonwhite on earnings is negative.

The impact of gender on earnings has also been the subject of numerous economic studies. Such studies find that women earn less than men. Differences in earnings may be attributed to less work experience, lower investment in human capital, job discrimination, and other factors. We expect to find an inverse relationship between being female and earnings.

Socioeconomic variables

The socioeconomic variables include years of schooling completed, client marital status, and reported earnings at referral to and closure from the program.

Marital status is a variable typically included in labor force participation estimations but not in earnings equation estimations. The theory is that, while being married will have some bearing on whether a person works or does not work, once that person chooses to work, marital status will not have any effect on the level of earnings. For a population that is predominantly mentally or emotionally impaired, it may be that marital status is a proxy for compatibility or commitment. Employers may value such attributes in the wage offer determination. To the extent that these attributes have an impact on earnings, we expect marital status and earnings to be positively correlated.

Returns attributable to education is another variable that has received considerable attention from economists. It is generally thought that the impact of education on earnings is positive but decreasing. This suggests a quadratic formulation of the years of schooling variable, similar to the relationship posited between age and earnings.

Perhaps the most important variables for our analysis, except for a measure of the disabling condition, are the client earnings upon referral to the program and after closure from the program. Unfortunately, current data collection methods do not give meaningful values for these variables. The earnings figures at referral and closure, if reported, are given only for the week before application for services and sixty days after termination of services. These figures are usually not indicative of either true prior or post VR earnings. (For a fuller discussion, see Chapters 6 and 7.)

The earnings at closure data must be interpreted cautiously. As shown in Chapter 7, an earnings figure sixty days after program termination may not be representative of the client's permanent earnings capabilities. Furthermore, the cohort not rehabilitated may report earnings at a later date, some of which may be attributable to the VR services received. To consider these clients "unsuccessfully" rehabilitated may severely underestimate the efficacy of the services rendered.

The magnitude of this problem can now be put in context. Almost

55 percent (910 clients) of the sample reported either zero earnings or did not report earnings at closure. Of these 910, 890 were either closed unsuccessfully—and thus by definition, had no earnings at closure—or were still enrolled in the program. By implication, then, 20 clients in the sample were closed successfully to homemaker status and therefore reported zero earnings.

Service variables

One of the unique attributes of this data set is the inclusion of the dollar amount of agency-purchased services on an individual client basis. Thirty-nine different types of services were provided by the Wisconsin VR Agency. These services can be aggregated into five major categories in accordance with the classification scheme used by the RSA: diagnostic, education, training, restorative, and other (a category that includes maintenance, transportation, and other miscellaneous services).

In estimating the impact of various services on earnings, we caution that some degree of simultaneity will exist between the client's impairment, the substance of the subsequent service regimen, and any outcome measure. Thus, in its ultimate impact on earnings, work adjustment training for a mentally retarded person would be quite different from vocational training for a physically impaired person.

The value of total services received averaged some $1,170 per client for the entire sample. These averages varied dramatically according to outcome status. For instance, the successful client received on average $875 of services, compared to only $450 for the nonsuccesses and $1850 for those clients still active in the program. Needless to say, these averages are significantly different statistically. Part of the explanation for the difference between cohorts may be that the nonsuccesses received the same types of services but left the program prematurely, for whatever reason. Another possible explanation is that differences existed in the type and duration of services received by the different cohorts.

DIAGNOSTIC SERVICES

The first type of service that would normally be provided to a client would be some form of diagnosis. This can consist of a medical, psychological, vocational, or even a rehabilitation engineering evaluation. Virtually all—85.3 percent—of the clients received diagnostic services. Excluding those that did not receive any of these services, the average amount received for the entire sample was just under $250.

RESTORATIVE SERVICES

The next group of services that a client could have received consisted of restorative services. These services include, in the main, providing adaptive and assistive devices such as hearing aids, as well as minor surgical procedures. Such services are invariably received by clients with physical or sensory impairments. About 10 percent of the Wisconsin sample had sensory impairment or some form of amputation, and so 10.2 percent of the sample received such restorative services. For those clients, the average amount per client was just over $430.

EDUCATIONAL SERVICES

After undergoing a regimen of diagnosis and possibly restorative services, the VR client may receive some form of educational service. This may consist of elementary, secondary, or university schooling; it may also consist of trade school training. These services were received by just over one-fourth of the sample. If a client received any such services, the average amount was just under $1,100.

TRAINING SERVICES

The next group of services for which VR clients could have been eligible consisted of training services. These services tended to be substitutes for education—a client received either one or the other but not both. Less than 20 percent of the full sample received services such as on-the-job, vocational, personal, or work adjustment training. For clients who received any such services, the average amount per client totaled over $590.

MAINTENANCE, TRANSPORTATION, AND OTHER SERVICES

A client invariably received supportive services while enrolled in one of the numerous programs prescribed in the Individual Written Rehabilitation Program (IWRP). These services varied greatly: examples include paying for modifications to a vehicle, providing transportation to and from a training program, paying the client a maintenance stipend during enrollment in the program, and providing counseling and related services to other family members. For the entire sample of Wisconsin DRS clients, just over 45 percent received these services. For those clients, the average amount received totaled $818.

RSA impairment classification

Because all clients must demonstrate a medically diagnosed impairment to be eligible for VR, we need to get a good handle on the composition of impairments in the sample. The Rehabilitation Services Administration (RSA) has defined six major impairment groupings, comprising over three hundred disabling condition classifications. The six major categories are visual, hearing, orthopedic, amputee, mental, and other (usually internal) impairments.

In our sample, 47 percent were classified as mentally impaired. Just under 28 percent were orthopedically impaired and 14 percent were classified as having other impairments. The remaining three classifications accounted for only about 11 percent of the sample. Of course, with only the condition classification, it is impossible to glean much useful information about the severity of the disabling condition. For this, we require a health/functioning measure, which the Wisconsin data set provides in the form of the Functional Assessment Inventory.

Functional assessment inventory results

In discussing health and functioning measures earlier in this chapter, we considered some of the strengths and weaknesses of the FAI. Here we look briefly at the design of the inventory and examine what it reveals about the Wisconsin VR client population.

The FAI consists, in part, of thirty questions designed to assess physical, mental, and emotional limitations. In addition, some questions address the client's vocational capabilities. The instrument is administered by the client's VR counselor. For each question, the client receives a score of zero to three, indicating no impairment, mild impairment, moderate impairment, or severe impairment.

For some categories scoring requires little judgment, but for others, rater discretion is important. For example, the vision variable relies largely on an eye examination, with different acuity levels assigned to FAI scores. On the other hand, the variable titled "effective interaction with people" requires the rater to distinguish mild impairment ("is somewhat awkward or unpleasant in social interactions") from moderate impairment ("lacks many of the skills necessary for effective interaction"). In spite of its reliance on counselor discretion, the FAI has been shown to exhibit a high degree of inter-rate reliability (Turner 1982).

In examining the results of the FAI, we must look at three different issues. First we ascertain whether or not a client has a particular impairment. It may be that the mere presence of an impairment has a significant impact on eventual client outcome. The prevalence of the various impairments can be found in Table 11.1.

The next issue is to determine the severity of the impairment for those clients with a given limitation. This measure can be reported in two different ways. The percentage of the entire sample with a given degree of severity for each FAI item is reported in Table 11.1. The percentage of clients with a particular degree of impairment severity, if they report some impairment at all, is then reported in Table 11.2.

Table 11.1 reveals that in six of the thirty categories, over 85 percent of the clients had no impairment. These categories include hearing and

TABLE 11.1

FUNCTIONAL ASSESSMENT INVENTORY RESULTS
FROM 1670 CLIENTS OF THE WISCONSIN
DIVISION OF REHABILITATIVE SERVICES

NUMBER & PERCENTAGE OF CLIENTS WITH NONE, MILD, MODERATE, & SEVERE IMPAIRMENTS

FAI VARIABLE	IMPAIRED: NONE	PERCENT OF TOTAL	IMPAIRED: MILD	PERCENT OF TOTAL
VISION	1516	90.8	86	5.2
HEARING	1567	93.9	57	3.4
AMBULATION-MOBILITY	1197	71.8	345	20.7
UPPER EXTREMITY FUNCTIONING	1454	87.1	139	8.3
HAND FUNCTIONING	1424	85.3	187	11.2
COORDINATION	1370	82.0	237	14.2
MOTOR SPEED	1217	72.9	340	20.4
CAPACITY FOR EXERTION	868	52.1	499	30.0
ENDURANCE	1152	69.1	375	22.5
LOSS OF TIME FROM WORK	1218	72.9	359	21.5
STABILITY OF CONDITION	635	38.0	699	41.9
LEARNING ABILITY	1134	67.9	260	15.6
PERCEPTUAL ORGANIZATION	1359	81.4	263	15.7
MEMORY	1377	82.5	229	13.7
LANGUAGE FUNCTIONING	1467	87.9	151	9.0
LITERACY	1278	76.5	231	13.8
SPEECH	1475	88.4	140	8.4
JUDGMENT	976	58.4	539	32.3
PERSISTENCE	1142	68.4	418	25.0
CONGRUENCE OF BEHAVIOR WITH REHAB GLS	1193	71.4	364	21.8
ACCURATE PERCEPTION OF CAPAB/LIMIT	1037	62.1	506	30.3
EFFECTIVE INTERACTION WITH PEOPLE	1090	65.3	397	23.8
SOCIAL SUPPORT SYSTEM	1153	69.1	412	24.7
PERSONAL ATTRACTIVENESS	1388	83.2	254	15.2
SKILLS	617	36.9	667	39.9
WORK HABITS	1141	68.4	362	21.7
WORK HISTORY	614	36.8	727	43.6
ACCEPTABILITY TO EMPLOYERS	621	37.2	746	44.7
ACCESS TO JOB OPPORTUNITIES	834	50.1	613	36.8
ECONOMIC DISINCENTIVES	1360	81.6	223	13.4

vision, speech, language functioning, upper extremity functioning, and hand functioning. For vision and hearing, less than 10 percent of the sample were reported to have any impairment at all. One possible explanation for the small number of clients with impairments within these largely physical or sensory functioning categories is that clients are assessed while "utilizing whatever adaptive equipment may be available" to them, such as eyeglasses, hearing aids, wheelchairs, or prostheses. It is also possible that the presence of these functional limitations does not make a client a suitable candidate for rehabilitation in Wisconsin. For instance, a blind client may be referred to an agency outside the purview of VR.

TABLE 11.1--Continued

IMPAIRED: MODERATE	PERCENT OF TOTAL	IMPAIRED: SEVERE	PERCENT OF TOTAL	MEAN VALUE	STANDARD DEVIATION
44	2.6	23	1.4	0.15	0.55
23	1.4	22	1.3	0.11	0.49
92	5.5	34	2.0	0.39	0.73
70	4.2	6	0.4	0.18	0.54
47	2.8	12	0.7	0.19	0.50
55	3.3	8	0.5	0.22	0.52
101	6.0	12	0.7	0.35	0.63
263	15.8	36	2.2	0.70	0.89
102	6.1	39	2.3	0.43	0.76
43	2.6	50	3.0	0.36	0.68
318	19.0	18	1.1	0.83	0.77
191	11.4	84	5.0	0.54	0.90
43	2.6	5	0.3	0.22	0.49
60	3.6	4	0.2	0.22	0.51
35	2.1	16	1.0	0.17	0.52
121	7.2	40	2.4	0.36	0.72
32	1.9	21	1.3	0.17	0.57
130	7.8	25	1.5	0.52	0.70
88	5.3	22	1.3	0.40	0.65
78	4.7	35	2.1	0.37	0.67
108	6.5	19	1.1	0.47	0.67
143	8.6	39	2.3	0.48	0.77
89	5.3	14	0.8	0.39	0.68
21	1.3	6	0.4	0.19	0.49
281	16.8	105	6.3	0.93	0.89
146	8.7	20	1.2	0.43	0.73
262	15.7	66	4.0	0.87	0.83
232	13.9	69	4.1	0.86	0.85
163	9.8	54	3.2	0.69	0.90
60	3.6	24	1.4	0.26	0.67

At the other end of the prevalence spectrum, in nine of the FAI categories more than one-third of the clients in the sample have some degree of impairment. These include mainly variables that assess emotional and vocational aspects of a client's functioning. Specifically, in areas of functioning such as skills, work history, acceptability to employers, and stability of condition, more than 60 percent of all clients sampled were assessed as having some impairment. Between 30 and 50 percent of all clients were assessed to have some impairment in the areas of economic disincentives, capacity for exertion, accurate perception of capabilities, and effective interaction with people.

From Table 11.2 we gain a different perspective. A closer look reveals that regardless of the prevalence of impairment, the degree of severity is generally mild. For twenty-nine of the thirty functioning categories, more than 50 percent of those impaired were assessed to have a mild degree of impairment. Only for those clients with a learning ability dysfunction were more than half assessed as impaired moderately or severely. Moreover, for twenty-eight of the thirty functioning categories, the percentage of those mildly impaired exceeded the percent of those moderately impaired, which in turn exceeded the percent of those severely impaired. Thus, the relative prevalence of severe impairment was low. For only seven of the categories was severe impairment assessed for more than 10 percent of the clients with some impairment; only hearing exceeded 20 percent (21.6 percent).

Interestingly, the categories with a lower percentage of clients having some impairment had a slightly higher degree of severity of impairment. Again, these are the sensory or physical functioning areas, such as hearing, vision, and upper extremity functioning. This may indicate that individuals must demonstrate more severe impairment in sensory functioning than that required for mental and emotional limitations in order to be eligible for VR. For the six attributes in which over 85 percent of the sample had no impairment, of those impaired, 56 to 76 percent had mild impairment. Meanwhile, for the nine attributes in which more than one-third of the sample were reported to have some impairment, the percentage of mild impairment ranged from 63 to 80 percent.

SPECIFICATION OF THE HEALTH VARIABLE
FOR THE EARNINGS EQUATION

No health variable

The result of preliminary estimation using an earnings equation without controlling for health (model 1, Table 11.3) gave rise to the expected sign on demographic and socioeconomic variables but unexpected (and significant) signs for training and education services. We can attribute three impacts to omitted variable bias. First, we cannot be confident of the sign or magnitudes of the parameter estimates. For instance, some of the estimates may be inordinately high, if omitted variables are collinear (nonorthogonal) with included variables. In this case the model attributes too much explanatory power to the included variables. Second, if the omitted variable is orthogonal to included explanatory variables, then the residual error term is not random, violating an assumption of the model, and the resulting standard errors for the remaining independent variables will be higher. Concomitantly, the explanatory power of the model as a whole will be reduced, evidenced by a lower R^2. The R^2 in model 1 is .23, low even for a standard earnings equation.

FUNCTION ASSESSMENT INVENTORY RESULTS FROM 1670 CLIENTS OF THE WISCONSIN DIVISION OF REHABILITATIVE SERVICES

FAI VARIABLE	NUMBER WITH SOME IMPAIRMENT	PERCENT OF ALL CLIENTS WITH SOME IMPAIRMENT (N = 1670)	IF IMPAIRED: PERCENT MILD	IF IMPAIRED: PERCENT MODERATE	IF IMPAIRED: PERCENT SEVERE
VISION	153	9.2%	56.2%	28.8%	15.0%
HEARING	102	6.1%	55.9%	22.5%	21.6%
AMBULATION-MOBILITY	471	28.2%	73.2%	19.5%	7.2%
UPPER EXTREMITY FUNCTIONING	215	12.9%	64.7%	32.6%	2.8%
HAND FUNCTIONING	246	14.7%	76.0%	19.1%	4.9%
COORDINATION	300	18.0%	79.0%	18.3%	2.7%
MOTOR SPEED	453	27.1%	75.1%	22.3%	2.6%
CAPACITY FOR EXERTION	798	47.9%	62.5%	33.0%	4.5%
ENDURANCE	516	30.9%	72.7%	19.8%	7.6%
LOSS OF TIME FROM WORK	452	27.1%	79.4%	9.5%	11.1%
STABILITY OF CONDITION	1035	62.0%	67.5%	30.7%	1.7%
LEARNING ABILITY	535	32.1%	48.6%	35.7%	15.7%
PERCEPTUAL ORGANIZATION	311	18.6%	84.6%	13.8%	1.6%
MEMORY	293	17.5%	78.2%	20.5%	1.4%
LANGUAGE FUNCTIONING	202	12.1%	74.8%	17.3%	7.9%
LITERACY	392	23.5%	58.9%	30.9%	10.2%
SPEECH	193	11.6%	72.5%	16.6%	10.9%
JUDGMENT	694	41.6%	77.7%	18.7%	3.6%
PERSISTENCE	528	31.6%	79.2%	16.7%	4.2%
CONGRUENCE OF BEHAVIOR WITH REHAB GLS	477	28.6%	76.3%	16.4%	7.3%
ACCURATE PERCEPTION OF CAPAB/LIMIT	633	37.9%	79.9%	17.1%	3.0%
EFFECTIVE INTERACTION WITH PEOPLE	579	34.7%	68.6%	24.7%	6.7%
SOCIAL SUPPORT SYSTEM	515	30.9%	80.0%	17.3%	2.7%
PERSONAL ATTRACTIVENESS	281	16.8%	90.4%	7.5%	2.1%
SKILLS	1053	63.1%	63.3%	26.7%	10.0%
WORK HABITS	528	31.6%	68.6%	27.7%	3.8%
WORK HISTORY	1055	63.2%	68.9%	24.8%	6.3%
ACCEPTABILITY TO EMPLOYERS	1047	62.8%	71.3%	22.2%	6.6%

TABLE 11.3

EARNINGS EQUATION ESTIMATION USING TWO DIFFERENT HEALTH VARIABLES

DEPENDENT VARIABLE -
LOG EARNINGS AT CLOSURE

VARIABLES	MODEL 1 NO HEALTH VARIABLE		MODEL 2 RSA HEALTH VARIABLE		MODEL 3 FAI HEALTH VARIABLE	
	PARAMETER ESTIMATE	T-RATIO	PARAMETER ESTIMATE	T-RATIO	PARAMETER ESTIMATE	T-RATIO
INTERCEPT	3.6085 **	14.6	3.557 **	13.9	3.5516 **	14.3
SEXM (MALE=1)	0.3267 **	6.1	0.3329 **	6.2	0.3295 **	6.5
RACEW (WHITE=1)	0.0099	0.1	-0.002	0.0	-0.0447	0.4
AGEREF (AGE AT REFERRAL)	0.064 **	5.3	0.0613 **	5.0	0.0628 **	5.4
AGEREF2 (AGE SQUARED)	-0.0001 **	6.0	-0.0002 **	5.8	-0.0009 **	5.9
EDYRS (YEARS OF EDUCATION)	0.0198 *	2.1	0.0206 *	2.2	0.0241 *	2.1
LURNACCP (LOG EARNINGS ACCEPT)	0.0462 **	3.6	0.0457 **	3.5	0.0266 *	2.1
SERVICE VARIABLES						
TRAIN ($ TRAINING SERVICES)	-0.0004 **	7.1	-0.0003 **	6.8	-0.0002 **	5.1
EDUC ($ EDUCATION SERVICES)	0.0002 **	3.5	0.0003 **	3.6	0.0002 **	2.9
RESTOR ($ RESTORATIVE SERVICES)	0.0001	1.1	0.0000	0.2	0.0001	0.9

TABLE 11.3--Continued

DEPENDENT VARIABLE -
LOG EARNINGS AT CLOSURE

VARIABLES	MODEL 1 NO HEALTH VARIABLE		MODEL 2 RSA HEALTH VARIABLE		MODEL 3 FAI HEALTH VARIABLE	
	PARAMETER ESTIMATE	T-RATIO	PARAMETER ESTIMATE	T-RATIO	PARAMETER ESTIMATE	T-RATIO
RSA IMPAIRMENT CATEGORIES ^						
VISUAL (IMPAIRED=1)			-0.0793	0.6		
HEARING (IMPAIRED=1)			0.2862 *	2.2		
ORTHOP (IMPAIRED=1)			0.1658 *	1.9		
AMPUTE (IMPAIRED=1)			0.4982 **	2.7		
MENTAL (IMPAIRED=1)			0.0734	0.9		
FAI HEALTH VARIABLES						
JUDGMENT (FACTOR 1)					-0.0580 *	2.1
MOTOR FUNCTION (FACTOR 2)					-0.0766 **	2.7
COGNITION (FACTOR 3)					-0.0885 **	3.2
PHYSICAL CONDITION (FACTOR 4)					-0.1792 **	6.1
COMMUNICATION (FACTOR 5)					0.0184	0.7
VOCATIONAL QUAL. (FACTOR 6)					-0.2142 **	8.4
VISION (FACTOR 7)					-0.0573 *	2.1
SAMPLE SIZE	710		710		710	
R-SQUARED	0.23		0.25		0.35	

* DENOTES SIGNIFICANCE AT 5% LEVEL
** DENOTES SIGNIFICANCE AT 1% LEVEL
^ THE REFERENCE CATEGORY IS INTERNAL IMPAIRMENTS

Most importantly, by excluding a measure of health in estimating the impact of services on earnings, one fails to distinguish among clients of different severity of disability. Equal amounts of treatment for individuals identical except for assessed level of functioning would be expected to result in very different earnings impacts. Conversely, to bring about the same enhancement of earnings in two persons of different severity of disability obviously requires different amounts of services. To the extent that levels of severity of disability differ across clients, the omission of a health variable will bias the estimates of the impact of services. In model 1, for every $100 of training services received, earnings are estimated to fall 4 percent. In the absence of a control for health, these results are not surprising. Specifically, the marginal impact of a dollar of services depends on the level of functioning of the client. The more severely disabled receive greater levels of services. Thus, the omission of a health variable would be expected to have a negative sign.

The RSA variable for health

These problems of omission of a health variable from an earnings or labor supply equation have been recognized in the economics literature in the past decade. But the solution to the problems—that is, the appropriate specification of a health variable—is not obvious. Typically, the ideal variable was specified theoretically, but its operationalization left much to be desired. The RSA health construct (model 2, Table 11.3) exemplifies the difficulty of properly constructing a health variable. The RSA health variable, described above, is a three digit condition classification code—thus a diagnostic classification. This variable was broken down into six categorical variables: visual, hearing, orthopedic, amputee, mental, and other internal impairments. By using other internal impairments as a basis, we can now interpret the impact of the other five impairment categories on earnings.

The R^2 of the regression was raised slightly from .23 to .25. Secondly, levels of significance did not change for the explanatory variables included in model 1, nor did the signs or magnitudes of the socioeconomic and human capital variable parameter estimates. However, there was a 25 percent increase in the magnitude of the coefficient for training services, although the sign was still negative. Also, the parameter estimate for education services increased by 50 percent.

For the RSA impairment categories, hearing, orthopedic, and amputee were all positive and significantly different from the basis group. A positive sign on these variables can be interpreted as measuring the impact of the presence of these impairments versus the basis impairment variable. As we explained above, this significance issue depends on the choice of basis variable and therefore cannot be given an absolute interpretation. For example, an amputee will have a 49 percent higher level of earnings than a person of similar nonhealth characteristics with other internal impairments. On the other hand, visual and mental impairments were not significantly different from the basis in their impact on earnings. Clearly, then, this health variable is not a particularly sensitive measure of the impact of health, or functioning, on earnings.

Raw FAI scores as health variables

The FAI scores consist of the thirty scaled responses assessing different aspects of functioning. The simplest use of this information as explanatory variables is to incorporate each of the thirty elements as continuous variables in the earnings equation. This model contains the usual battery of demographic and socioeconomic variables as well as the thirty FAI proxies for health.

The results of this estimation are unwieldy but are in some ways an improvement over model 1. Most of the demographic and socioeconomic variables are still significant and of approximately the same magnitude. Of the thirty functional assessment response variables, only hand functioning, coordination, endurance, and work history were statistically significant at the 5 percent level. Of these, three were of the expected negative sign, but coordination, inexplicably, was positive. The coefficients on the functional assessment variables can be interpreted as follows: a one unit fall in the level of, say, hand functioning brings an estimated reduction in earnings of $27. There is no a priori reason why, for example, work history would be expected to be significant while work habits or acceptability to employers— both related areas of functioning—would not. In the physical realm, upper extremity functioning and hand functioning are likely to be correlated. However, since these areas are related conceptually and thus potentially collinear, we would not be surprised to find that only one was significant, with the T-ratios of the others reduced.

This specification of the health variable lends little additional explanatory power to the earnings equation. The R^2 increased to .29, up from .23 in model 1. This result is expected from simply having added thirty more explanatory variables to the model. Furthermore, twenty-six of these thirty are statistically insignificant, some because of the multicollinearity problem mentioned above.

This specification is also unwieldy and of dubious interpretive value, due to the design of the FAI. The FAI was structured to measure functioning of different general categories. But within each category several aspects are assessed. Thus we would expect to be able to capture the impact of health, or functioning, or earnings in a more aggregative specification. The nonorthogonality of FAI categories indicates that data reduction might lead to a clearer interpretation of the impact of functioning on earnings.

Summing the FAI into one index

The simplest aggregation of the FAI response data is their summation into a single continuous index, ranging from 0, for absolutely no significant impairments, to 90, for severely limited functioning in all the measured categories. This model includes such a specification of the health index as well as the standard socioeconomic and demographic variables. The results of the estimation are similar to the completely disaggregated model 3 specification in overall explanatory power of the model and the sign, magnitude, and significance of the parameter estimates. Not surprisingly, the coefficient on the cumulative functioning variable is negative and significant at the 1 percent level. The interpretation of this coefficient is that a one unit change in the functioning index is associated with a 2.7 percent change in earnings at closure.

There are many problems with this specification of the health variable. First, as a linear specification, the model implicitly assumes that the marginal impact of a one-unit change in functioning is constant, that is, the same at all levels of functioning. For example, persons experiencing a decrease in the level of functioning from 10 to 11 are estimated to have their earnings impacted the same as persons experiencing a decrease in the level of functioning from 75 to 76. A priori there is reason to think that a log-linear specification, where the marginal impact of a one-unit change is increasing, and a sigmoidal representation, where the impacts increase, reach a threshold, and then decrease, are equally defensible as specifications for the cumulative index. More importantly, by summing the scores across functioning areas, we implicitly assume each variable has equal contribution to the change in earnings. For instance, the same decrease in level of functioning from 10 to 11 may be the result of a change in different aspects of functioning (such as physical, mental, emotional) for different clients; this change in aspects of functioning may have dramatically different impacts on client earnings. While we saw above that including all thirty FAI functioning attributes as explanatory variables was unwieldy and of limited interpretive value, the cumulative specification of a single linear scale masks the differential impact on earnings attributable to equal FAI score changes in different categories of functional capabilities. This gives us reason to believe that some intermediate level of aggregation of the FAI data may be a more appropriate specification of the health variable. Two possible methods of aggregation are principal components analysis and factor analysis.

Principal components of FAI scores as health variables

Instead of working with thirty FAI variables, we might transform these into a much smaller set of variables through a linear transformation. Ideally, we would want linear composites that have high correlations with the original variables and that explain much of the variation among the FAI variables. This is equivalent to maximizing the variance of the linear composite, that is, extracting the most amount of variance possible in a linear combination, given orthogonality of each successive principal component. The object of this method is to obtain components that account for most of the variation in the original variables. If successful, we will have reduced the dimensionality of the FAI without a significant loss of information. Furthermore, this may lead to a better understanding of the original variables, in that it gives underlying structure to a seemingly amorphous group of variables.

The purpose of principal components analysis is to represent the thirty FAI attributes in a smaller set of more basic or underlying functional categories. Thus principal components analysis attempts to reproduce, with a smaller group of variables, all the information contained in the original inventory. The first principal component extracts a certain percentage of the variance from the correlation matrix of the original FAI data. The second principal component is orthogonal to the first and extracts less of the remaining total variance. Each successive principal component is orthogonal to the previous ones and extracts successively less of the total variance. Since the variables were normalized to the unit variance, the total variance of the correlation matrix of FAI attributes is thirty units. If we extracted thirty principal components, we would account for all the variance in the standardized correlation matrix. Of course this defeats the purpose of the data reduction exercise. Using Kaiser's criterion, we decided to maintain a principal component as an explanatory variable only if it accounted for more than one-thirtieth of the variance—that is, more than one unit of variance. Following this criterion, we retained seven principal components for use as explanatory variables in the earnings equation.

The seven principal components extracted accounted for 61 percent of the variance of the FAI data. The first four principal components extracted 19.7, 14.1, 9.0, and 5.8 percent of the variance respectively, or 48.5 percent cumulatively. The remaining three extracted less than 5 percent each. In general, each principal component weights more heavily a different aspect of functioning, yet some of the principal components overlap. Thus we cannot claim that each principal component clearly represents a distinct aspect of functioning. For example, the first principal component had nearly equal correlations with thirteen FAI variables, ranging in value from .2 to .3 with such diverse aspects of functioning as emotional, mental, and vocational. Only physical functioning was not correlated with this component. Recall that the first principal component extracted roughly one-fifth of the total variance. Although this summarizes more of the information than that extracted by any of the subsequent principal components, it still only extracts 20 percent of the information, not enough to provide a strong interpretation, given the diffusion of the correlations between the component and the variables. The second principal component explains 14.1 percent of the variance, compared to the 20.1 percent of the first principal component. Ten variables are correlated .2 to .4 with the component. These comprise the areas of motor function and physical condition, variables different from the first principal component. Although this component explains a different aspect of functioning than the first component, it correlates weakly with too many variables to make clear interpretation possible—a problem similar to that associated with the first principal component.

The third principal component is orthogonal to the first two principal components but partly overlaps with the relative weights of the first principal component. Four of the variables with the strongest correlation with the third principal component are also among the variables most highly correlated with the first principal component. Again the correlation values range from .2 to .4 for these four.

The fourth, fifth, and sixth principal components account for a small amount of variance. They are negatively correlated with the FAI attributes with which the previous three components were positively correlated. Furthermore the magnitudes of the correlations are similar, albeit of the opposite sign—that is, in the range of −.2 to −.4. Intuitively, low FAI scores for clients should be negatively correlated with dysfunctioning. Thus it is not surprising that the later principal components are most strongly correlated inversely with the FAI data.

The seventh principal component correlates highly only with the vision variable. As we would expect, vision as a type of functioning appears to be unrelated to other measures of functioning.

Factor analysis as a health variable

The purpose of factor analysis is also to reduce the dimensions of the data to generate explanatory variables for the earnings equation. But while in principal components analysis we assume the entire variance can be explained, in factor analysis we make a prior assumption about the portion of the variance that is common to all variables (and implicitly the portion that is unique to each variable). In principal components analysis we seek to explain thirty total units of variance; in factor analysis some portion of this total variance is explained by a common structure, and the remainder is assumed to be attributable to unique elements of the thirty attributes.

The method of principal components involves generating an observable linear transformation of the variables such that the variance extracted from the data is maximized. All principal components must be orthogonal to each other (that is, independent). Beyond this, no formal model underlies this method of data reduction. As we have seen, the underlying components are not readily interpretable. In factor analysis, on the other hand, we estimate factor loadings, based on a model of the relation between underlying factors and the data. Furthermore, through various factor rotation techniques, it is possible to extract underlying factors that lend themselves to more meaningful interpretation than principal components. The concept of the underlying factor can be confusing, because of its unobservability and its hypothetical nature.

First we must specify the particular form of the factor analytic model to investigate the impact of FAI on earnings. The initial step is to make an assumption about the prior communalities—that is, about the amount of total variance common to all variables. Since the goal of the factor analysis is to derive final estimates of factor loads, we must first estimate the factor scores based on assumed communalities, then recalculate the final factor loads.

Using principal factor analysis with prior communalities set equal to one, a quartimax rotation method, and the Kaiser criterion of factor retention, factor analysis gave seven factors. The Kaiser, or mineigen, criterion specifies that a factor be retained only if it contributes to the explanation of more than the average amount of variance. Since the thirty FAI variables were normalized, the average amount of variance is one. Thus only factors extracting more than one unit of variance are retained. These factors have been assigned the names judgment, motor functioning, cognition, physical condition, communication, vocational qualifications, and vision, corresponding to the variables with the highest correlations with each factor. In general, we have applied the rule that a variable should be accounted for by the name of the factor if the correlation between that variable and the factor is greater than .5. This minimum level reflects the fact that the FAI attribute has a shared variance of at least 25 percent with the underlying factor (since a load is a correlation between a variable and the factor, which squared and summed yields the portion of the total variance explained by that factor). The seven factors explain 18.23 units of variance. Since there are thirty standardized variables, these factors explain 60.2 percent of the total variance.

Using the factors as explanatory variables in the earnings equation (model 3, Table 11.3) gives a much different picture of the role of health in explaining client earnings. First, the overall explanatory power of the model is increased by roughly 50 percent, from approximately .25 in the previous models to .35 in the current specification. This dramatic improvement indicates the importance of appropriately specifying health or functioning. Thus, with this more exacting specification, there is much less unexplained variation in earnings.

Six of the seven factors used as the basis for explanatory variables were significant at the 5 percent level; four of these were significant at the 1 percent level. For these six the parameter estimates were of the expected negative sign. Since greater loss of functioning corresponds to higher FAI scores, the negative sign on the health variables implies that an increase in the score results in lower earnings at closure. The perverse sign and statistical insignificance of the communication factor may be attributable to the limited dispersion in the scores for this regressor.

The magnitudes of the parameter estimates on the significant health variables range from -0.2142 (vocational qualifications) to -0.0573 (vision). The interpretation of these magnitudes is straightforward but instructive. A one-unit increase in the score on the vocational qualifications regressor, for example, results in a 21.42 percent fall in earnings at closure. While at first glance this sensitivity appears great, it becomes more plausible when we recall how the score is obtained. Formulated algebraically,

$$f = FR^{-1}x_i,$$

where f is the score data for each individual, F are the factor loads, R^{-1} is the inverse of the correlation matrix, and x_i are the FAI variable scores. The factor loads generally do not exceed 0.8, and the correlation matrix elements never exceed 0.5. Thus, using this extreme case as an example, we find that to have a one-unit increase in the regressor score would require a twenty-five point increase in overall FAI rating. Similarly a one-unit rise in the score on the vision regressor reduces earnings at closure by 5 percent.

The strong significance of the seven health variables generated from factor analysis indicates the superiority of this specification over the two previous specifications of the FAI analyzed. In the fully disaggregated case, only z variables were significant, and potential multicollinearity was high. The fully aggregated specification of the FAI health variable implicitly assumes an equal impact on earnings for a one-unit change in any of the FAI variables. From the factor-analytically based specification, we see that a one-unit change in the FAI score on two different variables will not, in general, have an equal impact on earnings. Furthermore, the fully aggregated and fully disaggregated specifications do not raise the R^2 of the model over the one exclusive of a health variable. Thus the specification based on factor analysis appears to be superior to the alternatives.

While inclusion of a health variable in the model may be justified on other grounds, it is our intent to use it as a control in order to isolate the impact of services on earnings. In models that do not include a health variable, health is picked up in earnings at referral, the other explanatory variables, or the error term. The factor-analytically based specification of the health variable appears to serve the function of a control and, at the same time, alters the estimated impact of other explanatory variables. The parameter estimate on the education variable increased in magnitude by roughly 20 percent. The earnings at acceptance parameter estimate fell dramatically, from 0.0457 to 0.0266, or almost 50 percent. Earnings at referral probably embodies much of this correlation. This is a desired result, since we feel that the inclusion of the earnings at acceptance variable on the right hand side of the earnings equation incorporates unobservable simultaneity with latent variables.

SUMMARY AND CONCLUSION

In our analysis, we employed a data set constructed from a sample of 1,670 clients accepted for services in Wisconsin in 1981. The data base consists of the Wisconsin R-300 data enhanced with specific case service costs and a Functional Assessment Inventory.

With an augmented data set of this kind, we could estimate the impact of specific services on earnings. Such estimates represent a vast improvement over assessments of the impact of "average" VR services on client outcomes. Clients with different disabling conditions receive qualitatively different types of services. However, the R-300 health variable—an impairment classification—yields no information about the severity of the impairment for these clients. In the absence of a severity indicator, it was found that certain services provided to clients *adversely* affected earnings.

By incorporating a more comprehensive measure of health, we were able to control for the severity of an impairment in an earnings equation. Using a factor analytic framework, we introduced seven measures of functioning into the earnings equation. Each of these measures of functioning was highly significant in explaining the earnings levels of successfully rehabilitated clients. It was also found that this model specification vastly improved the explanatory power of the earnings equation. Moreover, inclusion of the improved health measure corrected for the omitted variable bias that is inherent in the R-300 specification and that led to the perverse results for the impact of the specific services.

While our work in this chapter very clearly demonstrates the importance of a comprehensive measure of functioning, it also raises certain issues that merit further inquiry. It would be useful, for example, to investigate the extent to which a simultaneity problem may arise because of the correlation between the nature of the clients' disabilities and the service regimen they undergo. Further research into the problems of selection bias and the construction of comparison groups would also enable us to measure the efficacy of VR services with a greater degree of confidence.

WORKS CITED

Ashenfelter, Orley. 1978. "Estimating the Effect of Training Programs on Earnings." *Review of Economics and Statistics* 60:47-57.

Bartel, Ann, and Paul Taubman. 1979. "Health and Labor Market Success: The Role of Various Diseases." *Review of Economics and Statistics* 61.1:1-8.

Bassi, Laurie J. 1983. "The Effect of CETA on the Postprogram Earnings of Participants." *Journal of Human Resources* 18.4:539-56.

——— . 1984. "Estimating the Effect on Training Programs with Non-Random Selection." *Review of Economics and Statistics* 66.1:36-43.

Bellante, Donald M. 1972. "A Multivariate Analysis of a Vocational Rehabilitation System." *Journal of Human Resources* 7:226-41.

Berkowitz, Monroe. 1978. "The Search for a Health Variable." *Policy Analysis with Social Security Research Files.* Social Security Administration. Washington, D.C.: GPO.

Berkowitz, Monroe, and William G. Johnson. 1974. "Health and Labor Force Participation." *Journal of Human Resources* 9.1:117-28.

Boyle, Michael H., and George W. Torrance. 1984. "Developing Multiattribute Health Indexes." *Medical Care* 22.11:1045-57.

Chirikos, Thomas N., and Gilbert Nestel. 1981. "Impairment and Labor Market Outcomes: A Cross-Sectional and Longitudinal Analysis," in *Work and Retirement.* Cambridge: MIT Press.

Conley, Ronald W. 1965. *Economies of Vocational Rehabilitation.* Baltimore: Johns Hopkins University Press.

Crewe, Nancy M., and Gary T. Athelstan. 1981. "Functional Assessment in Vocational Rehabilitation: A Systematic Approach to Diagnosis and Goal Setting." *Archives of Physical Medicine and Rehabilitation* 62.

Crewe, Nancy M., Gary T. Athelstan, and Garland K. Meadows. 1975. "Vocational Diagnosis through Assessment of Functional Limitations." *Archives of Physical Medicine and Rehabilitation* 56:513-16.

Crewe, Nancy M., and Ralph R. Turner. 1984. "A Functional Assessment System for Vocational Rehabilitation," in *Functional Assessment in Rehabilitation.* Edited by Andrew S. Halpern and Marcus J. Fuhrer. Baltimore: Paul H. Brookes.

Granger, Carl V., and David S. Greer. 1976. "Functional Status Measurement and Medical Rehabilitation Outcomes." *Archives of Physical Medicine and Rehabilitation* 57:103-9.

Habeck, Rochelle, et al. 1985. "Functional Assessment Reflects Trends in Rehabilitation Practice, Technology." *The Interconnector* 8.1:1-4.

Haber, Lawrence D. 1970. "The Epidemiology of Disability: II. The Measurement of Functional Capacity Limitations," from the *Social Security Survey of the Disabled: 1966,* Report No. 10. U.S. Department of Health, Education, and Welfare, Social Security Administration, Office of Research and Statistics.

Halpern, Andrew S., and Marcus J. Fuhrer, eds. 1984. *Functional Assessment in Rehabilitation.* Baltimore: Paul H. Brookes.

Jette, Alan M. 1980a. "Functional Capacity Evaluation: An Empirical Approach." *Archives of Physical Medicine and Rehabilitation* 61:85-89.

———. 1980b. "Health Status Indicators: Their Utility in Chronic-Disease Evaluation Research." *Journal of Chronic Diseases* 33:567-79.

Keith, Robert A. 1984. "Functional Assessment Measures in Medical Rehabilitation: Current Status." *Archives of Physical Medicine and Rehabilitation* 65:74-78.

Kelman, Howard R., and Arthur Willner. 1962. "Problems in Measurement and Evaluation of Rehabilitation." *Archives of Physical Medicine and Rehabilitation* 43:172-81.

Lambrinos, James. 1982. "Health: A Source of Bias in Labor Supply Models." *Review of Economics and Statistics* 64.

Luft, Harold S. 1974. "The Impact of Poor Health on Earnings." *Review of Economics and Statistics* 57:43-57.

Manning, William G., Joseph P. Newhouse, and John E. Ware. 1982. "The Status of Health in Demand Estimation; or, Beyond Excellent, Good, Fair, and Poor," in *Economic Aspects of Health.* Chicago: University of Chicago Press.

Mincer, Jacob. 1974. *Schooling, Experience and Earnings.* New York: National Bureau of Economic Research.

Moriarty, Joseph B. 1981. *Preliminary Diagnostic Questionnaire: Introduction and Functional Assessment.* West Virginia Research and Training Center.

Nagi, Saad Z., and Linda W. Hadley. 1979. "Disability Behavior: Income Change and Motivation to Work." *Industrial and Labor Relations Review* 2:223-33.

Nagi, Saad Z., and Richard I. Haller. 1982. "Limitations in Function: Indicators and Measures." Prepared for the Social Security Administration, Dept. of Health and Human Services, under Grant No. 10-p98012-5.

Parsons, Donald O. 1977. "Health, Family Structure, and Labor Supply." *American Economic Review* 67.4:703-12.

———. 1982. "The Male Labour Force Participation Decision: Health, Reported Health, and Economic Incentives." *Economica* 49:81-91.

Scheffler, Richard M., and George Iden. 1979. "The Effect of Disability on Labor Supply." *Industrial and Labor Relations Review* 2:122-32.

Stewart, Anita L., John E. Ware, Jr., and Robert H. Brook. 1981. "Advances in the Measurement of Functional Status: Construction of Aggregate Indexes." *Medical Care* 19:473-88.

Turner, Ralph R. 1982. "Functional Assessment in VR Clients: A Pretest." Paper Prepared for Abt Associates, Cambridge, Massachusetts. Contract No. 105-78-4012.

Worrall, John D. 1978. "A Benefit-Cost Analysis of the Vocational Rehabilitation Program." *Journal of Human Resources* 13:285-98.

12 *David H. Dean and Robert C. Dolan*

ESTABLISHING A MINI-DATA LINK

The measure of client earning at closure used by VR agencies consists of the weekly earnings of clients at a point sixty days after they commenced employment. This reported earnings figure forms the basis for benefits estimation in benefit-cost analyses of the VR program.

Program analysts who use this measure to establish the benefits of a regimen of vocational rehabilitation services will encounter three types of problems. First, estimating lifetime benefits from a point estimate of earnings entails some questionable assumptions. Second, the R-300 data-base earnings figure does not permit the analyst to assign benefits to those clients classified as "not rehabilitated" because they have not reported earnings for the sixty day period in question. Third, the R-300 figure does not permit the analyst to examine the earnings levels of clients who apply for services but who are not accepted or the earnings levels of clients who subsequently drop out. This weakness relates to the control/comparison group issue that plagues any analysis undertaken in a nonexperimental setting.

Let us examine each of these problems in turn. What is wrong with assigning lifetime benefits from the earnings figure reported upon program closure? Even if we temporarily overlook that this measure is only applicable for those clients successfully rehabilitated, we must recognize that any projection is crucially dependent on the assumptions made. In the traditional analysis, the assumption is made that rehabilitated persons will work at the same job for the duration of their employment period. Further, it is implicitly assumed that the weekly earnings are for a forty-hour work week for the entire year. No allowance is made for periods of unemployment and job turnover. Finally, it may be assumed that there is a constant rate of increase in worker productivity, and thus earnings, over time. Such an assumption disregards the possibility that the human capital stock of the disabled population may depreciate over time because of their impairments. It is not at all clear that a positive rate of change in earnings can be assumed a priori. This becomes an empirical question that can be resolved by taking a better longitudinal look at the postprogram earnings levels of these people.

The second deficiency of this measure is the inability to ascribe benefits to those persons not rehabilitated. A statistical method to estimate the magnitude of such benefits is examined in Chapter 7. The empirical support for this procedure can be found in the SSA-RSA data link studies, which reported significant postprogram earnings for these clients on a macro level (Greenblum 1977). It would appear that a micro-level examination of the postprogram earnings of those clients not rehabilitated would be most useful in quantifying any such benefits.

The third problem in VR benefit accounting concerns the lack of control or comparison groups. Other authors in this volume have discussed the difficulties of establishing a control group. In this chapter, we will investigate appropriate substitutes for the ideal control group. One such substitute would consist of persons who apply for but are not accepted for services. This type of comparison group has been incorporated in a previous study for a small sample of clients (Nowak 1983). A second comparison group would consist of status 30 clients, the program dropouts.

Each of these shortcomings hints at a possible solution—namely, to resurrect the data link. Recognizing the difficulties of collecting data link information on the individual client level on a national basis, we looked for a more feasible alternative. Using data collected on earnings by states for unemployment insurance purposes, we were able to construct a state-level data link by merging this information with the data routinely collected by the state VR agency. In the next three sections of this chapter, we discuss the project in greater detail.

The first section describes how the data set was constructed and what additional data were generated. The second section examines the general results of the procedure and compares and contrasts the findings for the successes, nonsuccesses, and not accepted clients. Items such as the number of jobs held, earnings per job, number of quarters worked, and earnings per quarter are investigated. The fourth section looks specifically at earnings for subsets of the three groups. For instance, the earnings of persons classified as not rehabilitated because they moved can be contrasted with persons whose disability was judged too severe to justify further efforts at rehabiliation. In the final section, some conclusions and suggestions for further research are presented. While the data-link approach holds great promise, it should be noted that the data set we constructed covered only one year of postclosure earnings. Consequently, any conclusions must be interpreted cautiously.

CONSTRUCTING THE ENHANCED STATE DATA BASE

The augmented state data base that has been constructed consists of 17,622 clients closed from counselor's caseloads of the Virginia Department of Rehabilitative Services (VDRS) during the period October 1981 through September 1982. In order to track these clients' postprogram earnings through records kept by the Virginia Employment Commission (VEC), we needed to have a valid social security number for each client. Since 205 clients had been issued temporary numbers by the VDRS, these clients could not be tracked. This left a total of 17,417 records that were submitted to the VEC for matching with their employment records.

The VEC maintains on-line records of all persons working in UI-covered employment for a period of five quarters. For a record to be generated, the employer must contribute some portion of the employee's wages to the Virginia Unemployment Insurance Trust Fund. At the time of the data request, the time frame covered comprised all four quarters for calendar year 1984 and the first quarter of 1985. Thus the postprogram employment data obtained ranged from a minimum of fifteen months for clients closed in September 1982 to a maximum of twenty-seven months for clients closed from services in October 1981.

The information collected for each job reported consisted of the employer name and serial number, the quarters that the client may have worked for this employer during the five-quarter interval, and the total earnings reported during any of these quarters worked. Unfortunately, no data were recorded on either the hourly wage rate or the number of hours worked during the quarter.

Since some clients held several jobs during this interval, multiple records were reported for these people. With the file of 17,417 VDRS clients, the VEC was able to track 12,044 job records for 6,709 clients at an average earnings of $4,108 per job. Thus, five-quarter earnings data were generated from this procedure for 38.5 percent of the clients who were terminated from further VR services in 1982.

We can think of three possible explanations for the lack of reported earnings for the rest of the sample. First, it is likely that the people were either unemployed or had dropped out of the labor force entirely. Second, it is possible that the people were working but not in occupations covered by unemployment insurance. Third, some clients might be working out of the state and thus outside the jurisdiction of the VEC. In the absence of a more comprehensive earnings record, such as the Social Security Master Beneficiary Record, we can only speculate about the percentage breakdown of those not reporting into the respective categories. As a consequence, this report must necessarily focus on these clients who have reported earnings. We hope, however, that further data links will cover more than one year of earnings; the availability of client earnings data for a more extended period of time should lessen the problem of untracked earnings.

EXAMINING THE OVERALL RESULTS OF THE WAGE MATCH

One can fruitfully examine information on postprogram earnings in a number of ways. For instance, one can get some idea of worker movement by examining the number of jobs held by a worker during these five quarters.

One can get a crude proxy for worker productivity by investigating the quarterly earnings at each of these jobs. Information about labor force participation can be gained by looking at the number of quarters clients worked during this interval. Finally, some notion of worker skills and overall level of labor market success can be gleaned from an examination of the quarterly earnings for the clients who worked during any of the five quarters. Our findings on these aspects of employment are presented in Tables 12.1 through 12.4 below.

One of the more striking findings of the VEC-VDRS wage match is the transient nature of employment for these people. A client who worked at all during the five quarter period held an average of 1.8 jobs. Of course, this average figure is comprised of three distinct cohorts—those successfully rehabilitated, those not rehabilitated, and those not accepted for services. The number of jobs reported for each of these cohorts as well as the entire sample is reported in Table 12.1.

Before we examine the number of jobs for those who worked, it may be useful to look at the percentage of clients not working within each of the subgroups. We have already seen that less than 40 percent of the entire sample was tracked by the wage match procedure. By looking at the clients reporting positive earnings at their jobs, we found that 51.3 percent of the successfully rehabilitated (status 26) cohort reported at least one job with the VEC earnings file. This contrasts sharply with the 31.9 percent of those not accepted for services (status 08) who were tracked in the VEC earnings file and the 26.7 percent of those not rehabilitated (status 28 & 30) who were similarly tracked.

If one were to assume that those not on file with the VEC were not working, then one could conclude that a client in the success cohort was twice as likely to be employed as a client not successfully rehabilitated. On the other side of the coin, the fact that only half of the successes were working during a period starting from one to one and one-half years after they were closed status 26 might indicate that many in the success cohort lacked perseverance and were not employable in the long run. Of course, one must remember that the time frame being studied came in the midst of the 1982–1983 recession. Given that the last hired are usually the first fired, this low percentage of clients reporting any employment at all can be viewed in a different light.

Not only were the successes more likely to work, but when they worked, these clients tended to stay at the same job. The rehabilitated cohort held only 1.69 jobs on average. The typical nonsuccess and not accepted clients worked at 1.94 and 1.82 jobs respectively during this five-quarter interval.

This employment-transience indicator is illustrated in Table 12.1. It should be observed that just over 60 percent of the success cohort held one job. This is contrasted with 52 percent and 56 percent for the not

TABLE 12.1

NUMBER OF JOBS HELD FROM JANUARY 1984 THROUGH MARCH 1985 BY PERSONS
CLOSED FROM THE VIRGINIA DEPARTMENT OF REHABILITATIVE SERVICES
DURING FISCAL YEAR 1982, IF REPORTING ANY JOBS

Number of Jobs	Persons Rehabilitated		Persons Not Rehabilitated		Persons Not Accepted for Services		All Persons Closed from the Program	
	Number	Percent of Total	Number	Percent of Total	Number	Percent of Total	Number	Percent of Total
One	1583	60.6%	560	52.2%	1470	56.4%	3817	57.7%
Two	587	22.5%	256	23.9%	597	22.9%	1517	22.9%
Three	244	9.3%	127	11.8%	282	10.8%	686	10.4%
Four	120	4.6%	70	6.5%	144	5.5%	343	5.2%
Five	40	1.5%	30	2.8%	59	2.3%	133	2.0%
Six	22	0.8%	18	1.7%	30	1.2%	70	1.1%
More than Six	15	0.6%	11	1.0%	25	1.0%	53	0.8%
Total	2611	100.0%	1072	100.0%	2607	100.0%	6619	100.0%

TABLE 12.2

EARNINGS FOR EACH JOB HELD FROM JANUARY 1984 THROUGH MARCH 1985 BY PERSONS
CLOSED FROM THE VIRGINIA DEPARTMENT OF REHABILITATIVE SERVICES
DURING FISCAL YEAR 1982, IF REPORTING ANY JOBS

Number of Job Reported	Persons Rehabilitated		Persons Not Rehabilitated		Persons Not Accepted for Services		All Persons Closed from the Program	
	Number	Percent of Total (N=2617)	Number	Percent of Total (N=1097)	Number	Percent of Total (N=2649)	Number	Percent of Total (N=6709)
First Job								
Average Earnings	$7,012		$3,903		$5,328		$5,732	
# Reporting Earnings	2,583	98.3%	1,064	97.0%	2,567	96.9%	6,539	97.5%
Second Job								
Average Earnings	$3,506		$2,143		$2,676		$2,893	
# Reporting Earnings	1,023	38.9%	508	46.3%	1,130	42.7%	2,784	41.5%
Third Job								
Average Earnings	$2,147		$1,413		$1,762		$1,817	
# Reporting Earnings	443	16.9%	254	23.2%	548	20.7%	1,294	19.3%
Fourth Job								
Average Earnings	$1,603		$1,194		$1,410		$1,424	
# Reporting Earnings	203	7.7%	129	11.8%	264	10.0%	612	9.1%

TABLE 12.2--Continued

Number of Job Reported	Persons Rehabilitated		Persons Not Rehabilitated		Persons Not Accepted for Services		All Persons Closed from the Program	
	Number	Percent of Total (N=2617)	Number	Percent of Total (N=1097)	Number	Percent of Total (N=2649)	Number	Percent of Total (N=6709)
Fifth Job								
Average Earnings	$1,835		$923		$1,104		$1,319	
# Reporting Earnings	87	3.3%	63	5.7%	124	4.7%	281	4.2%
Sixth Job								
Average Earnings	$1,724		$1,072		$1,080		$1,310	
# Reporting Earnings	41	1.6%	31	2.8%	58	2.2%	132	2.0%
Seventh - 13th Jobs								
Average Earnings	$1,739		$1,065		$808		$1,187	
# Reporting Earnings	42	1.6%	27	2.5%	71	2.7%	147	2.2%
All Jobs								
Average Earnings	$8,861		$5,355		$6,906		$7,375	
# Reporting Earnings	2,627	100.0%	1,097	100.0%	2,649	100.0%	6,709	100.0%

rehabilitated and not accepted for services cohorts. Conversely, while almost one out of every four status 28 and 30 clients held more than two jobs durings this time frame, only one out of every six status 26 clients held more than two jobs. This may indicate that the successfully rehabilitated client experienced a longer period of job tenure after completion of the program. Without data for earnings in 1983, it is not possible to tell whether clients have switched jobs during the interval from the time of program termination through January 1984.

Not only were the successfully rehabilitated clients more likely to have a stable employment record after closure from the program, but they also earned more at these jobs. From Table 12.2 it can be seen that the average earnings for all jobs held during the five-quarter period were $8,861 for the status 26 closures. The reported earnings figures for the status 28 and 30 closures and 08 closures for the same period were $5,355 and $6,906 respectively. Taking the earnings for the three cohorts for the first job held during this period as a percentage of these total earnings, we see that 80 percent of the successful cohort's earnings came from their initial job reported. This figure is higher than those for the nonsuccesses and not accepted cohorts—73 percent and 77 percent respectively.

This same pattern holds for clients who held more than one job during this period. While rehabilitated clients were less likely to have more than one job, if they did work at other jobs during this interval they earned significantly more. These results must be interpreted with caution. It should be noted that the data only report on total earnings during a particular quarter. We cannot discern whether a client held jobs consecutively—demonstrating worker transience—or concurrently, in which case the client was moonlighting.

We can get some notion of overall labor force participation for clients who worked at least sometime during the five-quarter period by looking at the number of quarters worked. The successfully rehabilitated client was employed, on average, in just under four of the possible five quarters. The persons who were not accepted into the VR program worked in just under 3.5 quarters. Persons not rehabilitated only worked in 3.2 quarters, on average.

The pattern of labor force participation for the three cohorts and the combined sample is reported in Table 12.3. Note that almost 55 percent of the successful cohort worked at some time in each of the five quarters. This contrasts with under 40 percent for those not accepted for services and only 31.5 percent of the not rehabilitated cohort. Conversely, while over 38 percent of the not rehabilitated clients worked only one or two quarters, 31 percent of the clients not accepted for services worked in less than three quarters. Less than 20 percent of the successfully rehabilitated cohort who worked reported earnings in two quarters or less.

Perhaps the most telling statistic about the overall productivity of per-

TABLE 12.3

NUMBER OF QUARTERS WORKED DURING THE FIVE-QUARTER PERIOD
BEGINNING JANUARY 1984 BY PERSONS CLOSED FROM THE
VIRGINIA DRS DURING FISCAL YEAR 1982, IF REPORTING ANY JOBS

Number of Quarters Worked	Persons Rehabilitated		Persons Not Rehabilitated		Persons Not Accepted for Services		All Persons Closed from Program	
	Number	Percent of Total (N=2611)	Number	Percent of Total (N=1072)	Number	Percent of Total (N=2607)	Number	Percent of Total (N=6619)
Only One	291	11.1%	220	20.5%	413	15.8%	989	14.9%
Two	221	8.5%	191	17.8%	413	15.8%	873	13.2%
Three	281	10.8%	151	14.1%	323	12.4%	811	12.3%
Four	395	15.1%	172	16.0%	433	16.6%	1,049	15.8%
All Five	1,423	54.5%	338	31.5%	1,025	39.3%	2,897	43.8%
Total	2,611	100.0%	1,072	100.0%	2,607	100.0%	6,619	100.0%

sons closed from services during 1982 is their earnings for each quarter during the five quarters of the wage match. These results are found in Table 12.4. The status 26 cohort averaged earnings of just under $9,000 during this period. If such clients worked during any particular quarter during this interval, their earnings averaged between $2,121 and $2,427. The proportion of rehabiliated clients working during each quarter averaged about 80 percent, except during the last quarter when it dipped to only three-fourths of the cohort.

Note the general increase in quarterly earnings, which reached a peak in the last quarter of 1984 and then declined in the beginning of 1985. This may indicate an increase in hourly wages, hours worked, or both. One simply cannot tell with the given data. Given the prevalence of entry-level wages generally received by the disabled VR client, it would seem to indicate that clients were increasing the hours they worked and then cutting back on them for the first quarter of 1985.

Reported earnings were much lower for those clients closed not rehabilitated. Total earnings for the period averaged only $5,480 for the period, some 60 percent of what the successful cohort earned. This amounts to less than $90 per week. This low level, again, represents a combination of low wages and reduced hours of labor supplied. Further proof of the contention that this cohort worked fewer hours is provided by the lowered labor force participation rates during each of the five quarters. In only the last quarter of 1984 did more than two-thirds of this cohort report some earnings.

While average quarterly earnings increased at a higher rate during the first three quarters than for the successful cohort, they fell during both the fourth and fifth quarters for persons not rehabilitated. The labor force participation rates for this group mirrored this pattern, albeit with a lag of one quarter. In other words, the percentage of this cohort working rose from 60 to 68 percent during 1984 but then tailed off to 64 percent for the first quarter of 1985.

The reported figures for the cohort not accepted for services were somewhere between the other two cohorts with regard to both average quarterly earnings and labor force participation rates. While the average quarterly earnings were closer to the figures reported for the rehabilitated cohort, the labor force participation rates more closely resembled those of the not rehabilitated group.

In particular, the total earnings for the five-quarter period averaged just over $7,000, or just under $110 on a per weekly basis. This is less than 80 percent of the reported earnings for the status 26 cohort during the same period. However, for the individual quarters, the average earnings were closer to 90 percent of the earnings for the rehabilitated cohort. It is worthy of note that the reported earnings showed very little variation from quarter to quarter, ranging from $1,984 to $2,076. The latter maximum average earnings figure was reported during the last quarter of 1984.

TABLE 12.4

QUARTERLY EARNINGS AND NUMBER OF PERSONS WORKING DURING THE FIVE-QUARTER PERIOD BEGINNING JANUARY 1984 BY PERSONS CLOSED FROM THE VIRGINIA DRS DURING FISCAL YEAR 1982, IF REPORTING ANY JOBS

Period Worked, Average Earnings	Persons Rehabilitated	Percent of Total (N=2611)	Persons Not Rehabilitated	Percent of Total (N=1072)	Persons Not Accepted for Services	Percent of Total (N=2607)	All Persons Closed from the Program (N=6619)	Percent of Total (N=6619)
1st Quarter, 1984								
Persons Working	2,041	78.2%	643	60.0%	1,742	66.8%	4,628	69.9%
Average Earnings	$2,121		$1,610		$2,004		$1,985	
2nd Quarter, 1984								
Persons Working	2,089	80.0%	668	62.3%	1,840	70.6%	4,824	72.9%
Average Earnings	$2,230		$1,730		$1,984		$2,046	
3rd Quarter, 1984								
Persons Working	2,101	80.5%	699	65.2%	1,865	71.5%	4,895	74.0%
Average Earnings	$2,271		$1,810		$2,012		$2,090	

TABLE 12.4--Continued

Period Worked, Average Earnings	Persons Rehabilitated	Percent of Total (N=2611)	Persons Not Rehabilitated	Percent of Total (N=1072)	Persons Not Accepted for Services	Percent of Total (N=2607)	All Persons Closed from the Program (N=6619)	Percent of Total (N=6619)
4th Quarter, 1984								
Persons Working	2,058	78.8%	731	68.2%	1,887	72.4%	4,895	74.0%
Average Earnings	$2,427		$1,736		$2,076		$2,172	
1st Quarter, 1985								
Persons Working	1,982	75.9%	692	64.6%	1,731	66.4%	4,607	69.6%
Average Earnings	$2,283		$1,661		$2,012		$2,075	
All Five Quarters								
Persons Working	2,611	100.0%	1072	100.0%	2,607	100.0%	6,619	100.0%
Average Earnings	$8,915		$5,480		$7,018		$7,475	

The labor force participation rates of the not accepted cohort for the quarters comprising this interval ranged from 66.4 percent to 72.4 percent. These rates came during the first quarter of 1985 and the last quarter of 1984. There had been an increasing rate of labor force participation throughout 1984 for this group.

It is most interesting to note that for each group the highest earnings and labor force participation rates (except for those in status 26) were generated during the last quarter of 1984. Not only were more persons working, but when they worked they worked more hours—assuming entry-level wages. This is probably attributable to the seasonal increase in employment always observed for October through December. Again, such statistics indicate the tenuous nature of employment for persons who apply for VR services.

EXAMINING THE EARNINGS AND LABOR FORCE PARTICIPATION OF THE RESPECTIVE COHORTS

The previous section examined the entire sample of client VR records that were matched with the VEC wage records. By restricting the analysis to the separate cohorts composing the sample, we can glean a great deal of additional information from the data base. For the rehabilitated clientele, we can examine the earnings for the various work statuses into which these people may be classified by the VR agency. Since most of these clients reported an earnings figure upon leaving the VR program, we can compare their earnings levels with those reported by the wage match procedure. In the case of the other two cohorts, the records indicate the specific reasons why these persons were not accepted for services or, if they were accepted, why they were not rehabilitated. Since some of these reasons are the same for the two groups—clients moved, their disabilities were too severe, and the like—it may be fruitful to make comparisons by closure reason for these groups. Let us examine each of the cohorts in turn.

The greatest amount of information is provided for the rehabilitated group of clients. In addition to recording the weekly earnings upon completion of the program, the VR agency classifies the occupation of the person at this time. A client could be working in competitive employment, in sheltered employment, at self-employment, or in a Business Enterprise Program (BEP). Other occupational designations include unpaid family worker, student, trainee, or homemaker.

All told, 5,089 clients were rehabilitated in 1982. Eighty-one clients were in either the BEP or unpaid family member status. A total of 609 of the closures were into homemaker status. These clients did not have any wages upon completion of the program, nor did the 180 some clients who were closed as students or trainees. Since we seek to contrast the earnings at the two different periods, these persons were dropped from any further wage analysis. This reduced the relevant sample to 4,480 clients. The lion's share of clients were placed in competitive employment, with a small number in either sheltered or self-employment. The labor market outcomes for these three groups are presented in Table 12.5.

Since well over 90 percent of the rehabilitated sample was competitively employed, these figures will closely resemble those for the entire cohort presented in the last table. Overall labor force participation was 62.2 percent

TABLE 12.5

EXAMINING THE EARNINGS AND LABOR FORCE PARTICIPATION RATES
OF PERSONS SUCCESSFULLY REHABILITATED, BY WORK STATUS AT CLOSURE

Category	Competitive Employment (n=3936)	Sheltered Employment (n=345)	Self- Employment (n=226)
# Reporting Earnings	2450	92	67
% Reporting Any Earnings to VEC	62.2%	26.7%	29.6%
1st Quarter, 1984			
Average Earnings	$2,132	$1,164	$2,531
% of Total	49.7%	11.6%	18.1%
2nd Quarter, 1984			
Average Earnings	$2,244	$1,223	$2,576
% of Total	50.8%	12.2%	21.2%
3rd Quarter, 1984			
Average Earnings	$2,283	$1,292	$2,642
% of Total	50.9%	13.0%	22.1%
4th Quarter, 1984			
Average Earnings	$2,444	$1,518	$2,552
% of Total	49.9%	12.5%	22.1%
1st Quarter, 1985			
Average Earnings	$2,320	$1,046	$2,364
% of Total	47.7%	17.7%	19.0%
Average Total Earnings	$9,138	$3,100	$8,788
Average Weekly Earnings	$141	$48	$135
Average Number of Quarters Worked	4.0	2.5	3.5
Average Number of Jobs Held	1.7	1.3	1.6

for the competitively placed workers. Note that for the self-employed, total earnings, on average, were lower than for the competitively employed by some $350. However, quarterly earnings were higher for each of the five quarters comprising this interval. This is due to the lower labor force participation rates for the self-employed, who worked only 3.5 of the five quarters while the competitive cohort worked, on average, in four quarters of employment.

The earnings and participation rates for clients closed into sheltered employment were dramatically lower than the rates for their competitively-placed counterparts. Just over one-quarter of this cohort reported any earnings during the five quarters of the wage match. Total earnings for these persons were only one-third of the earnings for the competitively placed. Weekly earnings for the individuals in this cohort, if they worked at all, were less than $50.

Although earnings increased for each quarter for 1984, they fell precipitously in the fifth quarter, the first quarter of 1985. This may have been due to an influx of such workers—a development that increased the participation rate but lowered earnings as these individuals tended to work few hours. Note that these clients worked in only half of the quarters and that they tended to be at the same employment. One could surmise that these rehabilitated clients were placed into terminal workshops from which it was difficult to move into competitive employment. To verify this conjecture would require further investigation of the employer serial numbers.

A different line of analysis for rehabilitated clients involves transforming the quarterly and total earnings figures into weekly averages (by dividing by thirteen or sixty-five weeks). This figure can provide a crude measure of the change in earnings for clients from the time of closure to the time of the wage match.

At the time of program termination, the average weekly earnings for all 4,480 status 26 closures were $144. For those clients still working during the first quarter of 1984, the average weekly earnings were $163. These 2,041 clients averaged $153 per week when they were closed rehabilitated. Thus, these results could be cautiously construed as a $10 per week change in earnings, an increase of 6.5 percent. Similarly, for those clients working during the first quarter of 1985, there was an increase in earnings of $23 over earnings at closure. This represents an earnings increase of 15.1 percent during this roughly three-year interval.

When we look at the entire five-quarter interval, we find greater numbers of persons who worked at some point; that is, the chances of a client working at some time during the sixty-five–week interval were much greater than during a thirteen-week period. This increased the work prospects of persons with lesser degrees of labor force attachment. As a consequence, the transformed weekly earnings for the sixty-five–week interval for the 2,611 clients tracked by the VEC were only $137. Earnings at program closure for this group were just under $150. Hence we see that, overall, weekly earnings fell by $13, a decrease of 8.7 percent.

Of course this indicated decline in worker earnings could represent lower wages per hour, less hours worked per week than at the time of program closure, low labor force participation during this particular year and a quarter, or a combination of all three. In the absence of data on hours worked and wages for these hours, it becomes difficult to attribute this decline in earnings to any one facet of labor supply.

We can also learn a bit more about the nature of the earnings for persons who were not accepted into the VR program as well as persons who were not rehabilitated after being accepted. When any person is closed from the program, the VR agency requires that the counselor provide a reason for the termination. The agency has nine classifications to explain why an applicant was not accepted for services and a subset of seven of these to explain why the client was closed not rehabilitated. The two additional categories are concerned with eligibility criteria. It would be useful to examine these people's later earnings, or lack thereof, in light of the reason they were closed from the agency caseload.

To be accepted as a candidate for VR, a person must have a medically-determined impairment presenting a vocational handicap that can be remediated through the provision of VR services. Following well-defined guidelines, counselors can make the decision to not accept applicants if they find that the applicants have no disabling condition, that the condition does not present a vocational handicap, or that the disability is too severe for the agency to undertake a regimen of services to rehabilitate the applicants. A counselor may also transfer a case to another agency that is more appropriate. In addition to these counselor determinations, there are numerous ways in which a person can self-select out of the program. For instance, one could move, refuse services, be uncooperative, be institutionalized, or simply die.

Once a client has been accepted into the program, the counselor can only terminate that client by transferring the case to another agency or judging the client too severely disabled to warrant further expenditure of funds for services. Clients may opt not to continue to participate in the program for the same reasons that they may choose not to be accepted into the program. Termination from the program, whether initiated by the counselor or the client, can take place at two distinct time intervals. Clients terminated before the services specified in the IWRP have been provided are closed in status 30; such clients are essentially program dropouts. Clients terminated after the IWRP has been implemented are closed in status 28 and classified as nonrehabilitated. For purposes of constructing a comparison group, the distinction is critical. Nevertheless, since this section is primarily concerned with presenting longitudinal earnings and not with explaining earnings differences among the cohorts, these two groups are combined.

The results of the wage match process classified according to these reasons for closure are presented in Table 12.6 for those persons not accepted for services and Table 12.7 for those clients not rehabilitated. It must first be noted that the last column consists primarily of 595 persons who were tracked by the VEC wage match but for whom a reason was not reported for their disqualification from services. Slightly more than half of these people were tracked in the wage match. While this group had substantial earnings, averaging some $7,500 for the five quarters of the wage match, we can infer little else about them without knowing the reason they were not admitted to the program.

The highest earnings levels were reported by those persons not accepted because they did not have a vocational handicap. Participation rates for this group were also among the highest reported. Almost two-thirds of this group were successfully tracked by the VEC. This rate was higher than that reported by the competitively employed. For persons tracked, total earnings averaged over $8,500. On a weekly basis, this five-quarter figure translates into earnings of over $130.

One should remember that these people may indeed have had some disabling condition. In denying them eligibility, the VR agency judged that their condition did not impair their employability. Such people may have been temporarily off their lifetime earnings profile when they applied for services. After they were denied services, they returned to or found employment at a somewhat lower rate than rehabilitated clients. Therefore, it is not surprising to see that these people had earnings comparable to those of the competitively-employed rehabilitated cohort.

The group with the second highest average earnings as well as the highest participation rate were persons judged by the VDRS not to have a disabling condition. On a weekly basis their earnings were just over $116 for the five-quarter period. This cohort would also seem to have been temporarily off their expected lifetime earnings path. One might conclude that the individuals in this group had minor impairments and were down on their luck at the time of their application for services. After being denied VR services, they eventually returned to the labor market, earning about $1,000 less during the five-quarter period than those persons not *vocationally* disabled.

Each of the remaining reasons for not being accepted for services is also a legitimate reason for not being rehabilitated. Let us then compare the labor market experiences of persons who were not admitted to the program with the experiences of persons who were terminated from the program for the same reasons.

First we examine the individuals who moved or could not be located by the VR agency. Note that for the persons who moved after they had been accepted for services, the labor force participation rate is lower than that for persons who moved before acceptance—44 versus 33 percent. Both

TABLE 12.6

EXAMINING THE EARNINGS AND LABOR FORCE PARTICIPATION RATES
OF PERSONS NOT ACCEPTED FOR SERVICES, BY CLOSURE REASON

Category	Unable to Locate or Moved (n=872)	Disability Too Severe (n=849)	Refused Further Services (n=985)	Would Not Cooperate (n=450)	No Disabling Condition (n=399)	No Vocational Handicap (n=614)	No Reason Given, Transferred, Died, or in Institution (n=1220)
# with Earnings	383	231	532	225	265	404	618
% Reporting Any Earnings to VEC	43.9%	27.2%	54.0%	50.0%	66.4%	65.8%	50.4%
1st Quarter, 1984							
Average Earnings	$2,067	$1,547	$2,011	$1,584	$1,986	$2,194	$2,069
% Reporting	27.5%	15.7%	35.0%	29.8%	48.1%	50.7%	34.4%
2nd Quarter, 1984							
Average Earnings	$1,857	$1,739	$1,902	$1,758	$1,866	$2,196	$2,146
% Reporting	29.7%	15.7%	38.4%	33.1%	52.4%	50.8%	35.6%
3rd Quarter, 1984							
Average Earnings	$1,838	$1,732	$1,981	$1,782	$1,891	$2,238	$2,205
% Reporting	31.2%	17.6%	38.1%	33.1%	52.4%	50.7%	35.4%
4th Quarter, 1984							
Average Earnings	$1,943	$1,743	$2,004	$1,749	$2,143	$2,452	$2,125
% Reporting	30.8%	17.4%	39.0%	36.2%	51.1%	49.0%	36.6%

TABLE 12.6--Continued

Category	Unable to Locate or Moved (n=872)	Disability Too Severe (n=849)	Refused Further Services (n=985)	Would Not Cooperate (n=450)	No Disabling Condition (n=399)	No Vocational Handicap (n=614)	No Reason Given, Transferred, Died, or in Institution (n=1220)
1st Quarter, 1985							
Average Earnings	$1,957	$1,685	$1,919	$1,789	$2,104	$2,247	$2,088
% Reporting	27.8%	15.7%	34.9%	31.1%	47.1%	46.6%	848.0%
Average Total Earnings	$6,458	$5,082	$6,739	$5,668	$7,545	$8,525	$7,423
Average Weekly Earnings	$99	$78	$115	$87	$116	$131	$114
Average Number of Quarters Worked	3.3	3.0	3.4	3.2	3.8	3.8	3.5
Average Number of Jobs Held	2.0	1.6	1.9	2.0	1.9	1.8	1.7

TABLE 12.7

EXAMINING THE EARNINGS AND LABOR FORCE PARTICIPATION RATES OF PERSONS NOT SUCCESSFULLY REHABILITATED, BY CLOSURE STATUS

Category	Unable to Locate or Moved (n=1001)	Disability Too Severe (n=1181)	Refused Further Services (n=681)	Would Not Cooperate (n=630)	No Reason Given, Transferred, Died, or in Institution (n=198)
# with Earnings	326	151	269	283	43
% Reporting Any Earnings to VEC	32.6%	12.8%	39.5%	44.9%	21.7%
1st Quarter, 1984					
Average Earnings	$1,883	$1,149	$1,709	$1,475	$1,007
% Reporting	20.3%	6.4%	26.0%	25.4%	14.1%
2nd Quarter, 1984					
Average Earnings	$1,981	$1,344	$1,887	$1,462	$1,487
% Reporting	19.6%	6.4%	29.5%	26.5%	14.6%
3rd Quarter, 1984					
Average Earnings	$2,198	$1,240	$2,039	$1,401	$1,663
% Reporting	20.9%	7.2%	28.9%	28.6%	14.1%

TABLE 12.7--Continued

Category	Unable to Locate or Moved (n=1001)	Disability Too Severe (n=1181)	Refused Further Services (n=681)	Would Not Cooperate (n=630)	No Reason Given, Transferred, Died, or in Institution (n=198)
4th Quarter, 1984 Average Earnings % Reporting	$1,911 21.0%	$1,412 7.6%	$1,950 28.6%	$1,561 32.5%	$1,311 15.7%
1st Quarter, 1985 Average Earnings % Reporting	$1,910 20.8%	$1,247 7.5%	$1,860 26.3%	$1,481 29.8%	$1,066 14.1%
Average Total Earnings	$6,222	$3,513	$6,679	$4,702	$4,381
Average Weekly Earnings	$96	$54	$103	$72	$67
Average Number of Quarters Worked	3.1	2.7	3.5	3.1	3.3
Average Number of Jobs Held	2.0	1.6	1.8	2.1	2.1

groups earned between $6,000 and $6,500 for the five quarters of the VEC wage-match. This translates into earnings of slightly less than $100 per week. The not rehabilitated group also held slightly more jobs and worked fewer quarters than persons who moved before acceptance.

Given the paucity of information in the R-300 data set for persons who did not get into the program, we cannot make too many substantive inferences about differences between these groups. We do know one thing for certain. The people who moved after they were accepted received a significant amount of VR services (see Chapter 7). By tracking clients via the wage match, we now have data on both labor force participation and earnings. These data enable the researcher to estimate the efficacy of the menu of services received by these people. Traditionally, such persons were classified "not rehabilitated" and given no further consideration.

Let us next examine the groups that refused to be accepted into the program or refused further services once accepted. The only trenchant thing to note about these two cohorts is their remarkable similarity. Except for a lower tracking rate by the VEC for the not-rehabilitated cohort, there is virtually no difference in quarterly or total earnings, number of jobs held, or number of quarters worked. The total earnings for those refusing further services, $6,679, were the highest for all individuals closed in status 28 and status 30. The very fact of their refusal implies that they found a preferable alternative to the individual written rehabilitation plan (IWRP) offered by the VR agency. We can infer that this eventually led to their gainful employment.

The next population of interest includes those clients who were deemed uncooperative when they applied for services or after they started receiving services. Roughly half of both cohorts were tracked through the wage match. Note that persons who started the VR program earned significantly less for the five quarters of the wage match, some $900, than those who were uncooperative before being accepted. Both groups exhibited relatively low earnings and quarters worked. They also had difficulty staying at a job—averaging two jobs for the period under study. This should not be surprising given the implicit counselor judgment that such clients were difficult to deal with and probably had emotional problems that would tend to make them unemployable.

The final groups to be examined are those who were too severely disabled to be eligible for services or to continue further in the intended program. It should immediately be evident that such people are significantly worse off than the others. Their quarterly and total earnings, overall participation rates, and number of quarters worked if they worked at all were the lowest by far for all of the groups we have considered here.

One of the most perplexing findings is that the too severely disabled client who was terminated from the program did significantly worse than the similarly classified client who was not accepted. The overall labor force participation rate reported by the VEC for not rehabilitated clients was less than half that of those who were not accepted. Moreover, for the few status 28 and 30 clients who worked, earnings were much less than for those not accepted for the same reason. The former group had five-quarter total and estimated weekly earnings of $3,513 and $54. These are dramatically lower than the $5,082 and $78 for persons who did not enter the program.

This finding is anomalous for two reasons. First, the former clients of VR received large amounts of services. Given the outcome, one would have to question the efficacy of the service provision. Second, one would expect that the people who never got into the program would be more severely disabled and, other things being equal, have lower earnings than those who were receiving services. The only possible explanation lies in the large numbers of both groups that did not participate in the labor force during the time of the wage match. It may have been that persons terminated after receiving services were better off but were not able to obtain the necessary employment to demonstrate the improved functioning.

CONCLUSIONS

As we have seen, two major problems in evaluating the effectiveness of vocational rehabilitation services are the lack of meaningful data on postprogram earnings and the unavailability of a comparison group to gauge what a person with similar attributes would earn in the absence of the services. The introduction of longitudinal data on earnings for clients rehabilitated, not rehabilitated, and not accepted for services is one potential way to overcome these problems. To this end, a match linking quarterly earnings for 1984 of clients closed during 1982 was undertaken. While this particular data-link did not contain earnings before program acceptance, it did give some indication of client outcomes.

This data set contained information on the number of jobs held, the quarterly earnings, and the reason for closure for clients closed in status 08, 26, 28, and 30. This enabled us to examine not only differences in earning patterns between the various statuses but also differences within the groups.

We found that the status 26 cohort had the highest earnings and the highest labor force participation rates. Persons not accepted for services had slightly lower earnings depending on the specific reason they were not accepted. The status 28 and 30 cohorts had the lowest earnings and participation rates. However, these levels were not insignificant and demonstrate the usefulness of longitudinal data in estimating program outcomes.

The other use of the data-link is to make comparisons of earnings and participation rates within the groups. Thus, earnings for competitively employed status 26 clients were seen to be markedly higher than those who were employed in sheltered workshops. Persons not accepted because of lack of vocational handicap or lack of disability had earnings comparable to the competitively employed. Persons not accepted because they were judged too severely disabled had dramatically lowered earnings and participation rates. Finally, persons not rehabilitated because their disability was too severe had the lowest earnings.

This data set represents the first step in obtaining longitudinal information on the impact of VR services. Clearly, it would be desirable to have information on the earnings of clients before their application for services, in addition to the earnings information studied here. Future data-links will enable us to examine the earnings of persons for a period of up to three years before they apply for services. This data will then allow us to construct the valid comparison groups necessary for a sound evaluation of programmatic impacts.

WORKS CITED

Greenblum, Joseph. 1977. "Effect of Vocational Rehabilitation on Employment and Earnings of the Disabled: State Variations." *Social Security Bulletin* 40:3-16.
Nowak, Laura. 1983. "A Cost-Effectiveness Evaluation of the Federal/State Vocational Rehabilitation Program—Using a Comparison Group." *American Economist* 27:23-29.

Conclusion

In Part III of this volume, a survey of the evaluation procedures of several state agencies revealed that interest and activity in the area of benefit-cost analysis were declining. This development might indicate that the federal government has failed to provide the necessary direction, as the authors in Part III suggest, or it might mean simply that the energies of the state agencies have been diverted elsewhere, but the result is that we do not find states enthusiastically producing cost-benefit studies and using them to guide their programs. If there has been a lull in conducting studies, however, there has been no pause in the demands of those in legislative and oversight positions for some better social accounting of how funds are spent. It would be a tribute to the continuing resourcefulness of vocational rehabilitation if the program that pioneered in the use of real data were to regain its premier status in the evaluation arena.

For this to happen a number of things must be done:

1. Managers of the programs at the state level must have some motivation to conduct these analyses.
2. The data base must be adequate for the job to be done.
3. The models used must be convincing to those who have oversight responsibilities.

Let us look at each of these matters in turn.

MOTIVATING ADMINISTRATORS

The reason why program officials might distrust benefit-cost analysis is obvious. In a world where administrators compete fiercely for budgetary allocations and numbers of positions, the spectre of a possibly unfavorable or ambiguous benefit-cost ratio cannot be greeted with equanimity. This possible danger, a cost if you will, must be offset by benefits if the analyses are to get off the ground.

From the administrators' vantage point, the benefits must be found in two areas. One is the usefulness of benefit-cost studies in identifying program weaknesses. If the program has defects, if the program is truly one in which the marginal costs are greater than the marginal benefits, then the administrator responsible for the program ought to know of the problem before it is brought to his attention by others. Many measures could be taken to remedy the problem, and this brings up the second area in which benefit-cost evaluation can work to the advantage of program personnel— that area we have called "internal evaluation." Benefit-cost analysis in its broadest compass is a management tool that can be used by the counselor, the supervisor, and those responsible for the overall direction of the program to make some very basic decisions about the provision of services and the allocation of counselor time and program resources.

The analysis in Part IV is an initial effort to apply benefit-cost methodology to managerial problems. Even a casual examination of the program reveals that persons are treated quite differently once they are accepted as clients. The services given to clients differ in their intensity, duration, and type. The models presented by the authors in Part I and applied in Part IV show how it is possible to analyze the effectiveness of the mix of services received by clients with differing characteristics. The administrator of the program will always be less interested in an overall ratio than in the effectiveness of various types of service with different clients, and analyzing these in benefit-cost terms will serve to emphasize efficiency considerations. In the absence of a true experimental design, these examinations of the internal workings of the program inspire more confidence than do the external examinations of the program's overall costs and benefits.

One administrative concern that needs to be addressed if we hope to generate greater interest in benefit-cost analysis involves the source of the analysis. Who will be called upon to examine the program? It may well be more efficient to have independent evaluators come in to measure the effects of services. But at best this kind of assessment can take place only at infrequent intervals, and then it will probably be confined to some global look at the overall program. Such one-time evaluations are appropriate for short-lived programs, and they may even be inevitable, as in the case of the large national negative tax experiments. Evaluation probably yields the greatest dividends, however, if it takes place continually, so that its lessons can be absorbed and applied to the improvement of the program. For that purpose, evaluations conducted on a routine basis are preferable. Obviously such a procedure requires some integration with the ongoing process of serving clients. In the experiments with state data described in Part IV, the authors worked with information that had been collected by counselors; if the agencies themselves were to undertake such analyses at regular intervals, they could see to it that their findings were fed back to the counselors to assist them in making intelligent and informed decisions. If information could be circulated in this way within a particular agency or program, managers would be given some powerful motives to become concerned with benefit-cost matters.

THE PERENNIAL PROBLEMS OF DATA

What makes the case for regular in-house evaluation of the VR program is the vast amount of data regularly collected by the counselors and reported by the states to the federal government. The exact information to be reported has been the subject of some dispute in recent years, and the exact form used to elicit this information—a form that most of the authors in this volume refer to as the R-300—has been revised and given a different number. Still, this program has been a pioneer in tracking individual cases and reporting on the disposition of each case. Information on client benefits derived from this data base, together with reports on overall costs, supported the early claims of program personnel at both the state and federal levels that VR could truly be justified in economic terms.

Despite the wealth of information gathered, the examination of the data base in Part II of this volume showed that it still lacks some important elements. The information on client wages is insufficient. In order to judge the effects of program participation, one must know more than is currently being reported on the earnings and status of clients before they enter the program and after they leave. A longitudinal data base must be developed so that analysts are not dependent upon reports of client earnings at two points in time—immediately before acceptance into the program and sixty days after departure. Recent analysis of manpower training programs suggests that a record of earnings for a period of at least two years before program acceptance is necessary to obtain some notion of a person's true earnings capacity.[1] A work history of this kind would indicate whether some individuals accepted into the program are simply off their normal earnings curve; it is possible that a temporary drop in their level of wages or employment might have prompted the decision of these individuals to apply for VR services. VR clients differ, of course, from applicants to ordinary manpower training programs in that they are physically or mentally impaired. This circumstance makes the measurement of preprogram earnings even more problematical. It is necessary to have good information on preprogram earnings both before and after the date of onset of the client's disability condition. The authors in Part II also emphasize the need to trace earnings of both rehabilitants and nonrehabilitants over an extended period after they leave the program. Here again, confidence in conclusions about the effects of treatment will depend on the availability of better data.

Some additional efforts will, of course, be necessary to remedy these deficiencies in the data. Counselors may be asked to compile comprehensive job histories detailing the labor market experience of clients before they enter the program. Experience suggests that such efforts can be successfully undertaken: in a current study of VR programs in Virginia, Texas, and California, counselors have cooperated in recording detailed information on client earnings.[2] One incentive for such cooperation is that data collected for the purposes of evaluation can also be used by counselors to make decisions about their clients' future job prospects. Thus, the mechanisms of evaluation can be made less obtrusive and time-consuming if they are integrated with the normal responsibilities and case handling procedures of counselors.

A second data problem of considerable significance is examined in Part IV of the volume. The information available in the national data base on the physical and mental functioning of clients is inadequate. We have seen that health or functioning is an important variable in assessing the success of individual clients in the program and in judging the benefits attributable to the program. A condition classification of the client is recorded in the data forms but it fails to reveal the severity of the condition. The solution to this problem seems to lie in some direct method of assessing physical and mental functioning. One such instrument, examined at length in Chapter 10, is the Functional Assessment Inventory (FAI). The FAI is designed to reveal the extent of clients' physical or mental limitations at the time of their entrance into the program. Since one of the objectives of the vocational rehabilitation program is the improvement in the functioning of the client as a result of services received, the FAI could be administered at discrete intervals after the client has been accepted into the program. If the instrument proves sensitive enough, the results of these several examinations might reveal what progress the client has made in functioning. Such results would give an additional variable, besides earnings improvements, to measure the effectiveness of the program's services.

Obviously, having some measure of the severity of a client's condition is important in the vocational rehabilitation program, but an FAI-style measure would also serve a purpose in any manpower or human service delivery program. Clients entering such programs differ in their educational attainments and their demographic characteristics, and most program evaluation procedures will take these differences into account. But standardizing for these variables may not be enough if the entering clients differ as to their health status, a notoriously difficult variable to measure. The FAI does not measure health in a medically defined way; it measures another dimension, namely, the client's ability to see, hear, walk, carry, lift, and relate to others on the job. These capacities relate to functioning in a world of work, and if the FAI measures can be implemented in the analysis of human service delivery programs other than VR, they should provide an additional standardizing variable of great value.

Chapter 10 of the volume draws attention to certain additional data items that it would be desirable to have, over and above those now reported on the R-300 form. The authors note that counselors are required to report on each of the services given to clients but are not expected to indicate the amount of time spent on individual cases. In addition, the reports of services filed by the counselors are not sufficiently detailed, lacking precise information on the frequency, data, duration, and costs of service. Lastly, no report is made of the services received by the client from some other agency while the client is in the VR program.

These three data deficiencies can be remedied in several ways. The counselor can keep accurate track of the time spent on a case and can monitor the similar benefits received by clients. But the financial records of the VR agencies, containing information on services purchased and payments made, constitute another important resource. If these records are merged with client statistical files, they can provide the analyst with a more complete account of the services received and enable the analyst to distinguish the efficacy of the several kinds of services.

In view of the hundreds of types of services offered to clients of different ages and different levels of educational attainment and work experience, it is easy to appreciate the difficulties of interpreting the data to determine the benefits and the costs of the VR program. All of this information can only be understood with the aid of some model which will organize the variables.

MODELING THE PROGRAM

The authors in this volume have presented several kinds of models applicable to the VR program: models based on the behavior of individual clients and counselors, models assessing the overall costs and benefits of the program, and models designed to evaluate the efficiency of particular components of the program. The authors have also drawn attention to the conceptual weaknesses of some models and the practical difficulties that arise with their implementation. Much of the criticism has been directed at the benefit-cost models used to evaluate the VR program as a whole. It is our belief that the questionable design of these evaluation efforts deprives policymakers of the firm evidence they need to support increased public investment in vocational rehabilitation. We know, for example, that while overall disability expenditures in the United States run well over $122 billion a year, a mere 2 percent of that amount is spent on rehabilitation and prevention. Until it definitely can be shown that expenditures on the rehabilitation program significantly reduce disability cash transfers, this situation is unlikely to change.

One fundamental design flaw in the overall evaluation of the VR program has been the lack of control groups. The models implicit in the earliest studies of the program simply ignored the problem. If the individuals served by the program reported an increase in their earnings, this improvement was attributed to the program. It is apparent, however, that such an assumption about the role of the program is too simplistic. With more sophisticated evaluation methods becoming increasingly common, the question is more frequently asked: "What would have happened to that person had he or she not encountered the VR program?"

Ideally, researchers would obtain the answer to this question by conducting an experiment in which some individuals were randomly assigned to a VR treatment group and others were assigned to a control group. The ethical issues raised by such procedures, however, are very complex. Program officials are understandably reluctant to deny services for the sake of a cost-benefit experiment. Nevertheless, we do foresee certain developments that may justify the use of control groups to evaluate the program in the future. There are signs that the demand for the services of the program is increasing while the supply of services remains constant; as a consequence, administrators may be forced to decide which persons will be served out of the group applying. Under such circumstances, it might be acceptable to make choices of this kind on a random basis and to follow up those persons denied services as a control group.

A second method of assessing the effects of VR treatment, and a method that eliminates some of the ethical difficulties involved in denying services, would be to design experiments in which one group of persons would receive VR program services while a second group would receive alternative services. A variant of the method would give those denied admission to the VR program a voucher that could be valid for any service (at one extreme, the voucher could be exchanged for cash) or for some constrained set of services.

It is unlikely, however, that any experimental design for program evaluation will gain the approval of the rehabilitation community in the immediate future. Until such acceptance of experimental methods exists, we must find a way of compensating for the lack of true control groups. In Part II of our volume, the authors employ econometric methods of corrections as a substitute for a control group. Part III briefly examines some of the methods used by the states to adjust earnings data in an effort to isolate the effects of treatment. Finally, in Part IV, the authors show how additional data gathered by counselors and gleaned from financial records can give analysts greater confidence that they are measuring returns to particular inputs. These solutions, however, are only partial and, in all cases, the analysis would benefit by a properly selected control group.

The outlook is brighter for internal evaluation of the program. If sufficient data are available, researchers should be able to apply models for measuring the cost effectiveness of particular components of the program with reasonable confidence. Still, the use of comparison groups would result in more reliable estimates. A comparison group might be made up of individuals selected for the program who fail to complete it or who do not complete it successfully. These persons might be followed up and their postprogram experiences compared to those of successful rehabilitants. Still, this is only a second-best solution, since unobservable differences may exist between those who finish successfully and those who do not.

Another option would involve creating a data link between the VR program data and the earnings records of the Social Security Administration. A fixed effects model like the one described in Chapter 3 could then be used. Here again, however, the model would require the use of a comparison group consisting of persons who were referred to the program but did not complete it. Much the same type of model could be applied by the state programs using mini-data links that join program data with the earnings records of the state employment agencies.

In sum, it seems realistic to conclude that the outlook for a true experimental design utilizing a proper control group is not promising. This means that any dramatic announcement hailing the cost-beneficial nature of the VR program is unlikely in the near future. But if such external evaluations are not immediately possible, much can be done to improve and expand the internal evaluations. Program administrators should take full advantage of the findings of such evaluations to direct future changes in the program. Perhaps the real question for those who would assess the performance of VR is not "Does the program work or not?" but "What works in the program and what does not?" If this is the issue to be explored, then some progress has been made in this volume in pointing the way.

NOTES

1. See the following works: Ashenfelter, Orley. 1975. "The Effect of Manpower Training on Earnings: Preliminary Results," in *Proceedings of the Twenty-Seventh Annual Winter Meeting of the Industrial Relations Research Association*, pp. 252-60; Bassi, Laurie J. 1983. "The Effect of CETA on the Postprogram Earnings of Participants." *Journal of Human Resources* 18.4:539-56; Kiefer, Nicholas M. 1979. "The Economic Benefits from Four Government Training Programs," in *Evaluating Manpower Training Programs*, ed. Farrell E. Bloch. Greenwich, Connecticut: JAI Press; Lalonde, Robert J. 1984. "Evaluating the Econometric Evaluations of Training Programs Using Experimental Data." 1986. *American Economic Review* 76.4:604-20.

2. A report on this project, "Enhanced Understanding of the Economics of Disability," NIHR Research Project No. 133AH30005, is due in February 1988.

INDEX

Surplus: compensating, 34-35, 36;
  equivalent, 34-35
Switzer, Mary, 10, 20-21

Taubman, Paul, 205
Texas VR agencies, 179-81
Thornton, Craig Van Doren, 50
Thrall, Robert M., 52

Utility: cardinal and ordinal, 32; marginal,
  29
Utility function, 10; direct and indirect, 31
Utility possibility frontier, 38

Variables: demographic, 211-12; health,
  209-10, 218, 222, 223, 225-29; service,
  213-14; socioeconomic, 212-13
Variation, compensating and equivalent,
  34-35
Vartia, Yrgo, 35
Virginia VR programs, 180, 186-88, 197,
  233-34

Vocational rehabilitation: clientele changes,
  3; cost-benefit analysis, 1920s, 12-15;
  cost-benefit analysis, 1930s and 1940s,
  15-18; cure for disability, 12; evaluation
  methods, 4; goal of, 3; history, 9, 12-22;
  qualification for entrance into, 247; self-
  paying, 7

Wage gain, estimating, 50
Wage projections, 102-4
Wage time path, 47, 48, 49, 52, 185
Walras, Leon, 32
Wier, Roy, 25-26
Willig, Robert, 35
Willingness to pay, 8, 33, 34, 42
Wisconsin VR agencies, 185, 210; data base,
  199
Workers' compensation, 13
Worrall, John D., 8-9, 53, 55

Zero wages reported by VR referrals,
  119-23; corrections of, 123-28, 136-37